WHILE THE
GODS PLAY

WHILE THE GODS PLAY

*Shaiva Oracles and Predictions
on the Cycles of History and
the Destiny of Mankind*

ALAIN DANIÉLOU

TRANSLATED FROM THE FRENCH BY
Barbara Bailey, Michael Baker, and Deborah Lawlor

Inner Traditions International
Rochester, Vermont

Inner Traditions International, Ltd.
One Park Street
Rochester, Vermont 05767

First U.S. edition 1987

While the Gods Play was first published in French under the
title La Fantaisie des Dieux et L'Aventure Humaine by Editions du Rocher, Monaco, 1985

Library of Congress Cataloging-in-Publication Data

Daniélou, Alain.
    While the gods play.
    Translation of: La fantaisie des dieux et
l'aventure humaine.
    Bibliography: p.
    Includes index.
    1. Shaivaism.   I. Title.
BL1280.54.D3613   1987   294.5′2   87-10831
ISBN 0-89281-115-3

10 9 8 7 6 5 4 3 2 1

Printed and bound in the United States of America
Distributed to the book trade in the United States by Harper
& Row Publishers, Inc.
Distributed to the book trade in Canada by Book Center,
Inc., Montreal, Quebec

Note on the Transliteration of Sanskrit Terms

AS EXACT A PRONUNCIATION AS POSSIBLE IS AS MUCH essential for the ritual formulae and the magical sense of words as for establishing the parallels between different languages. The Sanskrit alphabet is a syllabic alphabet consisting of fifty-two phonetic signs. The syllables can be long (*â*) or short (*a*). The consonants are voiceless or aspirated (*t* or *th*). Certain vowels of the old phonetic system have disappeared from the pronunciation of modern Sanskrit. Such is the case with *ë* (as in the English word *above*), these days pronounced "ri," which is transcribed either as *e* or *ri*, and with *ü* (which does not occur in English, but is closest to the French *u* as in *vu*), pronounced "lri" and transcribed either as *ü* or *lri*. An *a* occurring at the end of a word is not pronounced in Sanskrit. It corresponds to the final silent *e* in English. It is denoted by *ä*. *Yogä* should be pronounced "Yog," *Shivä* as "Shiv." *Shivâ* is feminine, a name of the goddess.

The retroflex consonants are shown underscored: *t*, *th*, *d*, *dh*, *sh*, *n*. The palatal nasal is written *ñ*, the guttural nasal *ñ*.

The English sound *oo* (as in *book*) is represented by the letter *u*. The modern Tamil alphabet is based on the same phonetic system. Sanskrit words are written with a capital letter in the text, and the plural is neither shown by an *s* nor otherwise indicated. I have added an *(s)* for clarity.

In the translation of Sanskrit and Tamil texts I sometimes incorporated some explanatory words added by the scholars who quote them or taken from commentaries. Later I added some quotes from modern works that I noted in the course of my research.

In the exposition of the doctrines of Shaivism, I have followed the terminology of the Sanskrit versions of the Sâmkhyä(s) and the Ägamä(s). At times I have added Dravidian terms to the Sanskrit words or to their translation.

Contents

[vii]

CONTENTS

[ix]

CONTENTS

CONTENTS

[xi]

Introduction

WE ARE SO ACCUSTOMED TO REGARDING THE EVOLU-
tion of humanity as a constant progression, and the development of knowledge over the course of several centuries or
even several decades as a continuous forward movement, that
we sometimes have difficulty in realizing that contrary forces
also exist which periodically return peoples to states of incredible barbarism.

Important civilizations pass away, their highly developed
scientific knowledge suddenly annihilated. In such cases, the
only lingering echo is the vague remembrance of a Golden
Age, or sometimes a few monuments remain which reveal a
knowledge so evolved that our ancestors of only a few generations ago were not only incapable of deciphering it but
even of having any idea of what sort of knowledge they were
witnessing.

We use the rather vague term *tradition* to evoke the fragments, which have come down to us through secret and esoteric channels, of this ancient and prestigious knowledge,
whose substance we have lost even though we have preserved
its memory. There are periods in the course of history in
which we encounter attempts to recover something of this
ancient knowledge. The emperor Hadrian gathered together

a great number of scholars to try to recapture the science of the ancient Egyptians. Later on, in Italy, a group of artists, scholars, and philosophers formed the Accademia Vitruviana, then the Accademia Romana, providing the beginning impulse of what is called the Renaissance in Europe. This group had also sought to recover elements of the knowledge of the Egyptians, the Etruscans, and the Pelasgeans. Its members were tortured and massacred by the Borgia popes, and the survivors dispersed, leaving only a few enigmatic writings.

In India, around the time of Christ, there was an astonishing personality called Lakulishä who dared to stand in opposition to official Vedism and Buddhism, and enabled the ancient Shaiva religion to be reborn. With it the sciences and religious and philosophic concepts that had been "underground" for nearly two millennia came to the fore and provoked a prodigious effervescence in the domain of culture and the arts. Its representatives were likewise gradually eliminated, and modern Hinduism retains only a degraded remnant of it. The true knowledge is once again enclosed in esotericism.

Some texts dating from the pre-Aryan civilization of India were partially recuperated during the period of the Shaiva revival. I have attempted, often with difficulty, to study and understand the conceptions they present of ancient Shaivism concerning the nature of the world and the destiny of man, and to present certain aspects of these conceptions in this book. Obviously I can give here only a brief summary. The upholders of the tradition, always under threat, are reticent and secretive. Their knowledge is often fragmentary, and the level of the concepts sometimes goes quite beyond the scientific and philosophic notions with which I am familiar, posing arduous problems of comprehension and terminology. There remains, however, a vast corpus of texts, for the most part unpublished, which represent a body of knowledge coming from the depths of the ages. These texts deserve to be studied by people more qualified than I. I have limited myself to the texts that I thought understandable concerning cosmology, the nature of language, and musical semantics. I was not competent to approach the texts on mathematics, astronomy, or medicine, and hope that others will be able to explore them. What is important in such research is, first of all, to be conscious of the limits of our own knowledge and neither to reject nor to seek to bring to our level notions that seem bizarre or incomprehensible at first approach. The situation is analogous to that of a man of the eighteenth century being able, by a phenomenon of vision, to read certain texts of modern physics.

Vanity on the part of ethnologists and Orientalists often leads them to aberrant interpretations and absurd judgments.

My work will be useful if it succeeds in awakening the curiosity of even a few scientists at the forefront of research, several of whom have indicated to me their astonishment at the discovery, clearly expressed in this ancient knowledge, of concepts that they themselves hardly dare to envisage, such as the structural identity of the cells which form the galaxies and the cells which form our bodies, or the necessity of the omnipresence of consciousness as one of the essential components of interstellar and atomic matter, the relativity of time, and the purely energetic nature of matter, all of which are concepts familiar to the Sâmkhyä.

PART ONE

THE
HUMAN
ADVENTURE

※※※※

1

Origins

ACCORDING TO THE CHRONOLOGY OF THE PURÂNĀ, THE present humanity would have appeared about 58,000 years ago, a figure that corresponds to twelve and a half times what Shaiva cosmology calls the Age of the Ancestors (Pitri), that is, the duration of a lineage, a particular species of men. But men or similar beings existed before the present humanity. The human species that have succeeded each other on earth have each achieved a very high level of development and knowledge, then disappeared at the time of planetary catastrophes, leaving, however, traces that served as the bases for the development and knowledge of subsequent humanities, which, when they reach the limits of the knowledge permitted man in the plan of creation, are, in their turn, destined to disappear.

Creation is a continuous phenomenon. Species evolve. New species appear; others cease to exist. No species is born of a single couple. Even if a mutation can be the act of an individual, the appearance of a new species is always a global phenomenon. Man is no exception. Since the birth of the present humanity, four species of men have appeared at precise moments in the cycle. Thus they are in different ages of their development.

[3]

The history of humanity is not, therefore, a single phenomenon. It is marked by conflicts between peoples in different ages of their development. The principal problem for all civilizations is to know how to organize their coexistence.

To try to understand the history of man, anthropologists and archaeologists excavate, layer by layer, the places he has lived. They discover primitive forms of habitations, but also vestiges of civilizations prestigious for their arts and technology which are sometimes contemporaneous with them, belonging to lineages of men who are in different ages of their destiny. In any case, archaeology gives us information only about eras when humans used stone and metal, which are not indispensable ingredients for a sophisticated civilization. The spiritual decadence of man, according to Hindu tradition, goes hand in hand with progress in metallurgy from the Golden Age (Satyä Yugä) to the Iron Age (Kali Yugä). The scientific cautiousness that only recognizes the existence of man according to the material objects left surviving is a very unreliable method, since it depends on chance discoveries and only has value in respect to civilizations using stone or metal. It is very dangerous to draw any conclusions from such a method. After the destruction of the magnificent cities of the Indus by the Aryans, stone was not used in the construction of cities for a millennium. The eras that we call Stone Age are, in reality, ages of timber, of adobe, and of clay bricks.

Today in India, not far from Pondicherry, there are populations who construct the hulls of ships from curved wood, pierced in a fire and bound together with oakum, without any use of metal, and in which they are able to cross the seas. There are also artists there capable of constructing wonderful timber palaces covered with frescoes like those at Trichur in Kerala or in some Himalayan cities. The oldest temples dug into rock (at Ajanta), duplicate very elaborate timber architecture of which no trace remains.

In Africa, the sites of cities once famous for their splendor can no longer be found.

In Japan, it has been possible to save some timber temples thanks to the periodic replacement of damaged parts.

The men who decorated the cave sanctuaries of what we call prehistory did not live underground. They also painted frescoes on their earthen or timber houses, as is still done today in the villages of India.

When we see important vestiges of lost civilizations appear, it is often at a very high level of urbanism, art, literature, knowledge of astronomy, and philosophical myths, which represent a long past. Some megalithic monuments of India and Europe, as well as structures in certain forgotten cities of ancient America, necessitated the transport and polishing of blocks of stone so enormous that they required technical means that seem unachievable today. Their orientation implies a very advanced understanding of astronomy.

There exists no primitive language, a language that does not allow the expression of the most abstract notions. One cannot judge the level of culture of peoples or civilizations by the "permanent" vestiges that have survived or by the customs of new peoples wrongly called primitive. The astronomical, medical, mathematical, and physical knowledge of the Indians, but also of other peoples on various continents several millennia B.C., was, in some cases, more advanced than that of Europeans only two centuries ago. The modern world is much closer to Kapila, Pythagoras, Euclid, and Aristotle than to the theologians of the Middle Ages. Astrophysicists who study the birth, formation, and evolution of the world are coming closer and closer to the ancient theories of Shaiva cosmology whose elements India has retained.

The idea that modern civilization started practically from scratch, from a single source of ape-men several millennia ago, has distorted, or caused to be ignored, information that has reached us just as much by tradition as through archaeological finds. We are so fascinated by the technological advances of the last centuries of modern civilization that we simply forget the periods of obscurantism that preceded them and the differences in the level of development of the various peoples of the world. We tend to consider "progress" a continuous and general phenomenon stretching from the apes to Einstein. Yet the history of man is not one of regular development. It is characterized by a succession of developments and regressions related to astrological and climatic cycles. Barbaric races, still in their infancy, destroy civilizations that had been developed by older, more evolved populations, doing away with the sciences and arts, yet allowing some scraps of knowledge to survive which serve as the basis of the development of new cultures. On all continents we can find traces of outstanding cultures and advanced technologies belonging to bygone ages, followed by periods of barbarism and ignorance.

The Dravidians

THE first of the great civilizing peoples of the historic period seem to have been the Dravidians. According to the *Lugal-ud*, a Sumerian text inscribed on clay tablets six thousand years ago: "There were thick ice sheets everywhere . . . then a terrible fire . . . melting ice sheets, interminable rain, water covering the Earth, then, little by little, being absorbed." And the Book of Genesis (11:1) says: "Leaving the Orient, these men found a plain in the country of Shinear (Sumeria) and settled there." The present populations, called Dravidian, who, like the Sumerians, spoke agglutinative languages, appeared in India after the last Ice Age toward 9,000 B.C. According to tradition, they came from a continent that had been engulfed by the sea.

As M. R. Sakhare points out in his *History and Philosophy of Lingayat Religion*, the Dramilas or Dravidians, the Termiloi of Herodotus, belong to a race of the type called Mediterranean. They may have emigrated to India from Lemuria, a continent which extended from Madagascar to Indonesia and which was flooded by the sea. Their civilization spread in India from Cape Comorin to the Himalayas.

Starting from the sixth millennium B.C., during what the Hindu cosmology calls the Age of Doubt—the Dvâparä Yugä, which is the third age of the cycle that regulates the existence of the present humanity from its beginning to its end, the Dravidian civilization developed, reaching its peak in India between the sixth and second millennia B.C.[1]

It was the Dravidians who built, among others in the Indus Valley, the cities of Mohenjo Daro and Harappa, considerable traces of which have recently been discovered. The influence of the Dravidian civilization was very extensive. It affected the whole Indian continent, but also extended to the "Sumerian cities with which the people of the Indus were definitely in contact."[2]

The Dravidians were a seafaring nation. Large ports have been discovered on the Peninsula of Kathiawar and in the Gulf of Cambay, north of the present Bombay. Sizable necropolises belonging to a population called the Tortoise People, who were related to the people of the Indus, have been discovered in Oman and Arabia. The Indo-Sumerian influence on the first dynasty in Egypt is evident. The Cretan civilization is closely linked to that of the Indus.

The Sumerian deity called the Lord of the Animals corresponds to the Indian Pashupati (Lord of the Animals). The Sumerian goddess, the Lady of the Mountains, is called Parvati (Lady of the Mountains) in India. Nergal, the Sumerian god of the underworld, and his sister, Ereshkigal, call to mind Yama, the Indian god of the dead and his sister, Yami. The cult of the Bull, the symbol of the horns, and the story of the flood are found in the two cultures, as is the the symbolism of numbers. The mountain of cedars in the *Epic of Gilgamesh* is the Dâruvanä (the forest of cedars) of Indian myth. The Sumerians were called "Black Faces." The followers of the old religion are, throughout the course of history and still today, called the Kâlâmukhä (Black Faces) in India.

Isidore of Seville (sixth century), looking to very old traditions, mentions in his encyclopedia this migration of Indian populations, which he calls Garamantes and which, via Egypt, may have come to Spain and from there moved as far as to Great Britain.[3] According to a theory today supported by Soviet historians, this migration took place in the opposite direction, that is, from the Mediterranean toward India, thus linking it with the myth of Atlantis.

The Dravidian languages, which are agglutinative like Sumerian, formerly spoken in the whole of India, today survive essentially in the south. The main languages are Tamil, Kanara, Telugu, and Malayalam. However, in central and northeastern India as far as Baluchistan on the Iranian border, there remain pockets where Brahui is still spoken. Agglutinative languages similar to the Dravidian languages which have survived in the West are Georgian, Basque, and Peuhl, peripheral traces of an ancient culture surviving on the edge of the Aryan world. The Pelasgi of pre-Hellenic Greece were, in all likelihood, Dravidian.[4] Ligurian was a Euskaroid language related to Basque, as probably the Etruscan language was.

Recent studies on blood types have related the pre-Aryan origin of Caucasians, Basques, Sardinians, and Berbers.

Descending neither from Cro-Magnon man nor from the Celts, the populations living on the edge of western Europe and in some Mediterranean centers are therefore of Neolithic origin, their arrival taking place between the departure of the Cro-Magnon men, who set out for the North with their reindeer, and the Celtic invasions of the Bronze Age. . . . These populations . . . live in countries "at the end of the earth," the western extremity of Britain, a fringe of Normandy, Wales, North Scotland, Ireland, Iceland . . . [and also] certain Mediterranean regions, isolated or in refuge, like the inhabitants of the mountainous Massif of Sardinia, Corsica, several alpine valleys, the inhabitants of Liguria, some of the Berbers of the Saharan Atlas Mountains, some groups of Tuaregs. . . . the blood of these insular or isolated fringe populations is close to that of the Basques with a high occurrence of type O.[5]

Strangely, the blood of the American Indians is also type O. Their languages are agglutinative, and their religious symbols and the graphic principles behind their architecture are very similar to those of the Dravidians. They apparently belong to the same human species.

The Aryans

THE invasion of the Aryans, who came from the plains of the Ukraine at the dawn of the second millennium following climatic changes, was an unprecedented material and cultural catastrophe.

At first, the Aryan tribes only settled in the northwest of India. Their penetration into the Ganges Valley took place slowly. The south and the east of the continent remained independent for a long time, and they were able to save their languages, religions, and customs. The Aryans destroyed the cities of the Indus (about 1800), and also Sumeria, Crete, and Mycenae. They spread throughout the west. The Aryan Kassites settled in Babylon toward 1750. The Hyksos entered Egypt at the same time. The Persians, Achaeans, Dorians, Romans, Celts, and Germans were Aryan tribes.

ARYAN LINGUISTIC EXPANSION

Nothing has survived of the original Cretan language. We also know nothing about the Etruscan language, although many Roman nobles were sent to study in the universities of Etruria. The phenomenon of Aryan linguistic expansion continues on implacably today. Texts about the cultures of the peoples colonized by the Europeans survive only in Aryan languages (English, French, German, etc.). Even in India, whose ruling classes send their children to study at Cambridge, some aspects of Hindu thought are known today only through translations into Western languages, which are those of the new conquering Aryans.

By a curious falsification of history, the legend that the origins of civilization are Aryan, or Indo-European, was generally accepted until the discoveries of Egyptian and Cretan worlds, then Sumerian, Hittite, and Babylonian texts, combined to confirm the primacy of the ancient cultures whose languages and traditions India has safeguarded.

THE OCCULT TRADITION

The religion of the Aryans, which was introduced into India and also into Persia and Achaean and Dorian Greece, comes from a patriarchial society of nomads. The worship of the horse replaces that of the bull. The new religion, imposed by the conquerors, disturbed the order of Indian society, making men of Aryan origin a "master race" who considered themselves superior to other humans. Non-Aryans were treated as an inferior race, good for slavery (*dâsyu*) and deprived of civil rights. Many were driven into the mountainous or outlying regions and to the south of the country.

The Aryan conquerors destroyed cities, massacred populations, and reduced the survivors to slavery without regard for rank or learning. It was not only in Greek antiquity that scholars and philosophers were sold as slaves. The attitude of modern colonialists toward "native" scholars has scarcely evolved in this regard.

Therefore, it was in the classes considered inferior and used for the most lowly tasks that were found, mixed with artisans and farm laborers, the descendants of princes and priests, the holders of knowledge. Little by little, these latter organized themselves in the form of occult societies representing a parallel civilization, kept secret, in which the task of groups of ascetics was to pass on the various aspects of the ancient knowledge. This is not unique to India. Occult societies represent a force all over the world in maintaining the forms of knowledge that originated in the pre-Aryan world. In India, in order to escape persecution, these groups of initiates were often forced to feign madness. This explains some of the strange rules of conduct adopted by the majority of monastic orders, heirs to the ancient knowledge.

The Aryans, while maintaining their racial privileges, gradually absorbed some aspects of the technology and arts of the conquered people, as well as many of the philosophical and theological concepts of the ancient civilization of India. Vedism became imbued with the culture of a world that it was striving to subjugate. Non-Aryan princes and philosophers were raised to the rank of "honorary Aryans" and profoundly influenced the Aryan culture.

The first hymns of the _Rig_ Vedä, which represent the original religion of the Aryans, were in all likelihood composed before their arrival in India. The latest of their sacred books, the _Atharvä Vedä_, already reflects rites, beliefs, and religious and magical practices that no longer bore any relation to those of the first hymns of the _Rig_ Vedä. The Dravidian influence is also perceptible in the texts describing the great rituals, the _Brâhmanä(s)_; in the philosophy of the _Upanishad(s)_; and in "the tradition of Yogä, which begins with the Indus Valley and continues through the [non-Aryan ascetics called] Yatis of the _Rig_ Vedä and Vrâtyäs of the _Atharvä Vedä_."[6]

The teachings of the non-Aryan sage Kapilä (with brown skin), whose influence we see appearing toward the seventh century B.C., had already introduced some of the cosmological theories of the Sâmkhyä into the Aryan world. However, it was always an oral tradition whose extent and complexity we have difficulty in realizing.

Groups of the initiated, forming secret societies, were created everywhere that Aryan religions had been imposed, with the aim of safeguarding the threatened rites and forms of learning. Alchemy, astrology, and the powers of vision and prediction of Yogä were often considered to be diabolical and were persecuted by the official religions. It is thanks to the occult tradition that efforts could be made, in various eras, to salvage the ancient knowledge and cults. Thus, in the period when Lakulishä restored Shaivism we will see Gnosticism and Mithraism appear in the West.

Later, the emperor Hadrian tried to bring together a college of scholars to rediscover the ancient learning. A similar endeavor by Prospero Colonna was at the origin of the Renaissance in the West, whose philosophical and religious bases were destroyed by the savage persecution of the Church, allowing only the most external aspects to survive.[7] Despite Christianity, Dionysian practices and rites lasted for a long time in Europe in secret initiatory organizations. Sufi sects in the Middle East have protected an esoteric teaching and still practice ecstatic dances of Dionysian character despite opposition from orthodox Islam.

WRITING

Writing, a phenomenon linked to the Kali Yugä, appeared nearly simultaneously in India, Sumeria, and Egypt around 3300 B.C. The ancient writing of Mohenjo Daro, which has not yet been deciphered, seems to have disappeared after the invasion of the Aryans, who knew nothing of writing and probably considered it to be wizard's spells. Written texts probably survived for a long time in esoteric Dravidian centers, but subsist only in later versions. On the other hand, the tombs of the kings of Egypt have safeguarded precious documents, and it is thanks to a climatic miracle that original Sumerian texts, inscribed on clay tablets, have recently come down to us.

The Aryans, it is said, "loathed writing." (That is why we have no knowledge at all of the Druidic tradition.) Their religious texts and rituals, the Vedä(s), Upanishad(s), and the Brâhmanä(s), were, and still are, handed down with the help of very elaborate mnemonic techniques that assure the continuity of the oral tradition, even through individuals who do not understand their meaning. A text learned from a book is not, even these days, considered fit for ritual. Ancient writings survived in India only in a secret form, in places where dynasties of priests or scholars carried on the tradition of the ancient learning.

A new concept of writing with a commercial purpose appeared among the Phoenicians at the beginning of the first millennium B.C. It was introduced to Cyprus and Carthage in the eighth century, to Malta and Sardinia in the seventh. The Greek alphabet, derived from the Phoenician, was formed in the eighth century and spread among the Etruscan and Latin tribes from the seventh century onward. It was not standardized until the fourth century. Aramaic writing, which was to become Arabic writing, spread in Iran during the sixth century.

It was only in the sixth century B.C., the critical period in the middle of the Kali Yugä, that is, the period of the Buddha, more than a thousand years after the Aryans arrived in India, that Darius, who had annexed the Indus Valley and established a satrapy there, introduced into India a new form of writing, Aramaic, used by merchants, as was money. The ancient Sanskrit alphabets, the Brahmi and the Karoshti, are therefore of Semitic origin. The first inscriptions date from the third century B.C. The Vedic language had evolved, giving birth to various vernacular languages, the Prakrit(s).

Writing allowed the Aryans to fix the religious and philosophical texts until then passed on orally. It was on this basis that great scholars forged an artificial language called Sanskrit, the "refined language," devised to last forever, which, little by little, became the universal language of the culture.

In the fourth century B.C., the grammarian Pânini, summarizing earlier works, established in his famous grammar, the definitive form of Sanskrit, which has not changed since.

Apart from inscriptions and engravings on coins, writing was done on papyrus, palm leaves, parchment, and silk. Paper, which appeared in China at the beginning of our era, only spread to the West in the fourteenth century and in India a little later. The majority of Indian manuscripts are on palm leaves and must be periodically recopied.

NOTES

1. See Alain Daniélou, *Histoire de l'Inde*, pp. 32–33.
2. Thomas McEvilly, *An Archeology of Yoga*, I, p. 46.
3. See Alain Daniélou, *Shiva and Dionysus* (New York: Inner Traditions, 1984).
4. Ibid.
5. Jean Bernard, *Le Sang et L'histoire*, pp. 118, 120.
6. McEvilly, *An Archeology of Yoga*, p. 45.
7. See Alain Daniélou, "La sagesse assassinée," *Historia*, no. 440, pp. 37–40.

2

The Religions of the Kali Yugä

Shaivism

SHAIVISM, THE RELIGION OF THE ANCIENT DRAVIDI-
ans, was always the religion of the people. Its metaphysical,
cosmological, and ritual conceptions were preserved by communities of wandering ascetics living on the fringe of the
offical society, whom the Aryans scornfully called Yati(s)
(wanderers), Vrâtyä(s) (untouchables), or Âjîvikä(s) (beggars).

The *Vâyu Purânä* mentions the fact that these wandering Shaiva
ascetics "seem to have possessed the humble status of Shudras
(people of the servile caste or even of outcastes who were
forbidden to enter towns)."
  In practice, the term *Âjîvikä* applied to the whole of the
non-Aryan population. Communities of Âjîvikä laymen were
to be found in all the great cities of the Ganges basin (and
formed a parallel society). They included members of all classes.[1]

In the fourth century A.D., Amarsimhä, the author of a famous Sanskrit dictionary, still classes among the Shudrä(s)
(the low castes) the Devalä or Shaivas, who worship idols,

[15]

and notes among them the Pâshupatä(s), the Pâñcharâträ(s), and the Tantrikä(s), that is, the population groups who had been able to maintain the old religion, its rites, cosmology, myths, and practices. It is the members of these monastic orders who today still teach the disciplines and eroticomagical rites of Tantrism.

Aryan society practiced a punitive discrimination against them. In South India, even in the fourteenth century, the Âjîvikä(s), that is, the indigenous people, paid much heavier taxes than the rest of the population (as later on the Muslims imposed upon the Hindus).

The Return of Arihat

THE date 3102 B.C., which marks the beginning of the Kali Yugä, represents a cosmological reality linked with an alteration in influx from the planetary spheres; it is not an arbitrary date. Its influence is felt everywhere in the world. Differences in the estimation of this date derive from varying methods of calculation. In Sumer, it is the time of the flood. The Hebrew calendar preserved by certain sects begins in 3760 B.C., while the American Mayan calendar begins in 3313 B.C. After the events that mark the beginning of each period, a sort of characteristic climate is established, which, for the Kali Yugä, is an atmosphere of tensions, rivalries, conflicts, invasions, wars, and the like. Perverse conceptions, hostile to the tradition of wisdom and the harmony between the species which appeared during the Dvâparä Yugä, began, from the start of the Kali Yugä, to impose themselves with violence. It was at this time that the invasions of the Aryan barbarians, described in the Great War of the *Mahâbhâratä*, and the imposition of Vedism took place. At the same time, we can see the development of the moralistic and atheistic religion of Jainism.

It is at the midpoint of the Kali Yugä that the conditions are brought about which will lead to the final decline. The fifth century B.C. was then to see the forceful manifestation of the ideologies that would be the cause of humanity's decadence. And, indeed, we are seeing the reappearance, in conformity with the predictions, of the teachings of Arihat, which had caused the fall of the Assurs.

Gosâlä

THREE figures in India were to play a key role in the religious reforms that conditioned all subsequent religions. They are Makkhali Gosâlä (560–484 B.C.), Mahâvîrä (547–467 B.C.), and Gautamä (550–483 B.C.), whom his disciples called the Buddha, the Illumined.[2] The characteristic sign of this reversal of values was the Makkhali Gosâlä's attempt to reform the Shaiva tradition.

Gosâlä was one of those non-Aryan wandering ascetics of humble origin whom bourgeois society called Âjîvikä(s) (beggars). He was very early preoccupied by the activities of extremist sects such as the Kâpâlikä (Skull-Bearers) and the Kâlâmukhä (Black Faces), whose magical practices and antisocial attitudes shocked the urban society of their time. He sought to reinstate the philosophic and rationalist aspects of the ancient pre-Aryan culture, which were in opposition to popular ecstatic and mystical Shaivism. We find similar attempts to adapt Shaivism to the prejudices of bourgeois society with the Virä Shaïvä or Lingayat of the Middle Ages and later with the reformers of the British era. The Shaiva ascetics went about naked, their bodies smeared with ashes, practicing orgiastic dances. They refused to be participants in a society oriented toward productivity and puritanism. With matted hair and haggard eyes, they lived away from villages and towns and refused to take an interest in material well-being. In the same epoch, the sect of Cynics, of which Diogenes is a typical example, flourished in Greece and is clearly related to the Kâlâmukä(s) of India.

The *Bhagavatî Sûträ*, a Jaïnä work, has preserved for us

the most important description of the life and work of Gosâlä, his relationship to and his break with Mahâvîrä, and the circumstances of his death.

The father of Gosâlä was a Mankhä, a sort of roving bard, exhibitor of pious images. Of non-Aryan origin, he was considered to be a Dâsyu, an appellation corresponding to the term "native" in the period of European colonialism. This, in fact, meant that any position other than a servile one was prohibited to him in Aryan society. Nevertheless, he was a man learned in the philosophic tradition of the ancient culture, particularly in the materialist theories of the Vaïsheshikä and the cosmology of the Sâmkhyä, infinitely more evolved than the nebulous concepts of the followers of the Vedä. (In a similar context many centuries later, I myself knew a humble janitor at the French Consulate in Calcutta who was a poor Brahman who read the Upanishad(s) while operating the elevator for the sahibs, the Europeans, the new Aryan lords of India, as arrogant as they were ignorant.)

It was during the course of his father's peregrinations that Gosâlä was born, like Jesus, in a stable, not far from the famous university of Nalanda. After having practiced for several years the family business of dealing in images, Gosâlä joined a group of Shaiva ascetic-beggars. He soon acquired great renown for his asceticism and his learning. According to the *Bhagavatî Sûträ*, his disciples considered him the twenty-fourth prophet (Tîrthamkarä) of the Âjîvikä, in the Avasarpini Yugä (the age of secret messengers), and as the reformer of the old Shaivism, about which little was known at the time for the texts were only reconstituted later. "A great wave of spiritual unrest swept through the Ganges Valley in the sixth century B.C. The thirty-three great gods of the Aryans and the lesser earth spirits of the Aboriginals were too motley a company to correspond to the orderly civilization which had already emerged . . . and were inadequate to meet the spiritual needs of the rising class of merchants to the existence of which both Buddhist and Jaina texts testify."[3]

The wandering Shaiva sages, asocial and marginal, both

ascetic and lascivious, free from the tyrannies of society, held a great fascination for the bourgeois and aristocratic young people of the cities (a little like the hippies of modern times). Hence, the great bourgeois Mahâvîrä and the prince Gautamä became disciples of Gosâlä. (Plutarch reports that Alexander said of himself: "If I were not Alexander, I would wish to be Diogenes.")

The figure of Gosâlä is very important, for in presenting a different version of the old culture, until then ignored and rejected by Aryan society as the superstitions of despicable slaves, he attracted those, such as Mahâvîrä and Gautamä, who were dissatisfied with Vedic rigidity, and he aroused a sudden interest in the antique pre-Aryan philosophy within the good society of the period. The role of Gosâlä can be compared to someone such as Aurobindo, who, in the modern era, however contested by orthodox Hinduism, provoked considerable interest in the philosophic and religious conceptions that Europeans until then had regarded as the superstitions of backward populations.

Mahâvîrä traveled with Gosâlä for six years, and Gautamä joined them for three or four years. The commentary on the *Avashyâkä Sûträ* by Jîna Dâsä, which gives a rather complete picture of the life of Mahâvîrä, contains the story of his travels in the company of Gosâlä. Gosâlä finally argued with his two disciples over points of doctrine, and they separated. "After their separation, Gosâlä made his headquarters at Savatthi in the workshop of a potter-woman, Hâlâhalâ, and was surrounded by many disciples. At this time he was visited by six *dishâcharä* (missionaries of the six directions) in consulation with whom he codified the Âjîvika scriptures."[4] Gosâlä died in 484 B.C., a year before the Buddha. Mahâvîrä lived on until 467.

During his last years, Gosâlä observed a vow of silence (*vâcam pahâyä*) and lived in a state of trance. He practiced dance and drunkenness. A few moments before his death, one of his disciples asked him, "What is the nature of Hallâ [the principle of the world]?," to which he answered with the mysterious phrase, "The form of Hallâ is as the root of the bamboo. Play the *vînâ*, Friend." The *vînâ* is a stringed instrument made from a long bamboo. Music, the ephemeral harmony of sounds that evokes the harmony of the universe, comes forth from the bamboo. Its form and sonorous qualities are implied in its root, in its genetic formula, which like that of all other species is part of the plan devised by the Creator. Gosälä suggests here a subject for meditation on the tortuous route (*vakrä*) which links the world of appearance to the unfathomable origin of creation and thus evokes the fundamental problem of knowledge.

Hallâ is a mysterious term used by certain Shaiva sects to invoke the Supreme Being during ecstatic dances. It is difficult to avoid a comparison with *Allah*, the divine name adopted by the Muslims, together with the black stone of Mecca, which, according to the geography of the Purânä(s), is a Shivä Lingä situated in the ancient sacred site called Makhevshvarä (Lord of the Crocodile). Vestiges of an important colony of people from the Indus Valley have been discovered at Oman, on the Arabian Peninsula.

The teachings of Gosälä, which constitute the reformed doctrine of the Âjîvïkä(s), were gathered together in a work in ancient Dravidian called *Navakadir*. According to Nîläkêshi Tirattu, this work was translated into the Tamil language (modern Dravidian) under the name *Onbadukadir*, today lost, but of which the *Manimekhalaï*, a Tamil novel from the second century, preserves important extracts.

THE DOCTRINE OF GOSÂLÄ

We primarily know about the doctrine of Gosälä through the writings of his Jaïnä and Buddhist opponents. These texts must therefore be read with some caution. The essential element of the teaching of Gosälä is the doctrine of Niyati (determinism), which envisages a preestablished universal order by which the world evolves, at all levels, as do living beings, according to a plan contained in its seed. Progress and change are strictly determined by the "law of the process of development" (*parinâmä-kramä-niyamä*), which forms ruts or molds inside which individuals develop.

Gunaratnä, the commentator of the *Shaddarshana-Samucchayä* (condensed from the six systems) of Haribhadra, cites Gosâlä: "What makes thorns pointed and determines the innumerable forms of the animals and birds? All this originates from their nature (*svabhâvä*). Nothing is born of its own will or its actions. All beings develop according to the plan (*niyati*), to their nature (*svabhâvä*) and chance (*sangati*)."

Evil and suffering, attributed by others to the actions (*karmä*) of living beings, are, according to Gosâlä, determined by fate. "Just as a dropped spool of thread unwinds to its end, so will the madman, like the sage, follow his destiny and reach the end of suffering (*dukhântä*)."[5] "Human efforts are ineffective" (*N'atthi purisakare*) was the slogan of the Âjîvikä(s).

The doctrine of Gosâlä was divided into six parts: gains (*lâbham*), losses (*alâbham*), joy (*suham*), sorrow (*duham*), life (*jîviyam*), and death (*maranam*). It included the atomic theory of the Vaïsheshikä and the cosmology of the Sâmkhyä. We will see later with regard to the Vaïsheshikä, a summary of Gosâlä's materialist doctrine according to the *Manimekhalaï*. According to this doctrine, the number of souls, of "individual consciousnesses" in the world, is infinite.

A theory of cyclical liberation (*mandalä mokshä*) refers to the destruction of individual beings at the end of each cycle. The process of the development of life over 8,400,000 Mahâ Kalpä, the stages of evolution that represent the different species in creation, was later on interpreted as a series of reincarnations of the individual being.

All the Âjîvikä(s) used music and dance as ecstatic media and knew the secret of the technique of rescuscitating the dead by the transfer of their own vital energy, one of the Siddhi(s) (powers) obtained through Yogä. This power was called *paütta parihâra* by the disciples of Gosâlä.

Mahâvîrä

IT was in the Age of Doubt (*dvâparä*), with the development of agricultural, sedentary, and urban civilizations, that Jainism appeared, whose first prophet, Rishabhä, belongs to what we call prehistory. With him arose the notion of a moral, materialistic society with atheistic tendencies, which restrains individual liberty in the name of the common good and of the orderliness of the city, in opposition to Shaiva mysticism, which promotes the joy of living in communion with the divine work that the natural world represents.

It was Jainism that introduced vegetarianism and nonviolence, as well as the theories of transmigration and Karmä, into the Indian world. Jainism also advocated suicide by fasting.

The doctrine of Karmä, linked to that of transmigration, attributes differences between beings to their behavior in previous lives. Inequalities between living beings, and, in particular, between men, are due to an automatic retribution after death for actions committed in life. This theory tends to replace the responsibility of an impermanent "I," the transmitter of a genetic code that affects the species, with the evolution of a supposedly permanent "I." This has significant consequences, morally speaking, and also eliminates the notions of grace, of the whim of the gods, and of their freedom of action. It is basically an atheistic theory, contrary to the conceptions of the mystical Shaivism and ritualistic Vedism.

Mahâvîrä is considered to be the twenty-fourth and last prophet of Jainism. Pârshvä, the twenty-third prophet, lived three centuries earlier and had apparently liberalized the ascetic customs of the sect.

Mahâvîrä was, at a young age, outraged by the environment he lived in, which was essentially commercial. He became the disciple of the wandering monk Gosâlä, with whom he traveled, begging for his food, for over six years. Gosâlä did not practice or recommend the observance of chastity, as it was contrary to the principles of Shaivai Yogä. Antisexual moralism was introduced later in certain sects, such as the

Vîrä-Shaïvä. It was on these grounds and on that of Karmä that Mahâvîrä parted company with Gosâlä. "Mahâvîrä was almost certainly a twice-born Aryan who had been converted from the religious goal of sexual power to that of ethical celibacy. His reform of the religion of Pârshvä was precisely to impose the law of celibacy where earlier it had not been in effect. He was overall the most antisexual of the religious teachers of his time."[6] Mahâvîrä undertook to reform Jainism, which, since that time, has been divided into two sects: the Jaïnä "dressed in space" (*digambarä*), who are always naked, and the Jaïnä "dressed in white" (*shvetâmbarä*), which allows them to participate more easily in the social life of urban society.

Gautamä Buddhä

GAUTAMÄ belonged to a princely family of the Shâkyä clan of Nepal, who reigned over the rich city of Kapilavastu in the northeast of India. At the time, the families of the warlike aristocracy were in revolt against the authority of the Brahmans and the rigid ritualism of the Vedic religion. Immense sacrificial ceremonies, such as the sacrifice of the horse (*ashvämedhä*), through which the Brahmans imposed their power, ruined the states financially. Gautamä was at first attracted by the antisocial mysticism of Shaivism. For a time, he was also a disciple of Gosâlä and very close to Mahâvîrä, who was three years younger. For several years he practiced with them the austere and free life of a wandering monk. He eventually left them, however, and soon became their rival. He then undertook to reform Brahmanism on the basis of the fundamental atheistic concepts of the Jaïnä, in particular the prohibition of rites, nonviolence, reincarnation, the doctrine of Karmä, the negation of castes, the emphasis on moral values, and so forth.

His disciples called Gautamä the Buddha the Enlightened One. His doctrine, under the name of Buddhism, was to have a great influence, first in India, then in the Far East, South-east Asia, and Central Asia. Adopted by the aristrocratic and warlike class to which Gautamä belonged, Buddhism became a powerful instrument of colonialism and cultural expansion, justifying, under the pretext of religious propaganda, the most savage conquests, such as that of Kalingä, by the emperor Ashokä. Later, Christianity and Islam, other moralistic religions stemming from Arihat, were to serve in the same way as a pretext for a conquering imperialism. Buddhism was to play a major role on the Indian scene for more than six centuries.

The Religion of Nature and the Religion of the City

DURING the Dvâparä Yugä, the age of doubt and economic development, together with sedentary life and urban growth, new forms of religion emerged which sought to protect a conservative and puritanical social order. But it was not until the middle of the Kali Yugä that we witness the realization of the prediction of the Purânä(s). The teaching of Arihat, in the form of Buddhism and Jainism, as well as reformed Âjîvikism, attacks the old ecstatic, orgiastic, and mystical Shaiva tradition and, at the same time, the ritualistic and hierarchical structures of Vedic society.

The three heterodox sects that arose in this cultural climate, Buddhism, Jainism, and Âjîvikism, had much in common. All three alike rejected the sacrifical polytheism of the Aryans and the monistic theories of the Upanishadic mystics. The supernatural powers were relegated to an inferior or even negligible position. The three new religions represent a recognition of the rule of natural law in the universe, and the work of their founders may be compared with that of their approximate contemporaries, the natural philosophers of Ionia.[7]

The religious reforms in the middle of the Kali Yugä were to bring to the fore the conflict of mysticism and moralism, and of the religion of nature and love in contrast to that of the city and civic virtues.

In India, as elsewhere, we can, in the course of the Kali Yugä, follow the alternation, conflict, and sometimes even the complementary nature of the two tendencies. Beginning in the Dvâparä Yugä, in the limited spheres of what is called the intelligentsia of the cities, materialistic tendencies developed which were in conflict with Dionysian Shaivism, the religion of nature, hostile to the religion of towns, focused on man.

Jainism, an essentially moralistic religion, along with the forms of Hinduism derived from it, such as Buddhism and Vaishnavism, are still the religions of the city dwellers and commercial classes in India today.

The Kali Yugä in the World

A development similar to that in India took place in all the territories occupied by the Aryans. The legacy of vanquished Pelasgi and Cretans is at the root of the development of the Hellenic civilizations. The Indo-Sumerian sources of Hesiod and Homer have been proven.[8] Dionysian cults similar to Shaivism combine with the Aryan religion in Greek and Roman antiquity as they do in India.

The middle of the Kali Yugä is everywhere marked by great upheavals. Europe witnessed the spread of Celtic barbarians. It was the time of the destruction of Athens, Urarthu, and Babylon, and the Persian invasion of Egypt. In Italy, Rome developed at the expense of the Etruscans. We can observe, in different parts of the world, the simultaneous appearance of doctrines so similar to each other that they seem all to have the same source, which, according to the Indians, would be the Jainism of Pârshvä (817–778), the predecessor of Mahâvîrä. All these religions and philosophical movements are moralistic and puritanical in character, demonstrate a belief in transmigration, and also oppose polytheism and ecstatic practices.

Zoroaster (died 553 B.C.), a little before the occupation of the Indus by Cyrus (533 B.C.), had reformed the Persian religion (close to Vedic polytheism) and adopted the Jaïnä theory of transmigration and retribution for actions after death. Xenophanes, a Greek from Asia Minor, (c. 540 B.C.), opposed polytheism and anthropomorphism. In Greece, the naked Gymnopedists, who were Jaïnä missionaries, had a considerable influence. Pythagoras taught transmigration and set up a brotherhood in the same year that Gautamä became a monk (530 B.C.). He drew inspiration from the theories of the Sâmkhyä, while the School of Cynics is, in all likelihood, an echo of the teachings of the Âjîvikä(s).

In China, the fifth century is the age of the birth of Taoism (Lao-tse, 604–531 B.C.) and Confucianism (Confucius, 551–479 B.C.), whose ideas are very close to some of the Indian concepts. The great system of Tao, which tries to follow the natural movement of the universe, originally appears to be based on a poetic version of the concepts of the Sâmkhyä and of Yogä. The words *Yin* and *Yang* correspond to *Yoni* and *Lingä*. Breathing practices and the search for the sun and moon in the body recall Idâ and Pingalâ, the lunar and solar paths of breath in Yogä. The sexual practices (withholding the spermatic essence and trying to absorb the feminine essence) are identical to those of Yogä. The notion of immortality conceived as transmutation, in which "astride a white cloud the Sage or Yellow Emperor arrives at the region of the gods," is analogous to that of Shaivism. We again find the seven sages, the refusal of asceticism, the practices aiming at a long life (Ayurvedä, the Indian science of longevity).

Confucius, who was born ten years after Gosâlä, in 551 B.C., and died five years after him, in 479 B.C., was an agnostic who was against Taoism and sought to resolve all difficulties in the world through morality. He was, according to Max Weber, "a rationalist absolutely free of the metaphysical and of any religious tradition who . . . built up a morality based on the nature of man and the needs of society." His meeting with Lao-tse would have been in 517 B.C. It is apparently a Jaïnä influence that caused the appearance of the notion of transmigration in later Taoism.

With the development of urban, industrial, and capitalist societies, the doctrines of the kind attributed to Arihat—moralistic, materialistic, and atheistic—filtered through into all subsequent religions, including modernized forms of Hinduism and Shaivism. We find their influence in Zoroastrianism, Confucianism, Judaism, Christianity, Islam, and even Marxism, the last of the religions of the Kali Yugä.

The Shaiva Revival

THE period that corresponds to the beginning of the Christian era was everywhere a time when the official religions were being challenged. In India, Buddhism, which had considerably weakened the Vedic tradition, was on the decline, yet the authority of the Brahmans was not restored. Mendicant ascetics, despised and ignored by the ruling classes, had also undergone attacks from Buddhism, and it is only in the age of the decline of Buddhism, that is, at the beginning of our era, that we see the ancient pre-Aryan culture and its religion, Shaivism, reappear gloriously, scarcely affected by centuries of clandestine existence. The moment seemed favorable to the representatives of the ancient tradition to openly reestablish its precepts and react against all the foreign cults, including Vedism, and the new religions, Buddhism and Jainism.

Lakulishä

IT was an Âjîvikä called Lakulishä, one of those wandering monks who maintained the heritage of the ancient knowledge in an occult tradition, who judged the moment opportune to reveal it, causing a great revolution in society. This corresponds to the greatest period in Indian civilization, which was to last for more than a millennium. Lakulishä (the name means the "Club-bearing Lord") restored an extraordinary impetus to Shaivism, reestablished the pre-Aryan culture, and united, under the name of the Pâshupatä(s) (followers of Pâshupati, Lord of the Animals), the different sects that had survived in semisecrecy for centuries.

According to tradition, Lakulishä probably lived a little before and at the beginning of our era. He would be contemporary with John the Baptist. He is considered by his disciples to be the last of the twenty-eight manifestations of Shivä mentioned in the Purâna. The *Kurmä Purânä* (chap. 53), the *Vâyu Purânä* (chap. 23), and the *Lingä Purânä* (chap. 24) predicted that the Great God (Maheshvarä) would appear in the form of a wandering monk called Lakulin or Nakulishä, and that he would have four disciples named Kushikä, Gargä, Miträ, and Kanrushyä, who would reestablish the cult of Pâshupati and would therefore be called Pâshupatä(s). Lakulishä would have had a predecessor called Ulûkä. After teaching Maheshvarä Yogä, Lakulishä would return to the paradise of Rudrä (Shivä).

Lakulishä descended from a dynasty of non-Aryan priests called Jangamä. He belonged to the Kâlâmukha (Black Face) sect. He embarked on a work that conflicted with that of Gosâlä, reestablished the strictest conventions of the ancient religion, and violently opposed Vedism, Jaïnism, and most particularly Buddhism. Lakulishä reinstituted sacrifices, including human sacrifices, and restored respect for the practices of Hathä Yogä and Tantrism and the cosmological theories of the ancient Sâmkhyä.

According to M. R. Sakhare (*The History and Philosophy of Lingayat Religion*), the influence of Lakulishä was immense and spread like wildfire, first in the north and then in the south of India. The Shaiva revival, supported by the Bhârashivä and Vakatakä dynasties in central and northern India,

gradually spread in the south under the impetus of Shaiva
mystics, the Nâyanâr, who all belonged to the artisan classes.
During the first eleven centuries of the Christian era, Shaivism thrived and Buddhism was uprooted. This Shaivai and
Tantric revival coincides with one of the most important
periods of Indian civilization on a mystic, philosophical, artistic, and literary plan, which was to last until the Muslim
invasions of the twelfth century.

In the time of Lakulishä, the Akhâdâ(s) (regiments), which
were religious military orders, reassumed a great importance.
The order of the Dashanâmi Nâgä, which still exists, is the
oldest. Their organization had much in common with that of
Mithraism, which developed at the same time among the
soldiers of the Roman Empire, and which includes the cult
of the bull, sacrifices, Dionysian initiations, and communal
sacred meals.

In the fourth century, Chandrä Guptä, an adventurer of
Scythian origin, who had married a princess of the ancient
Shaiva tribe of the Lichavi, assassinated the last monarch of
Pataliputra and ruled from A.D. 319 to 330. It is from this
period on that representations of Lakulishä are to be found
in India. "These portray him as a naked yogin with a staff
(*lakula*) in his left hand and a citron (*matu-lingä*) in his right,
with his penis erect, and either standing or seated in the
lotus posture. At about the beginning of the eleventh century,
the Lakulishä cult seems to have shifted its activities to southern India.[9] In the north, the Kushänä emperors replaced the
pictures of Hercules on their coins with ones of Shivä, and
of Heracles with images of Lakulishä.

In A.D. 78 commences the Shakä (Scythian) era, which
is still in progress in India. The Vikrama era had begun in
58 B.C.

Mahâyanä

IN the second century, the Kushänä emperor Kanishakä embarked on a reform of Buddhism based on the ideas of Tantric

Shaivism. The canons of this new Buddhism, which is a disguised Shaivism and is called Mahâyanä (Great Vehicle), were defined in a great synod held in Kashmir. This synthesis of Buddhism and Shaivism was primarily the work of Ashvaghoshä, a Hindu converted to Buddhism. Mahâyana spread mainly in Tibet, where we find numerous practices of the Kâpâlikä(s) (skull-bearers) Shaivas, who also used a human skull to hold their food.

NOTES

1. A. L. Basham, *History and Doctrines of the Ajivikas*, pp. 131, 134.
2. These dates, which are approximations, are deduced from data given in the *Bhagavatî Sutra*. See Basham, *History and Doctrines of the Ajivikas*, pp. 74–78.
3. Basham, p. 285.
4. Ibid., p. 51.
5. *Dîghä Nikâyä* 1.53 (Buddhist text in Pali).
6. McEvilley, *An Archeology of Yoga*, I, p. 57.
7. Basham, *History and Doctrines of the Ajivikas*, p. 6.
8. J. Van Duk, *Introduction to the Lugal-ud*.
9. D. L. Lorenzen, *The Kapalikas and Kalamukhas*, p. 108.

3

Rediscovered Tradition

Texts

MANY OF THE ELEMENTS OF THE ANCIENT PRE-ARYAN culture that only survived in oral tradition or in Dravidian texts, now lost, were recovered, reconstructed, transcribed, and translated into various popular languages, but particularly into Sanskrit, which had become the universal language of the culture. It was then that numerous historical, philosophical, and scientific works appeared, mingled with legends, popular beliefs, and myths. Some versions of the Purânä(s) in the Tamil language are older than the Sanskrit versions.

Using this restored material as a point of departure, Shaiva monks and some traditional scholars have been able to reconstruct part of what survived of the ancient pre-Aryan heritage, rediscovering the bases of a wisdom, a way of living, and a path of knowledge originating in a golden age of humanity that had been for a long time safeguarded in an occult tradition.

This return to ancient knowledge and wisdom, advocated by Lakulishä, is considered by followers of Shaivism to be the last effort to check the evolution of a humanity racing toward destruc-

tion. Therefore, it was from the beginning of our era onward that the fundamental texts of pre-Aryan philosophical and religious tradition were reconstituted and translated into a fairly crude Sanskrit, with the aim of establishing a set of sacred texts to set up officially against the Vedä(s), which had themselves been recently transcribed.

The most important of these texts are called the Âgamä(s) (traditions) and Tanträ(s) (rules and rites). To these must be added the Purânä(s) (ancient chronicles), which deal with mythology and history, and philosophical and technical works about cosmology (Sâmkhyä), Yogä, linguistics (Vyâkaranä), astronomy (Jyotishä), medicine (Ayurvedä), mathematics (Ganitä), and so on—a vast literature, which, despite having been transcribed in a relatively recent era, nevertheless has sources in distant antiquity. Their rediscovery provoked a phenomenal revival of cultural, philosophical, religious, and artistic activity.

Almost all of what has come down to us of the religious and philosophical thought of India, including the texts and commentaries of the Vedä(s), Brahmä Sûträ(s), and Upani-shad(s), as well as those of Buddhism and Jaïnism, was only transcribed during the great age of liberalism and civilization which characterize the Shaiva revival.

The Hindu religion, as it is practiced today, is tantric in character, based almost exclusively on the Âgamä(s). Virtually nothing remains of the Vedic religion. The same applies to the Tibetan religion, itself also entirely tantric.[1] Hindu philosophy is wrongly considered to be of Vedic origin. Through contrivances of exegesis, attempts were made to link concepts originating from an older and more developed culture to Vedic texts.

If we wish to understand Indian thought, we must return to its sources, that is, to the great civilization that preceded the arrival of the Aryans, which has continued to the present time and of which the Shaiva religion, the cosmological theory called Sâmkhyä, the practices of Yogä, as well as the bases of what we consider to be the Hindu philosophy, are part.

Although the Âgamä and the Purânä texts that have come down to us are relatively late writings, we find their mark in all the philosophical and religious conceptions of the Aryans from the *Atharvä Vedä* onward. The disdain shown toward these texts by most of the modern Orientalists, who wanted to relate everything back to the Vedä(s) (as, moreover, the Western world does to the Greeks), has led them to make monumental errors in dating and describing the evolution of religious and philosophical concepts. Many passages of the best-known texts of philosophical and religious brahmanic literature written in the Sanskrit language are derived from the Âgamä(s). This is the case with, for example, the *Bhagavat Gîtâ*, of which over half the verses are borrowed from the *Parameshvarä Âgamä* and three of which passages are quotations from the *Shvetâshvatarä Upanishad*, which is itself based on the Âgamä(s).[2]

Sakhare also points out that already during the age of Vedic domination, five authors, considered to be Shaiva saints, called Arrivars, had compiled (in all likelihood in ancient Dravidian script) some elements of the pre-Aryan tradition in twenty-eight works, of which the subsequent Âgamä(s) are translations into fairly coarse Sanskrit. The four Brahmans mentioned in the *Chhândogyä Upanishad* turn to one of these Arrivars for teachings.

The Âgamä(s), taken together, constitute an independent literature that has no relation to the Vedä(s). The originals, in ancient Dravidian, are lost today. Some elements of doctrine and vocabulary have been inserted into subsequent versions to establish apparent similarities with the Vedic religion. In any case, the differences between the Vedä(s) and Âgamä(s) were recognized from then on, since the ritual practices of the Âgamä(s) are in conflict with Vedic rites, although, in the course of the centuries, a certain amalgamation has been achieved.[3]

In the everyday practice of current Hinduism, the Brahmans use the Vedic rite or the Tantric rite, established in the Âgamä(s), depending on the circumstances.

[33]

There are twenty-eight Shaiva Âgamä(s) and numerous secondary Âgamä(s) (Upâgamä). Thus, the *Kamikâgama* is followed by three Upâgamä(s) called *Uttarä*, *Bhairavottarä*, and *Narashimhä*. The *Yogâgamä* is supplemented by five Upâgamä(s), called *Vinashirottarä*, *Târaka*, *Sâmkhyä*, *Shânti*, and *Âtmayogä*.

The Âgamä(s) (traditions) and the Tanträ(s) (rules and rites) are part of a single system. In general, the texts that give preeminence to the cult of Shivä are called Âgamä(s) (*Kâmikâgama*, *Sukshmâgamä*, etc.), and those dealing with the cult of the goddess, Shaktism, are called Tanträ(s) (*Shakti Tanträ*, *Mahânirvâna Tanträ*, etc.). Those who venerate the conscious principle of the world in a masculine form are Shaivas. Those who venerate the divine power in a feminine form are Shaktä(s).[4]

The Tanträ(s) are classed in four groups: Shaïvä, Pâshupatä, Saumyä, and Lagudä, corresponding to four Shaiva sects called Shaïvä, Pâshupatä, Kâpâlikä, and Kâlâmukhä.

Already the *Mahâbhâratä*, which recounts the struggles that brought the Aryan invaders into conflict with the native populations of the second millennium, but which was only written down in its present form at the time of the Shaiva revival, lists the great philosophical and religious traditions of India in the age of its compilation. These are the Sâmkhyä, Yogä, Pâñcharâträ, Vedä, and Pâshupatä. We can see that the Vedic tradition does not occupy a predominant position: the other traditions are connected with Shaivism. This enumeration does not include sects considered to be atheistic, such as the Materialism of Chârvâkä and Jaïnism. The numerous sects stemming from Shaivism are, in principle, included among the Pâshupatä.

Few texts in ancient Dravidian languages still exist. The most important are the works of a sort of club of Tamil poets called the Sangam. These texts are neither philosophical nor religious but contain allusions to Shaiva mythology. The literature of the Sangam is divided into two periods: Puram (ancient) and Aham (more recent). In the Puram, we find references to the destruction of the three cities, the blue neck of Shivä, his third eye, and the crescent of the moon adorning the god's brow.

Later, four of the Nâyanâr (Shaiva saints) of the Middle Ages—Tirumular (c. 400–600), Sambandar, Appar (c. 650), and Sundarar (c. 800)—left works in the Tamil language, which are accepted as authoritative, on Shaivism, its principles and practices. The most important is the *Tirumandiram* of Tirumular, which is the foundation on which the philosophical system called Shaïvä-Siddhantä developed.[5]

The antiquity of the reconstructed texts of the Purânä(s), Tanträ(s), and Âgamä(s) has been disputed by the advocates of the Aryan origins of the civilization. However, the recent discoveries of Sumerian or Cretan parallels confirm their authenticity. Recent works have even made possible the identification of plans of Sumerian temples with those, described in the Âgamä(s), which serve as a basis for the construction of Shaiva temples.[6] A careful study of the texts of the Purânä(s) reveals important elements. From it we discover that at the time certain events occurred, the sages who meditated by the Ganges, at sunrise, saw the daystar substituted for Sirius in the constellation of the Hunter (Mrigavâchä) about 5500 B.C., or Orion in the constellation of the Antelope (Mrigä) (c. 4500), and then the Twins (between 4500 and 3400), or Aldebran (Rohini) in the constellation of the Bull (c. 4000). In other cases, it was the Pleiades (Krittikä) (c. 2500)[7]—following the precession of the equinoxes, a cycle of 26,000 years. These observations give us a clue that enables us to date the development of the great protohistoric civilization of India.

Hindu Decadence

THE Shaiva euphoria provoked by Lakulishä was to last for almost a millennium; then its expansion was crushed. India was once again in a period of conflict caused by invasions, first by the Huns, then of Islamized Arabs.

The Aryan Brahmans, who for centuries had represented the dominant intellectual class, tried gradually to take over, to their advantage, the philosophical and scientific conceptions inherited from Shaivism, while at the same time conflicting with them on religious grounds. With skillful exegesis, they tried to connect its ideas to a would-be Vedic tradition. As a consequence, from the sixth century onward, we see famous Brahmans present a modified version of the Sâmkhyä, the Vaisheshikä, and other philosophical systems inherited from Shaivism. Continuing the Jaïno-Buddhist moralistic and antiritualistic line, they were to create a philosophical and religious movement with monistic tendencies, which claimed to be connected to the original Vedism, but was profoundly influenced by Buddhism and Islam. Shankarâchâryä, Râmânuja, and Mâdhavä were to reinterpret the ancient texts. It is to them that we owe the great commentaries on the Vedä(s), Brähmanä(s) and Upanishad(s). However, they fought among themselves. Mâdhavä, the latest of this line of new philosophers, said of Sankarâchâryä that he was "a deceitful demon who had perverted the teaching of the *Brahmä Sûträ* to lead souls astray."

In parallel with what happened in the West with Mithraism or the teaching of Simon the Magician, the disciple of John the Baptist and the rival of Jesus, the Aryan scholars tried to obliterate the traces of the teaching of Lakulishä and to minimize the significance of the recovered texts. In this, they have been followed by modern Indologists, whether Indian or foreign.

The majority of Âgamä and Tanträ texts have still not been published, and only fragments have been translated. This vast amount of knowledge, which reflects the oldest traditions of India, remains systematically ignored. It is often through the writings of his opponents that we have some elementary knowledge about the teachings of Lakulishä.

From the age of Shankarâchâryä onward, a new religion, called Vaishnavism, developed in India, modeled principally on Jaïnism and linked to the cult of Vishnu. This devotional, sentimental, and puritanical religion suited an age troubled by the collapsing values brought about by Islamic invasions. "In many parts of India the Vaisnavas replaced the Jains in popularity and influence and in the process absorbed many Jain beliefs and practices, including hostility to the excesses of Tantric Shaivism."[8] What is today accepted to be the basic essentials of the philosophical, religious and moral ideas of India, in particular the Vedantä, and the theory of Karmä and reincarnation, therefore stems from a philosophical trend that, in the West, corresponds to the period following the fall of the Roman Empire and is situated between the eighth and twelfth centuries, inspired by Jaïnism, Buddhism, then Islamic and Christian influences. This new Hinduism has only a very theoretical link with the Vedism to which it claims to be related. Vaishnavism was subsequently, in the British period, profoundly influenced by Christianity, Protestantism in particular. New reformist movements attempting to present Hinduism in a form suited to Western prejudices, such as the Brahmosamaj of Râjâ Ram Mohan Roy and Devendranath Tagore (father of the poet), the Aryasamaj of Dayânandä Saravati, as well as doctrines expounded by Vivekânandä, Aurobindo, Tilak, and others, by claiming to return to the purity of a mythical Vedism, has merely succeeded in carrying on the negativist concepts of Jaïno-Buddhism, whose popular form was from then on linked to Vaishnavism, which had become the religion of the merchant class and of the new political power, Gandhi in particular. It is these ideas that so-called gurus teach today in the name of Hinduism, in ashrams where the tradition of Arihat is perpetuated.

The most obvious example of Jain influence on later Vaisnava attitudes is found in the philosophy of M. K. Gandhi. Although some of Gandhiji's ideas were inspired in part by European precedents, others—such as his faith in Ahimsa, asceticism, cleanliness and vegetarianism—owe more to his Gujarati Vaisnava background. From quite early times, Gujarat has been a center of Jain influence, and all these beliefs derive their original impetus more from Jainism than Hinduism.[9]

In India, as elsewhere, we can see social and economic preoccupations and puritanism take the place, in official religion, of the pursuit of communication with celestial powers through rites and mystical experience. A morality of toil, abstinence, productiveness, and civic conformity tends to become a substitute for a morality of love, ecstasy, happiness, and freedom.

A predominance of moralistic ideas marks the decline of a humanity given over to materialism and leads to despair, isolation, poverty, and drugs, for those who do not have the strength to stand up against it. Throughout the history of the Kali Yuga, we witness this conflict between mystical, erotic, intense, creative, orgiastic, ecological Dionysianism, protector of nature and the animals, and urban, exploitative, restrictive, puritanical moralism. The great ages of artistic creativity and mystical exaltation are related to the predominance of Shaiva or Dionysian tendencies. Economic progress, social order, detrimental power of states and tyrants are Vai<u>sh</u>_n_ava-Apollonian in character.

The West

AT the same time that Lakulishä caused the Shaiva revival, we see similar movements born in many other parts of the globe. In the West, Mithraism developed, and in the Middle East, Simon the Magician and Isha (Jesus) appeared, whose unconventional and liberating message approached that of Shaivism. Jesus opposed the mercenary mentality and the caste of Pharisee priests, and chased the merchants from the temple. He despised material possessions. He rejected puritanism and defended the prostitute and the adulteress. He never condemned physical love and was probably not unaware of its Platonic form (see Mark 15:51). He surrounded himself with the common people. He evoked, in the Last Supper, the rites of sacrifice and the consumption of the victim. His transfiguration and the transubstantiation of the Virgin are Shaiva concepts. He was born in a cowshed, like Gosâlä, near the ox, the sacred animal, and the ass, the impure animal. We know little of his teaching, which, soon after his disappearance, was distorted by the anti-Christ, Paul of Tarsus, who was to misrepresent his message, creating the exact opposite of it, and to give birth to a puritanical and tyrannical state religion, conflicting with the Gnostics of earliest times, in order to gradually seize political power. The Dionysian heritage was for a long time maintained in esoteric Christian sects as well as in Judaism and Islam in the occult traditions of Kabbala and Sufism, but has gradually deteriorated until it is no more than an intellectual game.

India Today

VIEWED from the outside, at the top of the social and cultural hierarchy of present-day India, we find the Aryan Brahmans, some of them great scholars, but many of them civil servants or political figures, and some artists. Then come the princely families and warriors serving in the army and in various occupations, except for craft and commerce. Real power belongs to the powerful caste of merchants, manufacturers, and shopkeepers, which constitutes the middle class of modern India. Two intermediate classes, foreign in origin, consider themselves to be superior to the rest of the population: these are the Muslims on the one hand and Europeans and Christians on the other. The pre-Aryans, who constitute the vast majority of the population, are considered by these various invaders as "natives" (in the colonialist sense of the word), good as a rule for manual, craft, or industrial work and for farm labor. In reality, they form a parallel civilization, albeit unofficial, in which the dynasties of priests, princes, and merchants are maintained. Princes often falsified their genealogy in order to claim Aryan origins, but they do not marry outside their clan. Guilds of architects, sculptors, painters, and musicians are part of the artisan castes. It is from among these allegedly inferior groups that most of the initiates to the monastic orders, who hand down the occult tradition of the ancient knowledge, are recruited. Sometimes they absorb members of other origins.

This world of ascetics, the Sadhu, the Sannyâsî, actually plays a major but secret role in contemporary Hinduism, where—although more often than not, caste Hindus feign ignorance of it—the tradition of Shaivism and Tantrism occupies a much more important place than the Vedic tradition in the religious practices of Indians of all castes.

NOTES

1. See M. R. Sakhare, *History and Philosophy of Lingayat Religion*, p. 192.
2. For these similarities, see ibid., pp. 159–165.
3. Ibid., p. 172.
4. Ibid., pp. 172, 192, 231.
5. Ibid., pp. 136–138.
6. See Karl-Heinz Golzio, *Der Tempel in alten Mesopotamien und seine Parallelen in Indien*, Brill, Leiden, 1983.
7. See Stella Kramrish, *The Presence of Shiva*, p. 43.
8. Lorenzen, *The Kâpâlikäs and Kâlâmukhäs*, p. 39.
9. Ibid., p. 39 n.

PART TWO

SHAIVA PHILOSOPHY

﷽

1

The Ways of Knowledge

Approaches (Darshanä)

DURING THE AGE OF THE SHAIVA REVIVAL, WHICH COR-
responds to the beginning of the Christian era, the age in
which the historical and religious texts of Shaivism were
published, we see the reappearance of philosophical, cosmological, and scientific concepts, the legacy, long kept a
secret, of the learning of the ancient world.

Apart from technical treatises, astronomy, mathematics,
medicine, architecture, and so forth, philosophical and cosmological thought is grouped into six major systems called
the Points of View or Approaches (Darshanä[s]).

It is thanks to the contrasts and contradictions resulting
from a diversity of approaches that we can evaluate and crit-
icize the value of the information given by the senses. The
main approaches by which we can attempt to understand the
nature of the world are arranged in pairs, each pair consisting
of an experimental method and a method of intellectual ra-
tionalization. The first two methods concern the impermanent world (*ksharä*), that is, the visible world: these are
Vaïsheshikä (study of the specific), or scientific observation,
and its counterpart, reasoning, or Nyâyä (logic). Then comes

Sâmkhyä (cosmology) and Yogä (introspection), whose object is the study of the permanent aspects (*akshara*) of the world, the universal laws that govern the cosmic world and the world of life. Sâmkhyä concerns the macrocosm, nature, and the universe, and Yogä the microcosm, the internal world of the living being.

These two methods are strictly coordinated and interdependent. They are the instruments of higher knowledge by which man is distinguished from other living beings. Yogä is the exploration of ourselves, this special body, this abode, in which our consciousness resides. Yogä seeks to analyze the structures of our interior universe, to study and develop the powers latent in it, and eventually to go beyond the barriers of the senses, the limitations of relative time and space that imprison us. The Sâmkhyä enables us to transpose the elements of Yogä to the universal plane and to establish correspondences between the macrocosm and the microcosm, between Universal Man (*purushä*) and individual man (*jivä*).

The last two Darshanä(s) are called Mîmânsâ (profound intuition). Their object is the hierarchy of creation, the relationships between the different levels of beings, between men, spirits, and gods. Every religious approach, whether ritual or mystic, is part of Mîmânsâ. Two sorts of Mîmânsâ are distinguished: the first, called Pûrvä Mîmânsâ (preliminary intuition), is, in a certain way, experimental. It concerns the efficacy of rites and the technical means, including invocation and prayer, which allow us to establish a contact with the celestial world and to influence it. We can judge their effectiveness according to the results obtained.

The second Mîmânsâ is called Uttarä Mîmânsâ (higher intuition). It includes cosmogony, theology, the study of the celestial hierarchies, and the description of the invisible world of spirits and gods. Included in the Mîmânsâ are the intuition of mystics, the supranormal perception of mediums, and all the relations between man and what is, to him, the supernatural.

By coordination of the basic ideas of the different approaches, or Darshanä(s), observations of the visible world linked with the extrasensory perceptions gained through Yogä, it has been possible to establish a general theory regarding the world and man, as well as the history of the universe and its destiny. The importance of the Darshanä(s) rests in their contrasts. It is because of their divergences, contrasts, and incompatibilities that we have some idea of the nature of the world. The transcendent or divine reality of the world is defined as "that in which opposites coexist."

The pre-Aryan theory of the Darshanä(s), whose concepts we can see showing through in all stages of Indian civilization, was not pieced together again in the Sanskrit language until after the decline of Buddhism and Vedism, at the time of the Shaiva revival. We have a first summary of it in Dravidian language (ancient Tamil) in the *Manimekhalaï*, a novel of the fourth century which expounds both the materialistic and atheistic theory, Lokâyatä, attributed to the mythical sage, Brihaspati, and his commentator, Chârvâkä, as well as the philosophical theories of Jaïnism and Buddhism. In this text Buddhism is considered to be derived from Jaïnism.

For the *Manimekhalaï* (book 27) "the six systems of philosophy are Lokâyatä (materialism) taught by Brihaspati; Buddha or Buddhism originating from Jaïnism (Jinä); Sâmkhyä (cosmology) codified by Kapilä; Nyâyä (logic) taught by Akshapâdä (alias Gautamä—not the Gautamä who founded Buddhism); Vaïsheshikä (physics) codified by Kanadä; and Mîmânsâ (metaphysics) taught by Jaimini. These people all lived before the writing of Sanskrit.

⊛⊛⊛⊛

2

Vaïsheshikä and Nyâyä

Science and Logic

THE CONCEPTS OF VAÏSHESHIKÄ AND NYÂYÄ WERE
handed down by monastic sects, in particular the Pâshupatä
and the Kâlâmukhä, who have sometimes given them a religious flavor. The materialistic theory of Vaïsheshikä was
considered as a sort of religion. Superstition of scientific reality and the near deification of science is not just a present-
day phenomenon.

According to Guṇaratnä, the author of a commentary on
the *Shaddarshana Samucchayä* (the six systems of philosophy)
of Haribhadrä, Vaïsheshikä and Nyâyä are part of the philosophy of Shaivism. Bhâsarvajñä, the author of the *Nyâyä
Sârä*, also wrote the *Gaṇä-Kârikâ*, a work that explains the
doctrine of the sect of Pâhupatä. The followers of Nyâyä
revere eighteen incarnations of Shivä, the last being Lakulishä.

Philosophers of the medieval period, such as Shankarâchâryä, acknowledge the Shaiva origin of the Darshanä(s).
When he discusses the doctrine called Ishvarä-Kartṛi-Vâda,
"the power of action of the divine principle," which sees the

divine person (Ishvarä) as the operative cause of the world, Shankarâchâryä attributes the teachings of Vaïsheshikä and Nyâyä to the Mâheshvarä(s), the sectarians of Shivä.

The Experimental Method (Vaïsheshikä)

VAÏSHESHIKÄ is the study of the impermanent (ksharä), the visible or apparent world (vyaktä). The word Vaïsheshikä means "study of particulars," that is, the observation of the perceptible world. With the aid of the methods of logic (Nyâyä), the Vaïsheshikä constitutes what can be called the scientific approach, which uses reasoning, deduction, hypothesis, and experimentation to analyze the information provided by the senses, whose perceptions are limited to the visible or impermanent world, also called the "world of movement" (jagat) since it is formed only of energy through which it manifests itself in the form of gravitation and pulsations.

Using observation as a starting point, by analyzing the data provided by our senses and noting the points common to various forms of observation, we can deduce some general principles. The scientific method calls for the development of the means of observation, the instruments that increase the power of the senses. Telescopes, microscopes, and radars today allow us to push our observations even further. Yet these remain limited by the very nature of the senses. We do not observe reality in itself but reality in relation to the limits nature imposes on us.

However, the development of psychic powers, which are part of physical man but are not usually developed, allow the addition of important elements of observation. These powers, developed by the techniques of Yogä, such as perception beyond the limits of dimension and of relative time, can eventually be used. They belong to the physical world and are in no way occult.

It is impossible to prove the existence of a deity by observation of the visible world. For this reason, all true science can be nothing but atheistic. All belief is, by its very nature, the opposite of science. One believes or one knows. The scholar who mixes his religious or moral ideas with his scientific work betrays both science and religion.

Related to Vaïshes̲h̲ikä is the very important school of atheistic and materialistic philosophers called Lokâyatä, whose best-known advocate was Chârvâkä, almost a millennium before our era. For Chârvâkä, science can acknowledge no evidence other than Pratyaks̲h̲ä (that which is before the eyes). As regards the materialism of Chârvâkä, only matter is eternal; thought and conscience appear as fermentations of matter. There are no gods, nor is there life after death. Materialist theory (*bhûtä-vâdi*) was part of the doctrine of the Âjîvikä(s), as taught by Makkhali Gosâlä, the master of Mahâvîrä and Buddhä. A summary of it is found in the *Man̲imekhalaï*.

Mixing yeast, sugar, and other substances results in fermentation, in the same way consciousness and the feelings are born of combinations of elements. When they disintegrate, consciousness disappears, as resonance disappears when the drum is dismantled. The Tattvä(s) (constituents of the world) are the same as those of the Lokâyatä(s) (materialists), for whom the only means of proof is Pratyaks̲h̲ä (visual evidence). What exists in the present and we enjoy in life is the only reality. There is no other life in which we can reap rewards for our actions. The *Onbadukadir*, the ancient Tamil work which summarizes the teachings of Gosâlä, deals with five subjects, which are life and the four elements, earth, water, fire, and air, which are made up of indivisible atoms. When they gather, these are perceptible; when they separate, they are invisible. It is agglomerates of these atoms that form a mountain, a tree, a living body. When they disaggregate, the atoms that make them up disperse. That which perceives these phenomena is called life . . . atoms are permanent, have no beginning, and are indestructible. They take on various appearances, depending on the circumstances. No new type of atom appears or is transformed into something else. Atoms are indivisible and do not evolve. They combine into conglomerations, to separate in the end, each keeping its own identity. They can assemble in such density that they become hard as diamonds, or take the light form of bamboo. When they spread over the earth, like moonlight, they take the form of different elements according to their relative density. They are therefore called by different names. They form the seed of the shoot which develops. They form the solid earth, the fluid water, the fire that burns, or the moving air. An atom can be seen only by those who possess the higher eye of knowledge. Others cannot see it. When combined to form the elements (*bhûtä*), they can be seen. In the same way, a single hair cannot be distinguished in the shadow of twilight, but a lock of hair is easily seen.

The combinations of atoms can be black, dark blue, green, red, gold, or white. These are the six forms that the combinations of atoms take, in order of superiority. Only combinations of pure white atoms can break up and attain freedom (*vîdu = mukti*). This represents the path of destiny. Those who wish to achieve the end of suffering must reach this stage . . . such is the teaching of Markali (Gosâlä). [*Manimekhalaï*, book 27]

The theory of Vaïsheshikä was explained in Sanskrit before Lakulishä, by Ulûkä, nicknamed Kanâdä (the atom eater). The texts of the Suträ(s) of Kanâdä which have come down to us were reworked in order to introduce certain conceptions of Brahmanism.

In the theory expounded by Kanâdä, the principle of the universe is the energy called Adrishtä (the invisible). The world is formed of nine substances, which are space, time, consciousness (or the soul), thought (*manas*), and the principles of the five elements, of which four (earth, water, air, and fire) are made up of atoms.

The two great moralistic and atheistic religions, Jaïnism and the original Buddhism, have been very influenced by Vaïsheshikä, the materialism of Gosâlä and Chârvâkä, and the philosophers of this school.

Logic (*Nyâyä*)

THE intellectual method that corresponds to Vaïsheshikä is logic (Nyâyä), by which, with the aid of analogies and deductions, the observed information can be coordinated in order to arrive at definite conclusions.

Nyâyä analyzes forms of reasoning and means of proof. According to the theory expounded by Gautamä, the author of the main treatise on Nyâyä, the elements of logical reasoning include a proposition (*pratijñâ*), the investigation of a cause (*hetu*), an example (*udâharanä*), a relationship (*upanayä*), and precedents (*nigamä*).

The means of proof (*pramânä*) envisaged by Nyâyä are:

Pratyakshä, direct evidence

Anumânä, deductive inference

Upamânä, similarity, analogy

Shabdä, the word, the authority of predecessors

Science only makes progress through the accumulation of knowledge over the course of generations.

The Sâmkhyä accepts as means of proof only Pratyakshä, Anumânä, and Shabdä, but adds Anubhava, experience. The Mîmânsâ also accepts Anupalabdhi, the absence of proof to the contrary, and Arthâpatti, assumption. Gautamä explains the forms of reasoning by means of illustrations that are well known, such as the real effects of an unreal cause, for example, the case of the snake and the rope: reacting to the sight of a snake, I break my leg (real effect); but the snake was only a rope (nonexistent cause). According to the *Manimekhalaï*: "The means of proof (*prâmanä*) are ten in number, but there also exist eight "semblances of proof" (*prâmanä abhâsä*), of which one must beware. The six basic means of proof are as follows.

1. Kâtchi,[1] direct experience (Skt. *pratyakshä*, in front of the eyes), is of five kinds, depending on the pleasant or painful experiences of the five sensory organs. When these come into contact with the vital energies (*uyir*; Skt. *prânä*) that serve as a means of communication (*vâyil*), they are conveyed to the mental faculties (*manas*), which, in a constant state of activity, become clearly aware of them, without any omissions, or any error or doubt concerning the place, form, type, quality, or effects.

2. Karudal, inference (Skt. Anumânä). Inference allows knowledge of that which is not directly perceived, but which can be deduced from what is visible. It has three forms:

   a. Podu (Skt. *sâmânyä*), deduction. When two things are by their nature dependent on each other, the reality of one is deduced from the perception of the other, as in the situation where we conclude that there is an elephant in the forest when we hear a sound that resembles trumpeting.

   b. Eccham (Skt. *sheshavat*) is the relationship of effect to cause. We deduce from seeing streams pouring into rivers that it has rained.

   c. Mudal (Skt. *purvavat*) is the relationship of cause to effect. At the sight of clouds, we predict rain.

3. Upamâ is the comparison between things with similar qualities: for example, fast as the wind.

4. Âgamä, teachings of the ancients. It is on such a basis that we assume that hell and heaven exist.

5. Arthâpatti, indirect indication. When we speak of a village situated on the Ganges, we mean it is situated on the banks of the Ganges. Saying that a fat man does not eat in the daytime implies that he eats at night.

6. Iyalbu, common sense (Skt. *svabhâvä*). When an elephant herder says, "Pass me the staff," he means the stick that is used to direct the animal.

7. Aitiham, tradition. There is a spirit that lives in the tree.

8. Abhavä, nonexistence. The assertion that something does not

exist in one spot does not imply that it does not exist elsewhere. Nonexistence has three forms: one thing in another (*pragâbhavä*) (there exists no metal in a cotton cloth); by destruction (*pradhvansâbhavä*); and absolute (*atyantâbhavä*), never having existed.

9. Mitchi, implication (Skt. Parisheshä). If one says that Râmä has won the battle, this implies that Râvanä, his opponent, has lost it.

10. Ullaneri, probability (Skt. Sambhavä). If a piece of iron moves, we deduce from this the presence of a magnet (*Manimekhalaï*, book 27).

The semblances of proof (*pramânä âbhasä*) are eight in number:

1. Suttunarvu, direct experience. Being aware of the existences of things through the experience of the senses, which, however, may be deceptive.

2. Tiryak kôdal: false appearances. We take mother-of-pearl to be silver.

3. Aiyam, uncertainty. We are not sure if what we see in the semidarkness is a man or a tree trunk.

4. Teradu telidal, the arbitrary assertion. We decide that the tree trunk is a man.

5. Kandu nâramai, evaluative error: not realizing that the approaching animal is a tiger.

6. Il-valakku, hare's horns. The two elements are real but the combination represented by the words is not.

7. Unardadai unardal, pretending to demonstrate something obvious, for example, that fire disperses fog.

8. Ninaippu, faith. You only know that a couple is your father and mother by their assertions or those of others (*Manimekhalaï*).

Aphorisms of the Nyâyä

IN his account of Vaïsheshikä, Kanâdä gives a number of aphorisms of the Nyâyä that are famous:

1. The blind man and the sparrow (*andhachataka*). A blind man cannot catch a sparrow. A fool cannot achieve what an enlightened man has difficulty in establishing.

2. "The blind leading the blind" (*andhä paramparâ*) refers to the disposition of people to follow someone who will lead them to disaster. This is often the case with political leaders.

3. Finding the polar star (*arundhati darshanä*). To see the polar star, you first look for a very bright star which is close to it. In the same way, one uses an approximation as a starting point in order to arrive at a more subtle truth.

4. The ashokä grove (*ashokä vanikä*). The demon Râvanä held Sita prisoner in a garden full of ashokäs. You cannot assume from this that he had a preference for these trees. In the same way, when a man is faced with various possibilities in which he has equal interest, you cannot assume that his choice corresponds to a preference.

5. The stone and the clod of earth (*ashma loshtä*). A clod of earth is hard compared with cotton but soft compared with a stone. An individual always appears important to his inferiors and insignificant to his superiors.

6. The flowering of buds on a tree (*kadambä korakä*). When you see buds flowering in one tree, you know that they will also have opened to others of the same species. What happens here also happens elsewhere.

7. The crow and the coconut (*kâkätâliyä*). Just when the crow is flying under a tree, it is killed by a coconut. There are possible but improbable coincidences.

8. Looking for the crow's tooth (*kâkädantägaveshanä*): wasting time looking for impossible things.

9. The crow's eye (*kâkâkshigolaka*). This aphorism is based on the belief that the crow has only one eye, which it transfers from one side to the other. This is used in reference to a word which, in a document, has two possible interpretations.

10. The motion of the water wheel (*kûpäyanträghatikâ*). The containers fill on one side and empty on the other. The same applies to the trials and tribulations of life.

11. The customs post and the dawn (*ghattkuti prabhâtä*). You take an indirect route at night in order to avoid the customs post, and at dawn find yourself right in front of it. You always come face to face with the thing you are trying to avoid.

12. The worm and the letter (*ghunâksharä*). A worm can by chance draw the shape of a letter on the page of a book. In court, misleading evidence exists.

13. The staff and the bread (*dandäpupä*). When a loaf of bread is tied to a staff and someone says that the staff has been eaten by rats, it is obvious that the bread has been too. When someone has close ties with another, what is said of one applies, in all probability, to the other.

14. The lamp on the threshold (*dehlidîpä*). The lamp lights up the interior and the exterior. One object can serve two purposes at once.

15. The king and the barber's son (*nripanâpiträputrä*). The king asks his barber to bring him the most handsome boy in the kingdom. After looking around, the barber brings his own son, who is particularly ugly. Everyone overestimates the value of what is his.

16. Washing the mud off (*pankâprakshâlanä*). It is better to avoid mud than to dive in and wash yourself afterward. It is better not to compromise yourself, even if you think you will be able to justify yourself afterward.

17. Grinding flour (*pishtäpeshanä*): Making an effort to achieve something that has already been done.

18. The grain and the seed (*bîjânkurä*). The grain produces the

seed, and the seed the grain. Two things are the mutual cause of each other.

19. Iron and the magnet (*lohächumbakä*). One thing attracts another.

20. Fire and smoke (*vahnidhumä*). There is no smoke without fire, nor effect without cause.

21. The worm and the poison (*vishäkrimi*). The worm bred in poison does not feel its effects. People born in a criminal environment feel at home there.

22. The poison tree (*vishävrikshä*). You cannot destroy a tree you have planted which bears poisonous fruits. When you put forward a harmful idea, you cannot then stop it from spreading.

23. One wave follows another (*vîchitârangä*). In the end, you are always replaced by someone else. The same applies to social movements.

24. An old maid's wish (*vriddhäkumârîvâkyä*). The old woman, whom the god Indra had told to make a wish, asked for a husband, children, wealth, corn, cattle, and gold. He who asks for too much receives nothing.

25. The branch and the moon (*shâkhâchandrä*). The ambitious person thinks he can catch the moon by climbing up a tree near it.

26. The lion's look (*simhâvalokä*). The lion chases a prey in front of him, but looks back in case there are any others behind him. This applies to those who, while throwing themselves into an undertaking, worry about what they are leaving behind.

27. The needle and the kettle (*sûchîkatah*). It is easier to make a needle than a kettle. When you have several things to do, it is better to start with the easiest one.

28. The rice and the saucepan (*sthâlïpulâkä*). When one grain is cooked, so are the others. You can judge the whole by looking at a specimen. (This is the principle behind opinion polls.)

29. Sinking a pillar (*sthûnânikhanä*). By dint of repeated blows, the

pillar becomes stable. The same applies to the spreading of an ideology, even if it is false.

30. The master and the servant (*svâmîbhrityä*). The master feeds the servant, the servant feeds the master. This refers to the interdependence of persons and things.

NOTE

1. The *Maṇimekhalaï* has only partially been translated. I am striving to indicate the Sanskrit equivalents of certain terms by using information given by S. Krishnaswami Aiyangar in his incomplete English translation of the text.

⠶⠶⠶⠶

3

The Sâmkhyä: The Study of the Macrocosm

The Quest for Constants (Ak*sh*arä)

THE WORD *SÂMKHYÄ* MEANS "THE SCIENCE OF THE NU-
merable," since the potentials of human knowledge and the
mechanisms of thought, like the forms of matter, are linked
to what can be expressed in mathematical terms. All the
structures of the material or psychic universe are considered
to be determined by harmonies, patterns created from numerical relationships that exist between energetic elements.
The science of the measurable therefore refers to aspects of
knowledge that can be expressed in mathematical or geometric terms. It is, moreover, a generally accepted definition
of knowledge.[1]

We find the mark of the Sâmkhyä in all the aspects of later
Hindu thought that deal with works of a philosophical or
ritual character, such as the Upani*sh*ad(s) and the Tanträ(s),
or with scientific and metaphysical investigations such as
linguistics, astronomy, physics, mathematics, and physiol-
ogy.[2]

We do not have the original texts of the ancient Sâmkhyä,
which were not in the Sanskrit language, but we are ac-
quainted with its Dravidian terminology thanks, in particular,

to the *Manimekhalaï*, which is written in the Tamil language. The first texts seem to date from approximately the same period as the *Manimekhalaï*.

The Texts of the Sâmkhyä

THE teachings of Kapilä, the dark-skinned sage who was the first to teach the Sâmkhyä in the Aryan world, were collected by his spiritual heir, the magus Asuri, in the form of a set of 256 aphorisms called *Sâmkhyä Pravachanä Sûträ*, which was then summarized into 22 aphorisms under the name *Tattvä-Sâmasä*.

The practice of expressing knowledge in the form of very concise verses, which can be passed on even by individuals who do not understand their meaning, is one of the fundamental methods of the oral tradition. Proverbs are often vestiges of this traditional form of teaching.

It would have been on the basis of the aphorisms of Asuri that, much later, the philosopher Panchashikhä wrote a great number of works including 60,000 verses, concerning the nature of matter (*prakriti*), the nature of the self, the faculties of perception and action, and supra normal powers. The work of Panchashikhä is mentioned in the Chinese *Tripitaka* (the Buddhist canon). The *Shashti Tanträ*, of which fragments remain, was probably part of the work of Panchashikhä. It was Panchashikhä's disciple Ulûkä, humorously nicknamed Kanâdä (the atom-eater), who was the author of the *Vaïsheshikä Sûträ* and who taught Ishvarä-Krishnä. Toward the third century of our era, this latter summarized the theory of Sâmkhyä in seventy aphorisms called *Sâmkhyä-Kârikâ*. Commentaries on this text were made by various authors. A Chinese translation has given us the commentary of Vârshaganä. Vasubandhu, a Buddhist, wrote another commentary, called *Sâmkhyä-Kârikâ Bhâshyä*.

Gaudpada, who taught Shankarâchâryä, also wrote, in about A.D. 700, a commentary on the aphorisms of Ishvarä-Krishnä,

based on the commentary of Vârshaganä. Later, the Arab
scholar al-Bîrûnî, who lived in India from 1017 to 1030,
claimed to have translated a text of Sâmkhyä, probably that
of Gaudpadä, into Arabic.

Concepts of the Sâmkhyä

ACCORDING to the concepts of the Sâmkhyä, the universe is
made up of two fundamental elements, consciousness and
energy, which are complementary and interdependent. Matter is merely organized energy. There is no material element
that exists without being inhabited by consciousness. No
element of consciousness exists without an energy-giving support.

Space represents pre-matter, the substratum in which energy can be manifested in the form of vibratory waves and
magnetic forces which give birth to the elements, to the
appearance of matter.

Time is born of consciousness, since measurement only
exists through the perception of duration.

Consciousness is present everywhere from the moment that,
from an initial point (the bindu or boundary point) an immense mass of energy appears, which gives birth to the universe. The formation and development of the visible world is
related to the principle of Time, which is omnipresent and
is expressed in the form of rhythms. These determine not
only the structures of matter but also the cycles of the history
of the world, and the life and death of stars, galaxies, and
also life forms, whether they be vegetable or animal species,
which includes men or beings of a more subtle form, which
we call spirits or gods. The Sâmkhyä envisages 84,000 degrees
of the manifestation of consciousness in matter, starting with
infinitesimal particles, then atoms, then simple organisms and
bacteria, and ending at the higher life forms, animals, men,
spirits, and gods.

This idea, largely misunderstood, has been interpreted by

Buddhists as a reference to 84,000 reincarnations of the individual soul.

For the Sâmkhyä, the laws that govern the formation of atoms, cells, matter, and life are not the result of a stroke of luck, but are the implementation of a preexisting plan. The universe develops in accordance with a code contained in its seed, as a plant develops from its seed. These laws are based on archetypes, formulae which are the same whether they concern the whole universe or its individual elements or parts.[3] The galaxies, which are the cells of the body of the universe, behave like the cells that form the living being, independent and yet cooperating with the whole, even when there does not appear to us to be any communication between them. The laws which govern perception, intelligence, and thought cannot be separated from those which rule over the formation of matter.

What we perceive as objects is simply made up of galaxies of atoms, centers of energy separated by enormous spaces. The appearance of objects is merely the result of the limits of our perceptions. The living being, seen as a center of autonomous perception, is a witness whose whole role it is to give a visible reality to the divine dream that is creation. This appearance is illusory since it is formed from combinations of atoms that are nothing but centers of energy lacking substance. An infinitesimal being would see the human body as we see the solar systems and galaxies, which are the atoms of the Puru_sh_ä, the complete organism that the universe is.

A coherent universe can only develop in accordance with a plan, a system, which comes before it. *In the conception of the Sâmkhyä, thought precedes matter, the subtle precedes the concrete*, possibility precedes reality, and the laws which govern the universe precede their manifestations or applications. The laws of gravitation precede the birth of the atoms and constellations whose formation results from these laws. This is true for all aspects of the world. The laws that govern the mechanisms of perception, life, thought, and communication, including the principle of language, precede the formation of the organs that make them possible in the living being. This applies to all the physical or sensory functions, individual and collective, as well as to the social laws that govern vegetable, animal, or human groups. The only true science is the search for understanding of these laws, which constitute the permanent aspect (*akshara*) of the world. Life, perception, and thought are born of the same archetypes as matter, and are strictly coordinated and interdependent aspects of the development of the visible world. The slow development of the states of matter, then of life, in infinitely diversified forms, as well as that of perception, sensation, and the mechanisms of thought, depend on increasingly complex combinations of simple energetic forms, whose "signature" we find at all levels. We speak of physical laws, heaviness, density, gravitation, and compounds of elements, all of which science tries to understand, but we sometimes forget that all aspects of life, the structure of individual or collective beings, human or animal, all also obey these laws.

There is no fundamental difference, with precise limits, between what we consider to be inert matter and living cells. It is simply a matter of an additional dimension which we call life, but which is only apparent under certain conditions related to duration and to certain potentials of perception. An element of intelligence and perception is present, in a form that may be more or less latent, in every atom, every cell, every molecule, every astral system, every organism. It is this element of intelligence that guides the logic of their affinities, behavior, and inclinations, and allows them to play a consistent role.

In its conception of the world and its origins, what characterizes the cosmology of the Sâmkhyä is that it does not separate matter from consciousness and perception. The conscious principle, which characterizes the planning of the world and the potential of perception, necessarily precedes the appearance of the energetic material from which the corresponding matter and mechanisms of perception and thought will be made. The plan precedes the formation of the world and is an integral part of it.

Thought and consciousness do not issue from matter as the materialist theory of the Lokâyatâ maintains. According to the Sâmkhyä, it is matter which is born of a thought, an organic plan. This is implied in the notion of creation and of a creative principle. A thought, a consciousness, is at the origin of the laws that govern the universe and remains present everywhere in all aspects of its manifestation.

> In the phenomenal world, there is nothing absolutely conscious or absolutely unconscious. Consciousness and unconsciousness are always intermingled. Some things, however, appear to be more conscious and some more unconscious than others. This is due to the fact that *Cit*, which is never absent in anything, yet manifests itself in various ways and degrees. The degree of this manifestation is determined by the nature and development of the mind and body in which it is enshrined. [Woodroffe, *The Serpent Power*, p. 30]

The principle of perception precedes the formation of what is perceived. The principle of the senses precedes the differentiation of the elements that are perceived. The perception, consciousness, and thought of living beings reflect the first aspect of universal being. They are mirrors in which the creator contemplates his work. An unperceived universe does not exist, any more than a perception without an object does. The world only exists to the extent that it is perceived. Aspects of the world perceived by senses other than our own, or according to other norms of time or dimension, appear completely different, and reflect other facets of the game of creation. The entity that thinks the world needs this mirror to give a visible reality to his dream. Different kinds of beings play this role at different levels. For this reason, multiple forms of plants, animals, men, spirits, and gods exist.

If we want to try to understand the structures of the universe, we must first establish the potentials and limits of the instrument of understanding, that is, man himself. This is why the counterpart of the Sâmkhyä is the method of Yoga, which is the study of the inner man, his nature, potentials, latent powers, and limitations. This is how the pair Sâmkhyä-Yoga is formed to allow the study of the macrocosm and the microcosm of the individual being and the universal being, in relation to one another. An understanding of the conclusions of the Sâmkhyä concerning the nature of man and his place in the universe is indispensable to explain how the methods of Yoga have contributed to this end.

Nature and Perception

ABSOLUTE being is the only reality. It is external to existence, to the worlds it invents. It is neutral, nonactive, without substance, duration, or place, and is beyond the perceptible or conceivable. Although indescribable, it is called Paramä-Shivä (beyond the creative principle); although without dimension, Parä-Brahman (the beyond-infinity); although impersonal, Paramâtman (the beyond-self).

It escapes human understanding, is not identifiable. It is not part of the Tattvä(s), the definable. It is outside what has been created. It cannot be represented by any symbol, verbal or visual. "Absolute being *is* beyond Prakriti (nature), substance, and creation; is without form, color, name, evolution, or effect; does not suffer deterioration; is indestructible and unchanging. All that can be said of it is that it *is* and that the universe rests on it" (*Vishnu Purânä*, 1.2, 10–13).

When within this unknowable being, the "desire to create" (*sishriksha*) is born, like a kind of dream, this represents the first form of dynamic tendency, of potential energy. From the uncreated comes the "possibility" (*avakâshä*), the conditions that will permit the development of creation. This possibility is the principle of space (*âkâshä*). Space is not an absolute. It is merely the specific condition in which the world we know can develop. Space is neither eternal nor limitless. It is the receptacle in which the plan or model of the universe will be able to develop. This plan is called Universal Man, Purushä. "Prakriti, nature, only works because it has as a support or basis the pure Intelligence present everywhere in the form of the plan represented by Universal Man, Purushä" (Shashti Tanträ, cited by Gaudpadä in his commentary of the Sâmkhyä-Kârikâ, p. 16). Therefore, the first stage of creation is not the appearance of matter or energy, but the appearance, or creation, of space.

The principle that will permit the visible universe to evolve in the spatial receptable emanates from the "desire to create" (sishrikshâ). Desire is a directed force, the principle of Energy (shakti).

Time and everything that will be established in the universe are forms of energy. The various forms of time are simply the relative measurement of dynamic tendencies (vritti), the vibratory or gravitational movements that constitute matter, the perceptible substance of the universe. It is from the sudden explosion of an incredible mass of energy that all the elements, including the corresponding forms of perception and life, are gradually released. The world is only created from forms of energy coordinated in Space-Time. Matter is merely appearance. All the energetic relationships that we perceive in the forms of matter, electricity, radioactivity, magnetism, or gravitation constitute the substance of things. The principle of Energy (shakti) is called the Nature (Prakriti) of the world, or Pradhânä, "the basic element." We could represent the pair Purushä-Prakriti (form and substance) by saying that the Universal Man, Purushä, is the plan, the model of the world, and Nature, Prakriti, constitutes its material, its substance.[4]

In this way, we will symbolically take as the principle of the world, as the original cause, Universal Man, Purushä, the symbol of the plan, and Energy (Shakti) or Nature (Prakriti) as the material of its realization.

The Three Tendencies of Prak*ri*ti, the Nature of Nature

THREE fundamental tendencies are the basis of the energetic relationships that form the substance of the world. These tendencies can be found in all aspects of the universe. They constitute the nature (*svabhâvä*) of Nature (Prak*ri*ti).[5]

The first of these tendencies is called Tamas, expansion (centrifugal force); it is responsible for the birth and destruction of the worlds, and the life and death of universes like those of the atoms or conglomerates that make up galaxies and living beings. Tamas is also the principle of unmeasured unidirectional time (*mahâ-kâlä*).

The second tendency, called Sattvä, is attraction. This is the centripetal force that causes particles and stars to be attracted to each other rather than repelled. It is this tendency which, by allowing condensation, is the principle of the formation of stars, the source of light.

From these two conflicting tendencies the current that causes both vibratory movement and gravitation is born. It forms the magnetic field that links together the particles and stars and gives birth to the formation of atomic and stellar systems. This third tendency, called Rajas, is the basis of the formation of matter but also governs the activities of the subtle energies such as perception and thought. Symbolically, these three tendencies are personified, cosmogonically speaking, by three divine personages: Shivä represents Tamas, creative and destructive expansion; Vi*sh*nu represents Sattvä, coagulation or attraction, and Brahmâ represents Rajas, activity, movement, gravitation, and orbiting. Therefore, from the point of view of matter, Brahmâ is the initial point of the visible world and is called the Creator, even though he is only the fifth principle in the order of manifestation.[6] Nothing exists, nothing can exist in the universe that is not governed by these three tendencies, by the three characteristics or "qualities" (*gunä*[s]) of Nature, or Energy. We will come across them everywhere, at all levels, material or subtle, intellectual or sensory, spiritual or social, in the animate and the inanimate worlds. It is gravitation that gives rise to the measurement of relative time and space. In cosmogonic myth, the sun is the center of the cosmic cell of the world we live in. It is its attraction that keeps the planets in orbit. Sattvä-Vishnu is therefore identified with the sun, light, illumination, knowledge, and order, everything that allows man to make progress in the world, to develop and to improve himself, but also everything that links people together: society, conventions, virtues, and so forth.

Tamas-Shivä is the opposite force. It is the source, the primary impulse, the explosion that gives birth to the world, but it is also the force that tends to disintegrate or disperse the atomic or cosmic cells into endless obscurity. Shivä therefore represents darkness, the black hole that precedes and engulfs light and the diffuse night where it dissipates. Shivä is at the same time the source of life and the power of time, of death. He is liberation, detachment, everything that distances us from the organized world, society, conventional order, duration, possessions, and acquired virtues. He is the god of pleasure, the enemy of all human conventions.

Rajas-Brahmâ is the power of organization, the force of gravitation, the result of conflicting forces. It is the equilibrium of these forces that controls both atoms and astral systems, all the molecules and cells of matter and the life of all individual and collective organisms. This is why Brahmâ is called the modeler, the craftsman of creation. In the human being, he represents activity, power, organization, and social order.

In living beings Shivä appears in everything masculine, and Vishnu in the feminine, while Brahmâ is neuter.

The Definables *(Tattvä)*: The Twenty-five Constituents of the World

FROM the different combinations of the three tendencies, the "primordial elements" or "distinct and identifiable principles" are formed, called Tattvä(s) (from *tad*, that) in the Sâmkhyä, to show that they can be designated as "something." The slightly pretentious word *quiddity* has sometimes been used.

The number of Tattvä(s) in the Sâmkhyä is twenty-five, but the addition of subdivisions of some of the basic constituents results in thirty-six or even sixty-six Tattvä(s) being envisaged. The universe is made up of these constituents or "identifiable ontological elements," which originate from one another in a given order, a given hierarchy, in the same way that the geometric diagrams, Yanträ(s), which symbolize them variously combine lines, curves, proportions, and numbers.

The Plan *(Purushä)*

PURUSHÄ, or Universal Man, the plan, the model, is the first of the Tattvä(s). It (or he) is a sort of complex equation, a set of formulae, intentions, and archetypes out of which the universe will be formed. Purushä will only achieve its fullness when, materialized in energetic substance, it has filled the void of space and the universe reaches its limits. It is preexistent, abstract, but "it is present in all aspects of the nonperceptible *(avyaktä)* or perceptible *(vyaktä)* universe" (*Vishnu Purânä* 1.2.14).

Originally the Hebrew concept of Adam, the first man, seems to be derived from the notion of Purushä, the Universal Man. In fact *Adam*, like *Purushä*, simply means "man" and not one man in particular. The vast body of this primordial Adam stretched from earth to sky.

The World-Substance (*Prakriti*)

THE second of the Tattvä(s) is the energetic principle from which thought, perception, matter, and life stem. This principle is called Prakriti, Nature. "It is also given other names: the fundamental element (*pradhânä*), boundless Being (Brahmâ), Potentiality (*avyaktä*), the principle of Multiplicity (*bahudhâtmä*), the Power of Illusion (*mâyâ*)" (Gaudpadä, Commentary on the *Sâmkhyä Kârikâ*, 22).

Nothing exists that is not made from the energetic material which Prakriti represents. But the universe is not eternal: all that we perceive is, in the final analysis, only composed of unstable and immaterial combinations of elements that continually transform themselves and will one day cease to exist. This is why Prakriti is also called Mâyâ, the Power of Illusion. The reason for the existence of Prakriti is to put Purushä, the plan, the set of laws that will enable the primordial energy to be manifested in the multiple aspects of creation, into a concrete form. The universe therefore originated from two complementary and contrary fundamental entities, which are not derived from each other. On the one hand is the plan (Purushä) and on the other the material (Prakriti). According to Gaudpadä: "Purushä, Universal Man, the transcendent consciousness (*vijñânä*) (which represents the plan of the world), is inactive, immobile, external to the visible world. Primordial Nature (Mûlä Prakriti) does not stem from Purushä, it is autonomous." The formation of the revealed world starts with seven principles derived from Prakriti, which are Mahat, the universal omnipresent intelligence; Ahamkarä, the principle of individuality; and the five Tanmaträ(s), the modes of the interaction of matter, the origin of the senses and the elements. Materialism attributes the conception of the world to Prakriti alone by ignoring the ordering principle, the omnipresent universal intelligence, Purushä.

Cosmic Intelligence (Mahat)

The set of archetypes (which are to be found in all forms of existence) is used and regulated by Cosmic Intelligence, the "Great Principle" (Mahat), a manifest form of Purushä, also called the object of Knowledge (*khyati*), the Idea (*mati*), or the Intelligence (*buddhi*). It manifests itself in living beings in the power of knowledge (*jñânä*) or consciousness (*prajñâ*). It is also given the name Magic Power (*asurî*). [Gaudpadä, Commentary on the *Sâmkhyä-Kârikâ*, 22]

Mahat is given the name "magic power" because the universe is only an appearance stemming from the Power of Illusion (*mâyâ*). Like a magician, Mâyâ makes a world appear which has no permanent reality. Mahat, Cosmic Intelligence, represents the presence of the plan, of consciousness, in all aspects of what has been created, consciousness (*cit*) is present in matter at all levels. The unmasking of an aspect of Mahat, the intelligent organization of the world, is called Revelation.

The Principle of Individuality (Ahamkarä)

"FROM Mahat comes the notion of identity, individuality, the Self (*ahamkarä*), which makes differentiation and multiplicity possible" (Gaudpadä, Commentary on the *Sâmkhyä-Kârikâ*, 3). All development implies multiplicity, but this can only exist if the different entities each have a separate identity. For this reason, the first of the principles that stem from Mahat, universal Intelligence, is the principle of identity, the notion of self (*ahamkarä*).

The interplay of the three tendencies of Nature allows for the formation of energetic cells, atoms in which the notion of individuality, autonomy, and "self" will blossom.

The awareness of being autonomous is the characteristic

of atoms, as well as solar systems, or individual beings, men, or gods. Every cell in the world, whether infinitesimal or gigantic, gathers around a "self." This self is inhabited by consciousness (*cit*), which is part of the omnipresent universal consciousness (*mahat*). It is this element of consciousness, apparently individualized, which allows the cells to detect each other, to communicate, to collaborate and organize themselves.

The notion-of-self (*aham*) is universal and primordial. It is found in all forms of matter and life. "Depending on the situation, it is called the principle of identity or sense of self (*ahamkarä*), the subtle origin of elements (*bhûtâdi*), the sense of difference (*vaïkritä*), the radiance (*taïjas*), vanity, or pride (*abhimânä*)" (Gaudpadä, Commentary on the *Sâmkhyä-Kârikâ*, 22).

Each atom or group of elements is therefore going to see itself as an autonomous and independent center. This is the self of living beings. It is via this notion of individuality and autonomy that the world substance differentiates itself, manifests itself in innumerable entities, each having its own personality, which will become atoms, different elementary chemical substances, but also conglomerates, whether solar systems, galaxies, chemical bodies, or living beings. Each conglomeration forms around its notion of identity, of its self. An atom of hydrogen forms around its notion of being an atom of hydrogen and defends its identity. It possesses a "self" just as does a man, who himself is also only an assemblage of various molecules. We all say "I" without really knowing to which part of ourselves this "I" corresponds. Yet the self is a fiction.[7] In living beings, it is seen as a knot temporarily formed by the different constituents of the transmigratory or subtle body. The self is the nucleus of every object conceived of and shaped by the creative thought. Like the nodes of the lunar orbit that causes eclipses, the self is a precise but abstract and insubstantial place where magnetic lines intersect.

The Modes of Interaction of Matter (Tanmâträ)

ALL the structures of the world are founded on the five modes of interaction (*tanmâträ*[s]) between particles (*aṇu*) or atoms (*paramaṇu*). These modes of interaction, of varying intensity, are electrical (*vidyut-shakti*) or magnetic (*mohakä*) in nature. They give birth to the different elements and also to the organs that permit their perception. "The five modes of interaction stem from the principle of differentiation, that is, the principle of individuality (*ahamkarä*)" (ibid.).

It is from these modes of interaction, experienced in living beings through corresponding five forms of perceptions, that the perceptible elements (*bhûtä*) are born.

> Space or ether (*âkâshä*) is the field of the vibratory principle, also called the Word (*shabdä*). The gaseous state (*vâyu*) is governed by the principle of touch (*sparshä*). The principle of smell (*gandhä*) determines the solid state (*pṛithivi*). The principle of sight (*rûpä*) is the reason for existence of the igneous state (*tejas*) of light. The principle of taste (*rasä*) determines the liquid state (*apä*). Not only do these modes of interaction (*tanmaträ*[s]) give birth to the perceptible elements, but their repercussions on the individual self, the Sattvä Ahamkarä, is the cause of the organs (*indriyä*[s]) of the senses. [Ibid.]

The Principles of the Senses (Mahabhûtä)

THE Mahabhûtä(s) are the different modes of interaction that determine the different states of matter called elements (*bhûtä*[s]). They are only truly differentiated with respect to the centers of perception within the given limits of relative time and space. The differences, obvious to us, among the vibratory, igneous, gaseous, liquid, and solid states of matter are merely the varying behaviors of the atoms that comprise them, and are not transformations of these atoms. It is only differences of perception linked to the duration of the time span that make conglomerations of atoms appear to be in a vibratory, gaseous, liquid, igneous, or solid state.[8]

The atoms of matter are therefore organized according to variable degrees of concentration corresponding to the different forms of relationships, modes of interaction, or communication. The elements appear on the physical plane according to an organized hierarchy. First the substratum appears, which permits the manifestation of vibratory (*spandanä*) or magnetic (*âkarshanä*) forms, and which is called ether and has space as one of its properties. Everything that we perceive can, in the final analysis, be reduced to a vibration of ether, but in order to gain an intelligible idea of it, we liken it to the invisible vibration of air which we call sound. It is from "primordial sound" (*nâdä*), the inaudible vibration (*anâhatä nâdä*), that the other visible states of matter originate, although they too are only formed from different organizations of energetic elements and are not different in nature. It is from this aspect of the nature of the world that the symbolic image of creation by the Word is born.

From the vibratory or magnetic state the atoms of the various elements are formed, which first appear in a diffuse, extensible form, a gaseous form that fills the universe, the simplest image of which, for us, is air. Molecules in a gaseous state communicate by contact, by a magnetic sensation of proximity, which, for us, corresponds to the sense of touch and keeps them at an equal distance from each other. Without this ability to communicate, they could not organize themselves. Touch is therefore the form of perception, the sense, related to the gaseous state. It is in this state that the gaseous clouds give birth to the stars.

With the concentrations of atoms caused by gravitation, visibility and heat, the igneous state, appear. It is then that the suns and the constellations are formed. Light waves are only characterized as such with respect to our organ of vision. Essentially, they are no different from other waves (which we today call infrared, radio, gamma rays, etc.), not normally perceived by man but perceived by other species. It is through light and similar waves that constellations communicate with each other, just as living beings detect each other by sight.

The liquid state depends on temperature, therefore on the igneous state. It is at the level of the melting or liquid state that the principle of life appears. It is especially perceived by man in the element water, which plays a fundamental role in the structures of living beings. It is associated with the sense of taste and the phenomenon of assimilation. Life originates from water. The characteristics of life are the consumption of energy and its transformation, which is expressed in man by the functions of feeding and reproduction, from which comes the importance of the sense of taste. Nonliving cells gather and combine. Living cells devour one another and reproduce themselves. It is in this sense that the sun is a living being, like all the stars, in a liquid state of consumption, production, and dispersion of energy.

Finally, the solid state appears, called earth, perceived by all the senses, to which the sense of smell is added. The sense of smell is related to the phenomenon of attraction and repulsion. The earth is seen as a womb, the starting point from which will develop all the forms of life in the world of which we are a part. It is called the mother. But it is also the prelude to death, for when all elements are reduced to the solid state, the universe becomes a desert without light or life.

The Powers of Perception and Action (Indriyä)

FROM the point of view of the human being,

> the universe appears to be formed from only sixteen Tattvä(s), sixteen indentifiable aspects stemming from the principle of individuality. These are the five modes of interaction (*tanmaträ*[s]), the five forms of perception, and the five forms of action that correspond to them. To these fifteen constituents

is added a sixteenth, which coordinates them, the mental (*manas*, seat of consciousness and thought). [Ibid.]

All living species possess senses and organs of perception and action that are developed to different degrees. Their relative predominance varies according to the species. As far as man is concerned, both types of senses are five in number. The number five is an essential characteristic of the structures that constitute the state of life. This is why man possesses five organs of perception of matter, which therefore appears to him to be formed from five elements which he perceives and which, from a certain point of view, he creates. (The importance of the factor five is not unexpected, since the living being is born from the association of a ternary masculine principle and a binary feminine principle.)

Particular species, subtle or living, can have another vision of the world, possess other organs that refer to a more or less extensive perception of the vibratory spectrum. In fact, all the senses are potentially present from the beginnings of existence, but are developed to a lesser or greater degree. In man, the five organs of perception and the five organs of action are as follows: for sound, the organ of speech (the vibratory element of ether) whose receptor is the ear and whose organ of action is the mouth; for touch (corresponding to air), the receptive organ is the skin, and the organ of action is the hand; for sight (the igneous element), related to directional movement, the receptive organ is the eye, the organ of action is the foot; for taste (related to the aqueous element and to the phenomenon of assimilation and reproduction), the receptive organ is the tongue and the organ of action is the genitals; for the sense of smell (related to the solid element and to the phenomenon of repulsion), the receptive organ is the nose and the organ of action is the anus.

In man, the sense organs work in association with the treble internal organ (the mental-intellect-ego). Perception can be instantaneous or gradual. The same applies to the perception of the invisible (distant, past, or future). The impulses of the senses (*vritti*) only function with a view to the realization of man's reason for existence (Purushârthä) (such as being a witness, etc.). They are an expression of the universal plan (Purushä) but are not directly controlled by it. [*Sâmkhyä-Kârikâ*, 30–31]

The Living Being

ALL beings issuing from Prak_r_iti, Primordial Nature, display comparable characteristics and are organized on the basis of a definite number of archetypes, fundamental mathematical graphs (*mudrâ*[s]), or geometric patterns (*yanträ*[s]), according to which all the structures of the universe are formed. However, all beings are not necessarily in similar conditions of materiality, or relative time or space. "The gods, spirits, men, and animals were originally born of the same formulae, of which they are different applications" (Commentary on the *Sâmkhyä-Kârikâ*, 40). "The thirteen constituents which are the basis of the development of all beings are the same" (Commentary on the *Sâmkhyä-Kârikâ*, 44–45)—whether we are speaking of a cell, a bacterium, or a complex being, a plant, animal, or man.

Animals perceive the elements, the stars, the harmony and beauty of the natural world, and possibly sense the presence of subtle forces that govern it. Animals anticipate earthquakes, the approach of death, and disasters. Man, like animals, perceives a particular aspect of the external world and has an intuition of the existence of the subtle world. Genetically, he inherits the senses, faculties, and modes of individual and social conduct necessary for his survival and his continuation as a species. But this set of abilities and knowledge is limited to the external aspect of things.

The role of living beings in creation is one of witnesses. It is their perceptions that give a visible reality to the divine dream. They form the audience for the divine play (*lîlâ*) of creation.

The principle of consciousness, of perception, is therefore the center around which living beings are constituted. However, the potentials of perception and knowledge operate within narrow limits corresponding, in each case, to a specific vision of the world. For this reason, the senses are instruments of perception, but also barriers that restrict its range. Beings living in conditions of different duration and dimension inevitably have different images of the world, which allow them to testify to another of the many facets of the divine game. Man's role as witness is more extensive than that of other living beings. It is man who possesses the potential to perceive, to try to figure out, the inner nature, the plan, of creation. He is an intermediary being between an animal and a god.

NOTES

1. Number now appears to be the only entity in physics that is sufficiently stable to really be taken seriously by science. Bernard d'Espagnat, *La Recherche du réel*, p. 12.

2. The relationship between the numerical factors of frequencies in musical intervals and the psychophysiological effect of music is a fundamental element of the theory of the râgä(s), or musical modes. It is on this basis that I have attempted to establish a general theory of aesthetics and of the expression of music in my *Sémantique musicale*.

3. The conception of the earth as a whole system, an organism in itself, has only recently appeared in the field of scientific research . . . (Jonathan Schell). For the mathematician Freeman Dyson of Princeton, "Somewhere the universe knew that man was going to come. It was programmed to lead to a complex and intelligent molecular being" (*Disturbing the Universe*).

4. In terms of modern industry, we could call these two aspects software and hardware. We can sell the plans of a machine to Japan, this is the software, while the machine itself is the hardware. As far as the universe is concerned, we can either consider the software as a point of departure, the plan prior to matter, to the reality of the object, or the realization of the plan in the substance of which the world is made.

5. In Chinese translations of the texts of the Sâmkhyä, Svabhâvä and Prakriti are represented by the same character. We also find this ambiguity in Western vocabulary.

6. We find a simple illustration of the three principles in a car battery: the positive terminal (Tamas) and the negative terminal (Sattvä) create the magnetic or energetic field (Rajas), which provides power for the headlights and makes the starter-motor work.

7. The human body is made up of an immense number of cells, each having an independent self. Each cell, each organ of the body, has its own identity, which means that a transplanted organ can be integrated into another collective self, a different individuality.

8. One of the problems with the return of spacecraft is that the gaseous atmosphere of Earth, when penetrated at a certain speed, behaves like a liquid or even a solid.

4

The Exploration of Man's Inner Universe

The Being of Flesh and the Being of Knowledge

MAN HAS A DOUBLE NATURE, A DOUBLE ROLE IN CRE-
ation; he is at once actor and spectator. Like other animals,
he is the representative of a species whose harmony and
beauty make up part of the spectacle, the theatrical diversion
(*lîlâ*) of the creator. He transmits and develops the characteristics of his species through the genetic formulae contained
in what the Sâmkhyä calls his Sexual Body (*Lingä-Sharirä*)
or Transmigrant (or Transmittable) Body. On the other hand,
he is inhabited by a consciousness and is the bearer of a
heritage of knowledge that enables him to play his role of
witness at the different stages of his evolution, to become
aware of the various aspects of the world spectacle, and to
discover little by little their secret nature. He thus accu-
mulates a knowledge that he formulates and transmits from
individual to individual by means of the symbols of language,
thereby giving an overall role to his species.

Himself impermanent, man transmits his physical and mental
characteristics through the genetic chain and, in parallel with
this, the basis of his understanding of the cosmic world and
its laws through the initiatic chain. There is an evolution on

the one hand of his physical being and on the other of his cultural being.

The evolution of the physical being, the growth of the human species, like the progress of knowledge, does not occur in a single day. The development of the human animal takes place in the course of a long evolution, which follows a route parallel to the progress of knowledge.

There exists a concordance between the physical being and the intellectual and moral being. To be able to receive and transmit the heritage of knowledge, the individual must be qualified (*adhikâri*), that is, possessed of a physical harmony, and the moral virtues and capacities that form part of his genetic heritage, his transmittable Sexual Body. This is why man's destiny is determined by two factors, his membership in a physical line, which makes a good receptacle (*pâträ*) of him, and an initiatic line, which makes use of this receptacle.

Within man's destiny, it is the progress and transmission of knowledge that predominate and determine his destiny.

The Sexual Body (Lingä-Sharirä) or Transmittable Body

THE permanent transmittable element, the code that defines the possibilities of development of each individual, each link, is contained in the seed that transmits it. It is part of the plan, considered as a male principle, realized in the female matrix. Similarly, the universe is considered as issuing from the Lingä, the divine phallus fecundating Prakriti, the world substance. This is why the Sâmkhyä calls the living being's set of transmittable characteristics the Sexual Body.

The principle of life is symbolized by a column encircled by a serpent. The column, or phallus, is the image of Purushä (the male principle), that is, the plan or program; whereas the spiral, or serpent, represents Prakriti, substance, the feminine principle.

The moral, intellectual, and spiritual characteristics of the human being are profoundly linked to his physical being and cannot be separated from it.

The Lingä-Sharirä, the Sexual Body (as the plan or model of a species) preexists the physical development of its carrier. It emigrates and evolves. But it can only function when it becomes incarnate, although it remains independent of the body. It is characterized by a Dharmä, a goal to be accomplished, which continues when it leaves one body to take on another. [*Sâmkhyä Kârikâ*, 40]

The Lingä-Sharirä cannot subsist without a material support, without a physical body which lodges it, without a series of impermanent carriers, just as a picture cannot exist without a support, a shadow without a pillar. [Ibid., 41]

The Sexual Body is formed essentially of innate elements, but can, to a certain degree, acquire new ones. (This is why species can evolve. The development of the innate elements is achieved by the age of sixteen in the male. After this, one can only add acquired elements to them.) The capacities, tendencies, and intelligence of the living being are thus innate but can be modified by knowledge and virtue (*dharmä*), that is, by the conformity or nonconformity to the role given to the species. Furthermore, the habitat of the sexual body, the physical and mental substance of the living being which develops starting from the food it receives as an embryo, is perishable. [Ibid., 39, 43]

The individual depends for his development upon the terrain which nourishes the seed, which materializes the plan, that is to say, upon the maternal breast, then upon the fruits of the earth. The earth continues the role of the mother. The earth is identified with the female principle. It is the nourishing mother of living beings.

It is fundamental Nature, Pradhânä, present in the feminine aspect of all things, which determines the manner in which the data of the genetic code, the Lingä-Sharirä, unfold, more or less favorably, in the physical body. [Gaudpadä, Commentary on the *Sâmkhyä Kârikâ*, 40]

To accomplish the goal which is assigned to it in the creation . . . the Sexual or Transmigrant Body, incarnated by the power of Nature (Pradhâna), behaves like an actor who plays one role after another. [*Sâmkhyä-Kârikâ*, 42]

The Nature of the Transmigrant Body

The Transmigrant Body is formed of thirteen components: the mental (*manas*), which discusses and invents; the intelligence (*buddhi*), which enregisters, chooses, and decides; and the notion of the "I" (*ahamkarä*), to which are added the five modes of perception manifested in the five senses and the five principles of the elements or states of matter. [Gaudpadä, Commentary on the *Sâmkhyä-Kârikâ*, 39]

This group of faculties forms "the internal organ" (*antah-karanä*). "Discussion (*sanchayä*), decision (*nishchayä*), memory (*smaranä*) and pride (*garvä*) or the sense of the "I", are the activities of the internal organ" (ibid., 40).

Intelligence, the organ which registers, selects, and retains the data of perception, is called Buddhi. Memory is a part of Buddhi.

The Mental (*manas*) is the organ that discusses, combines, and utilizes the data accumulated by Buddhi. It is the organ of thought, cogitation, and the formation of ideas.

Buddhi and Manas are physical organs. They form part of the body, and their structures are transmittable through the genetic code, although their contents, memory in particular, are, with rare exceptions, destroyed with the death of the physical body.

Consciousness (*cit*) also makes up part of the internal organ, but the Sâmkhyä considers that consciousness, the principle of all perception, remains an integral part of Mahat, the omnipresent universal consciousness found in every atom, every cellular organization, every astral system, every living organism. Although present in the Transmigrant Body, it is not a part of it. It can be compared to the space enclosed in an urn, which is never really distinct from the space which surrounds it and into which it dissolves when the urn is broken.[1]

Normally, we have no control over the functioning of the different organs of the enormous machine that constitutes our body. We can at the very most remedy the poor functioning of some of its wheels, oil a joint or two, aid the healing function of an injured organ, and practice physical and mental exercises to prevent the machinery from becoming rusty. The organized cells that form our body, acting in a totally independent manner, each play their role with a remarkable intelligence and autonomy over which we have no power and of which we have no consciousness. In fact, our consciousness, as an entire being, only concerns our social role.

Our internal organ can be compared to the driver of an automobile who is completely outside of the functioning of the motor's organ, constructed according to a preestablished plan, but which he must treat with care, nourish with fuel, and drive in the traffic among the dangers of terrestrial life. This "I" drives several cars, just as the Lingä-Sharirä guides one body after another and perfects the art of driving in the course of its transmigrations. The used cars are sent to the demolition site to become parts for other machines. The driver in due course also dies. This marks the end of a line, a species. The elements that compose the Lingä-Sharirä then return to the general store, since, for the Sâmkhyä, the "I" is but a temporary knot that forms between the various materials which constitute the internal organ. It dissolves at the time of death. Nevertheless, certain acquired elements have been able, accidentally, to impress the genetic memory and can be transmitted with it. This gives rise to the experience of *déjà vu*, impressions of previous lives, and the like.

For the person who has no descendents, who breaks the

lineage of his ancestors, the "I" disappears at death, although it may sometimes attach itself for a time to certain subtle elements, producing phantoms.

At the end of a lineage, when the genetic plan is not transmitted, each subtle element returns to the general stock: the intellect to the universal intellect, the consciousness to the universal consciousness to be reused, just as the matter of the body returns to be used again in other bodies.

It is in regard to the nature of what eventually survives and the duration and density of the group of faculties which constitute the human person that, in India as elsewhere, the profound divergences between religions and theological and philosophical systems appear.

NOTE

1. The triad of the Sâmkhyä—consciousness, internal organ, physical body—corresponds to the gnostic triad *spiritus-anima-corpus*, which the Council of Constantinople (869) reduced to the Catholic dualism of soul and body.

5

The Being of Knowledge

Universal Law (Sanâtanä Dharmä) and the Heritage of Knowledge

CERTAIN FORMS OF KNOWLEDGE, ALONG WITH THE SE-
cret of the rites and practices that connect man to the different levels of the natural and supranatural world, make up
part of his role in creation. This role varies for the different
ages of each of the species, thus presenting different mirrors
in which universal consciousness contemplates its work. In
order for humanity as a whole to play its role, an intellectual
heritage must be transmitted in parallel with the genetic
heritage, even if its transmission can only be made through
a few individuals under a veiled and secret form in what is
called the occult tradition. However threatened this knowledge, together with the principle of language which is its
vehicle, may be, it can never completely disappear.

The name Sanâtanä Dharmä, the "Eternal Law" or "Perpetual Tradition," is given to the group of fundamental notions that permit the Being of Knowledge to play, from its
inception to its end, its role. Shaivism attributes the teaching
of these basic elements of knowledge to the <u>Rishi</u>(s), the Seers
of the first ages.

According to the teachings of Shaivism, one can decline to postulate the hypothesis of a god, either personal or impersonal, unique or multiple, but one can never believe that the universe is the result of chance, that it is not subject in all its aspects to certain laws. It is in reference to this notion of a law which goes back to the origin of things, and in fact precedes it, that one speaks of the "primordial tradition." The expression "primordial tradition," however, has the disadvantage of placing the accent on the transmission of a certain knowledge rather than on its contents.[1]

The Hebraic notion of Torah (Law) seems originally to come from the notion of Dharmä (the universal law that governs matter and life) but has degenerated so that it no longer applies to anything but a more or less arbitrary human "rule of conduct." The potentiality and the limits of all knowledge, of all science, of all knowledge accessible to man at the various stages of his development is included in the plan of the species. The mechanisms of thought, its relations with perception, are, like the development of the physical body, determined by the Chakrä(s), the geometric patterns or models which are found in the vital centers and which nothing can modify. These patterns serve to differentiate the physical and mental capacities of individuals and determine their role in the various stages of their evolution as well as their access to knowlege.

Each species, each lineage, is realized, and progresses, through the chain of physical paternity, according to the information of the Lingä-Sharirä, the genetic code. The development of the Knowledge Body is made in a parallel way, that of the spiritual paternity, through the accumulation and transmission of knowledge. This is the initiatic way, which leads to the discovery of the subtle nature of the world and which enables man to realize his spiritual destiny. All evolution, whether it concerns the intellectual or the genetic heritage, is subject to cycles that give the rhythm of their progress and decline. At certain epochs we can observe a remarkable development of knowledge followed by periods of obscurity during which true knowledge is only transmitted in a secret form by initiates who once again unveil it in favorable periods, giving birth to periods of creativity, to the liberation of mankind, to the great periods of art, love, beauty, the harmony of beings and things again taking a predominant place.

The Seers (_Rishi_)

CERTAIN aspects of the nature of the physical or metaphysical world are revealed to men at determined moments in the maturation of the human species. These "revelations" are the work of the Seers, the _Rishi_(s), who are the intermediaries, the mediums gifted with the perception of the higher levels of creation. Some of them are subtle beings; others are incarnate beings. Vision and speech are of a transcendent order while the body remains destructible. Shaivism does not, like Vaishnavism, envision physical incarnations of the divinity, but only mental incarnations of a prophetic nature in the persons of the Seers. At the beginning of each cycle of humanity, the god Skanda inspires in the Seers the knowledge necessary for the reestablishment of a tradition of knowledge that enables the new mankind to play its role.

Seers can reappear during the course of the cycles to ensure the maintenance of the tradition and the discovery by man, at the opportune moment, of the secrets of the nature of the world.

Great discoveries are always inspired, programmed. This is why they generally take place simultaneously in several regions of the world. For, in the Seers, it is perception that is inspired. Its formulation can be inadequate. In any case, the relationship of the vision to the words that express it is only valid for a particular moment.

❀

The Sacred Books

AS we have seen, writing is an urban phenomenon, characteristic of the Kali Yugä. *To freeze the teachings of "prophets" in books regarded as sacred is to paralyze the spirit of research; it fixes so-called established truths and tends to create blind faith instead of the search for knowledge.* The nature of knowledge is to evolve. Like other aspects of the human being, it knows periods of progress and decline. The teaching of the <u>Rishi</u>(s) is a living thing that enables the species to realize its role at various stages of its evolution. It can only be transmitted by initiation through qualified individuals. The fixation in Writings of the visions and perceptions of Seers, which represent the forms of knowledge necessary at a certain moment of the evolution of the species, whether it be a matter of cosmological, scientific, religious, or moral ideas, presents grave risks. The sacred book valid for all time and all people is a fiction.

The new Sâmkhya sometimes replaces the word Âgamä (tradition) by the word Vedä (from the root *vid*, knowledge) to represent permanent information (*akshara*), the plan that is at the basis of all aspects of creation, the object of all research, all science, all metaphysics, all true knowledge. Taken in this sense, the word Vedä has nothing to do with the religious texts known by this name. The notion of Vedä represents the belief in a universal law, the object of knowledge. This implies the acceptance of the idea that there exists a divine order of the world of which it is possible to have a fragmentary glimpse, an "approach" (*upanishad*), even though this order remains on the whole unknowable. No one can pretend to possess the "truth" in any domain. A dogmatic teaching can be neither scientifically nor philosophically nor morally justifiable.

The advent of writing has allowed for the substitution of conceptions of religious or social reformers, in the guise of inspired prophets, for the teachings of the Seers. This has given birth to the religions of the book that characterize the Kali Yugä.

The superstition of the written word is an obstacle to the development of knowledge in the domain of scientific or religious information. The religions of the book have been one of the most effective instruments of man's decadence during the course of the Kali Yugä and have been used by urban oligarchies, both religious and secular, as instruments of domination.

To take texts, whether called Vedä, Bible, or Koran, as an expression of reality or of divine will is puerile and dangerous. This is part of the antireligion which lowers the concept of the divine to the human scale.

NOTE

1. I discussed this question with René Guénon in the course of translating certain sections of his works into Hindi. He fully recognized this difficulty. Cf. Alain Daniélou, *René Guénon et la tradition hindoue*, Dossier H, 1984.

※※※※

6

Yogä

Yogä: Study of the Microcosm

IN PARALLEL WITH THE SÂMKHYÄ, WHICH SEEKS TO understand the laws governing the universe, the secrets of Universal Man, Yogä attempts to explore the human being, the microcosm, and to discover, within this particular universe which forms each living being, the applications of these same laws.

Man cannot understand the world without understanding himself, and he can only know himself in relation to universal structures, to his role, to his raison d'être, to his place in the play of creation. For this reason, Sâmkhyä and Yogä are interdependent and interconnected. Yogä represents the experimental method that will, first, help to establish and, second, confirm or invalidate the theories of the Sâmkhyä. For, in the measure that it allows us to go beyond the limits of the senses, Yogä gives us an increased perception of the structures of the universe. The techniques of Yogä are a heritage of pre-Aryan Shaivism. Its teaching is attributed to the god Shivä, the Great Yogi. Representations of Shivä-Pashupati, the Lord of Animals, in yogic posture, have been found at Mohenjo-Daro and the other cities of the Indus Valley. "The techniques of

Yogä, which are an essential element of the ancient Shaivism, were totally unknown in Vedic literature" (M. R. Sakhare, *History and Philosophy of Lingyat Religion*, p. 175). They gradually penetrated into the Aryan world, just as today they have penetrated into the Western world.

Method

YOGÄ is a method of introspection that permits the exploration of the subtle centers, dwelling places of those inner faculties which receive, enregister, and analyze the perceptions of the senses, but which are not limited by the barriers of the senses. The part of the human being that can be called physical includes, besides the body, certain faculties such as thought and memory which are of a material nature and which function within the relative and oriented temporal scale of a given time span. By contrast, the higher human faculties, such as intelligence and conscience, together with the information that constitutes the codes governing the evolution of the species and forms part of the plan coming forth from Purushä, are not limited by space and time. They are as though imprisoned in the body.

> The physical sense organs are the openings, the doors through which the Internal Organ perceives exterior objects (but which, at the same time, by confining them, limit the possibilities of perception). Consciousness and the other inner faculties are like spectators gazing through these doors. [*Sâmkhyä-Kârikâ*, 35]

With the aid of yogic methods we can reach, then control, the faculties that constitute our Transmittable Body or Sexual Body—this permanent aspect of ourselves, whose nature and functioning are not tied to the duration of our life, and are not limited by the barriers of relative space and time. Starting from there, we can develop powers called Siddhi(s) (accomplishments), which enable us to "see" beyond our limits what the barriers of the senses normally mask. Being born of Prakriti, "the physical organs [exist only within time and] function only in the present. The subtle organs (the principles of consciousness and of perception) are not limited by time and can equally perceive past, present, and future" (ibid., 33). They can also perceive, beyond dimension, the infinitely small or the infinitely large. Only the limits of our senses and the rhythms that determine for us the dimension of relative space and time prevent us from contemplating the interiors of atoms or the exteriors of celestial spheres, from seeing objects far away from us in space and time, or from entering into contact with the subtle forces of nature.

Freed from the barriers of the senses and the limitations of space and time, our Internal Organ can have a prodigiously amplified perception of reality, of the macroscopic and microscopic structures of the world, see the invisible, hear the inaudible, perceive what dimension or distance hides from us, transport us into the past and the future.

The methods of Yogä will also enable us to become aware of what is inconscient in us, and to reach the mechanisms that constitute our faculties, and not only their applied forms; to perceive matter's own modes of communication (the *tanmâträ*[s]), and not only their limited aspects, which give birth to the Bhûtä(s), the elements perceived by our senses. Through the methods of Yogä, we can go beyond the normal possibilities of the living being, emerge from his limitations, and thus obtain the powers of knowledge and joy that belong in principle to levels of being above the human state.

The methods of Yogä have permitted the development of knowledge concerning the structures of the world and the nature of the living being which seem otherwise inexplicable in a world destitute of modern means of investigation.

The word *Yogä* means "link." The English word *yoke* or the French *joug* have the same root. The word *religion* is most probably its translation. All the relations that the individual being has with the different levels of existence, with the forces that govern the world, with the spirits and the gods, are included in the investigations of Yogä. Yogic techniques enable man to develop himself and to explore his latent possibilities and to obtain thereby a less confused picture of the extrasensible, extratemporal, extraspatial world. By cultivating his possibilities of extrasensory perception, man can go beyond the limits of time, space, and materiality. He then comes into contact with other forms of beings and can explain, rationalize, and instigate these contacts. It is through lack of rational data and experience that we meet in most religions such absurd theories concerning the nature of spirits, angels, divinities, demons, phantoms, or even of God himself.

The Structure of Living Beings

THE living being is formed of galaxies of cells that are all bearers of a message, of a function that is assigned to them. A living body is analogous to an ordered society in which each individual fulfills a distinct function independently but in coordination with the others. These activities are grouped, according to the Sâmkhyä, around the five vital functions called prânä(s) (breaths): "The organs of the body are constituted in view of the functioning of these five activities" (*Sâmkhyä-Kârikâ*, 29). The first stage of Yogä consists in perceiving and controlling these functions.

The Five Vital Energies (Prânä)

THE first and most characteristic of the vital functions is a power of combustion, of animation. Life only exists by devouring, by consuming matter and life, and transforming it into energy. This function is fulfilled in man by respiration (*prânä*) but also by digestion (*prânä* in another sense). This power of combustion is in relation with the element Fire.

The second function is the power of rejection, or elimination (*apânä*), the expulsion of wastes, particularly evident for us in the fecal functions, but which also takes place in each cell. This function is related to the element Earth and to the sense of smell.

The third function is distribution (*samânä*), that is, assimilation or nutrition, which impartially distributes the energy produced by food to all the organs. This function is related to the element Water, the sense of taste, and the circulation of the blood.

The fourth function is reaction, the vigor (*udana*) or force that enables each organ to act by itself, to possess an independent activity. This function is related to the element of movement, Air, and to the sense of touch.

Finally, Vyânä (present everywhere) is the activity of verification, planning, attribution, and specialization, which distributes and separates the functions of the different organs, causing the body to function as a society whose different cells have distinct attributes, even though they are basically similar. Vyânä is related to the element Ether, the sense of hearing and speech.

These five activities are to be found in every organism, whether individual or collective. We find them again at the basis of every social organization: alimentation, elimination, distribution, force, and specialization, or, in other words, attribution of functions.

Vyânä, planning, is the last of the vital functions to disappear at the time of death. It is what enables certain specialized processes, like the growth of nails or hair, to continue. The first sense to disappear at the moment of death is sight, then the sense of smell vanishes, then taste, then touch. Hearing is the last sense to disappear. People who are apparently dead can hear. Vyânä, the central activity, subsists long after apparent death. This explains the possibility of the reutilization or transfer of organs, as well as the resurrection of a corpse by a transfer of psychic energy. Illnesses of the body, like the disorders of a society, come from the fact that certain cells quit their role and infringe on that of another group. Normally, the vital energies function independently of the will, of the "I." But the methods of Yogä can enable them to be controlled.

Man, as a finished object, as the end product of an evolutionary sequence, thus possesses external organs adapted to each function. But this does not prevent each of his components, each cell, each organ, from possessing, in a more or less effective manner, the same possibilities of absorbtion, rejection, communication, action, and so on.

Magic Powers (Siddhi)

THE exploration and control of his inner universe, by making use of the faculties that are not limited by the barriers of the senses and by mastering physical functions, vital rhythms, and mental mechanisms, enables the adept of Yogä to develop powers that are normally latent in man. These powers are called Siddhi(s), accomplishments or "godly powers" (*aïsh-varyä*).

These are the powers of Yogä that have made possible the observations on which the cosmological theories of the Sâmkhyä are based. The Siddhä(s), or persons who know how to develop the Siddhi(s), have been able to "see" the functioning of atoms, or view the exterior of galaxies, better than the most sophisticated observational equipment allows.

It is not necessary to cross the oceans with a chronometer to know the time differences between India and the Mayan cities as the geographer Aryabhata precisely shows us; it is sufficient to be in the two places at the same time, somewhat as the radio allows us to do today.

The possibilities of Yogä and the texts that describe it cannot be understood without taking into account the fact that the exploration of the secrets of the world and the development of supranatural powers that permit this exploration are its first objective.

The Yogi who has perfected the Siddhi(s) thus acquires powers "which belong to the gods" (*aïshvaryä*) and which are essentially the power of vision (*dṛikshakti*) *or power of knowledge* (*jñânâ-shakti*), that is to say, omniscience, as well as the powers of action (*kriyâ-shakti*), which are nine in number:

Animâ (atomization), enabling the perception of the infinitely small, the structures of atoms

Mahîmâ (immensity), enabling one to see the exterior, the structures of the galaxies

Garimâ (gravity), permitting one to assume an enormous weight

Laghimâ (lightness), permitting levitation

Prâpti (obtainment), permitting one to obtain an object wherever it might be

Prakâmyä (at will), enabling one to transport oneself to any location

Ishitvä (dominion), the power of control over the natural world, enabling one to arrest wind, provoke rain or storms, etc.

Vashitvä (holding in one's power), permitting one to have power over any being; hypnotism is an elementary form of it

Yatrakâmâvasâyitvä (transformation at will), allowing the adept to take on any form, that of a god, a giant, a blade of grass [Commentary on the *Sâmkhyä-Kârikâ, 23*]

The Yogi can enter into other bodies and bring corpses back to life by taking possession of the Vyânâ, the vital activity which regulates the vital functions and subsists for a certain time after apparent death.

Among the additional powers acquired by the Siddhä (adept) are those of incantation and enchantment. "The Yogi acquires the power of destroying or injuring his enemies through the aid of imitative magic, as, for example, by making images of an enemy and practicing magical rites and enchantments on them" (L. Chakravarty, *Indian Historical Quarterly* 6:114). The Yogi can, with a single glance, reduce all those who oppose him to ashes. He also acquires the power of acting with the speed of thought (*manojavitvä*) and the power of acting without physical organs (*vikaranä-dharmitvä*). Among the attributes of divine beings obtained by means of the Sid-dhi(s) are also the absence of fear, the absence of aging, and the absence of death.

The Yogi enjoys during his terrestrial existence all the voluptuous delights that others promise after death in a hypothetical paradise.

The Yogi does not pass his time in some vague meditation. He is constantly occupied by an intensive work which is the exploration, in ever-increasing depth, of this image of the Universal Being that is his own body. He explores all the nooks and crannies in which reside the mechanisms that regulate his physical and mental activities. He investigates and gradually enlarges the narrow and secret passages that will enable his higher faculties to escape from their corporeal prison. He must force certain passages, but he must be careful not to damage this marvelous dwelling place which is his body and which he must maintain with care and love. All asceticisms, all brutality toward himself, is forbidden. The Yogi, through his own power, controls the effects of time and prolongs his existence indefinitely. He acquires a perpetual adolescence, preserves this adolescent body, which he will one day transmute, if he succeeds in his enterprise, into a celestial body. He remains mortal, for the gods themselves are mortal, even though attaining prodigious longevity (sometimes confused with immortality). It is through the efficacy of his powers that he arrives at a suprahuman knowledge of the nature and structure of the world.

❧

Reincarnation

THE theory of reincarnation, which promulgates the continuity of the "I," seeks to replace the stages of evolution of a
lineage by the adventures of an individual being wandering
from species to species.

It is a strange pride, exploited by religious sects, which
persuades man to desire the permanence of the individual
instead of the continuity of the species, and to imagine a sort
of post-mortem eternity of human individualities while en-
visioning nothing of the sort for the other species.

Apart from the very particular cases of possession or of the
occupation of an apparently resuscitated corpse, the migration
of the Lingä-Sharirä is envisioned only as a phenomenon of
hereditary transmission and not as reincarnation, which would
be a vagabondage of the individuality through the most diverse
bodies. The theory of reincarnation, such as it appears in
later Hinduism, was a part neither of the old Shaivism nor
of Vedism. It derives from Jaïnism, which transmitted it to
Buddhism and then into modern Hinduism.

Belief in the survival of the human individuality in infernal
or celestial worlds, like the theory of reincarnation, is tied
to the doctrine of Karmä, which assumes the permanence of
an "I" which the Sâmkhyä, by contrast, considers ephemeral,
and an automatic retribution of actions committed in the
course of terrestrial life.

Prasâdä, divine Grace, is an essential element of the Shaiva
doctrine. The destiny of living beings depends essentially
upon the Creator's imagination and not upon their Karmä,
or automatic retribution of their actions, good or bad, which
would limit the absolute power of the Sovereign Principle
(Maheshvarä). *Shaivism does not accept the theory of Karmä
because it limits the omnipotence of the divine Being, his right to
injustice.* All that exists in the universe depends upon the
whim, the grace, of Shivä. This is why Shaivism orients
people toward devotion, Bhakti, and not toward moralism.
One does not barter with the gods.

Transubstantiation

SHAIVA Yogä is directed toward making use of the powers acquired at the far reaches of knowledge: the mastery of natural forces, magical action. It is through the force of his will, his power of knowledge, the power that he acquires, that the adept of Yogä can launch himself toward the conquest of the celestial worlds, surpassing the limitations of the human state and elevating himself to the level of the subtle powers that direct the world.

It is by a transubstantiation, which is the ultimate object of the practices of Hatha Yogä, that the realized Yogi (the hero, Vîrä) succeeds in elevating himself, body and soul, to a higher level of the hierarchy of creation. At this point he ceases to be a man, having transposed the harmonies, the characteristic patterns that constitute his physical nature, into another state of matter. What he seeks is to leave the animal state (*pashu*), to liberate himself from the snare (*pâshä*) of the material body, which imprisons the plan or group of faculties that constitute his Transmigrant Body or Sexual Body containing all the elements of his physical and mental personality. By virtue of the Siddhi(s) or powers acquired by Yogä, he comes to realize an ascension in the hierarchy of beings, which culminates in a transubstantiation that transforms the entire body into a celestial body without passing through death. The living being is thus transferred to a higher, more subtle level of existence, free from the constraints of materiality. Christian mythology, in speaking of the Assumption of the Virgin, alludes to this same phenomenon of transubstantiation.

It is thanks to a particular technique that the body made of corruptible matter (*ashuddhä-mâyâ*) is made to correspond to incorruptible matter (*shuddhä-mâyâ*) and transubstantiation takes place . . . the human body becomes liberated from the requirements of the animal economy when the transfer from corruptible Mâyâ to incorruptible Mâyâ occurs. It is then no longer subject to death . . . it is transfigured into a body of glory and power called Jñānā-tanu or spiritual body. The living liberated man (*jīvan-muktā*) leaves the domain of matter and with his body disappears suddenly into light. [V. V. Ramanan Shastri, *Cultural Heritage of India*, pp. 307–308]

Transubstantiation, by which the living being can transmute himself into a being of a more subtle essence without passing through death, is a completely different phenomenon from a post-mortem transmigration. The entire structure of the living being, in which resides the notion of "I," the persona of individual being, can be transmuted into another form of substance and subsist in proximity to (*samīpyā*) the divine beings, in what we imagine as paradise. On the other hand, when death takes place, the group of elements that consitute the human person disperses and the "I" ceases to exist. There exists no immortal soul independent of the body and the Internal Organ. It is omnipresent consciousness (*cit*) that is immortal, but although it inhabits the Internal Organ just as it does all the cells of the body, it is not a part of it. Confusion between consciousness (*cit*) and the notion of the "I" (*ahamkarā*) has given birth to the belief in the immortality of the "soul." The word *soul*, from *anima* (that which animates), is furthermore connected with the notion of prânä, of breath, regarded as the principle of life.

Liberation (Mok*shä*)

WHEN a created being, at whatever stage he finds himself, that of man or of god, reaches the highest level of awareness and perceives the nature of the world, he identifies himself with the plan, with Puru*shä*, and goes beyond the stage of Prak*ri*ti or nature. He leaves what is created and makes his way back to the Bindu, the initial point. This is what is called the final passage or liberation (*mok*shä*), also called the "instantaneous or total end of the world" (*atyantikä pralayä*) from the point of view of the individuality. In all events, the individual sooner or later ceases to exist and is dissolved into the various entities from which he was formed and which themselves will cease to exist when the universe is reabsorbed and returns to nonbeing.

Immortality

IMMORTALITY does not exist. Everything that has a beginning must one day have an end. When the universe is reabsorbed, when space and time no longer exist, when there is no longer either matter or harmony or plan or consciousness or thought, no form of survival, of existence, is possible or conceivable at any level.

All the same, within the hierarchy of creation there exist forms of consciousness, of matter, of organized complexes whose duration appears immense (or infinitesimal) with respect to our perception of time. Some of these forms of being are what we call the immortals.

Formed at levels of more subtle combinations than those perceived by our senses, spirits and gods still are within the domain of the multiplicity, the domain of Prakriti. Thus, the gods are mortal even if their life might seem of very long duration measured against the norms of time that human beings perceive.

When the divine dream becomes extinguished, when desire is obliterated, space and time, which are only the determining elements of what is "measurable" in the world, will be reabsorbed and cease to exist.

Yogä and Tantrism

YOGIC method makes use of the vital energies as sources of energy, particularly the combination represented by respiratory energy (*prânä*), but also sexual energy, connected with the very principle of life. Starting from the center where the

Transmigrant Body's models are manufactured, that is to say, the sexual center, by means of particular exercises and practices, the methods of Yogä can lead to the control and utilization of sexual energy.

When the adept seeks to attain knowledge by means of the Siddhi(s) or powers, he makes use of the practices known as the "left hand," centered around the genital functions. He transforms his procreative force into creative force. For this reason, the development and mastery of the sexual power plays a central role in the practices of Hathä Yogä. All the forms of shamanism are based on these techniques.

Shaiva Hathä Yogä is therefore tied to the magic rites of Tantrism, to the Yogi's grasping of the subtle plan according to which both his physical body and his mental image of Purushä—Universal Being—develop. The body in its entirety becomes the instrument for the realization of the higher powers of knowledge and for going beyond the limitations of the apparent world. It is in exploring the most secret regions of the body, developing the powers hidden in them, that the Hathä Yogi succeeds in transgressing natural laws and, by a transubstantiation of the entire body, elevates himself in the hierarchy of beings. Having then acquired the status of the subtle beings, he integrates himself into the company of spirits and gods.

He becomes equal to the gods, a god himself; but before realizing this ultimate stage, the disciplines that he must follow isolate him from other mortals. He becomes, with respect to human society, a strange being, disturbing, marginal, who has no place in materialist society. He leads a life both ascetic and lustful, for the sources of his power are in the Sexual Body. He is respected but feared.

Aryanized Yogä

THE religions of the Kali Yugä have endeavored to recapture the amazing methods of Yogä by adapting the teachings and practices to the modes of thinking of the urban cultures. The result is that there exists a Taoist Yogä, a Buddhist Yogä, a Zen Yogä. The Râjä Yogä of Patañjali is an intellectual path, while modern Shivä Yogä finds itself reduced to a devotional path based on the veneration of images and the hypnotic repetition of formulae or Manträ(s). The adepts of these new conceptions of a "civilized Yogä" have little in common with the marginal society of magician-sages practicing the ancient Hathä Yogä. "The entire yogic process is seen as a preparation for the pure mentalism of the Vedantä" (Thomas McEvilley, *An Archeology of Yoga*, 1, p. 58).

The goal is no longer knowledge or the exploration of the secret of the nature of the world and the conquest of heaven, but a negative conception of liberation that is nothing more than the destruction of the Transmigrant Body. The influence of Christian dualism, which separates body from soul (readily identified with the "I"), will find expression in the spiritualist conception of Vedantä and of an aseptic Yogä.

In modern times, Svâmî Vivekânandä, the founder of the Râmakrishnä Order at the end of the nineteenth century, was particularly active in the propagation of a theory of Yogä and of Vedantä adapted to the concepts and prejudices of Anglo-Saxon puritanism. He was followed in this path by Aurobindo and other recent commentators on Hinduism writing mostly in English. These new forms of Yogä extol negative methods such as abstinence, nonviolence, vegetarianism, chastity, and nonpossession. Certain essential practices of Hathä Yogä are eliminated. The "six acts" are replaced by mental attitudes. Symbolic elements are substituted for the material rituals of Tantrism. The attitude of the new Râjä Yogä is alien to the general conception of the world and the hierarchy of creation. Words such as *spirituality*, *transcendental meditation*, and *liberation* remain vague and often devoid of meaning, for the principle which dreams the world is beyond creation; it is in any event unknowable, unattainable.

The intermediate powers, on the other hand, are multiple, very diverse, and very defined. The world of the gods is part of creation; it is not in essence different from the world of men; it is only at another level of reality. It is through the Siddhi(s) that it is possible to contact, to communicate with, the individualities of the celestial world, then to become assimilated to them. The Siddhi(s) also make it possible to control the nature of the invisible forces with which certain practices permit contact.

PART THREE

THE MÎMÂNSÂ: THE RELIGIOUS, RITUALISTIC, AND MYSTICAL APPROACH

1

The Two Mîmânsâ

THE THIRD METHOD OF INQUIRY ENTAILS THE INVES-
tigation of contacts with the world by the subtle powers who
represent the various levels of consciousness within the hierarchy of creation, and whom we call spirits or gods. It
involves on the one hand experiment and intuition, the elementary approach (*pûrvä*), and on the other hand theory and
theology, the higher approach (*uttarä*).

Pûrvä Mîmânsâ, primary intuition, tries to establish, by
means of symbols, rites, sacrifices, and magical practices,
contacts with the powers which inhabit the subtle worlds but
which cannot be identified by any other means. We are able
to create, with the assistance of the symbols, images, and
rites, meeting points which allow contact between the different levels of existence and which help us to better understand through direct experience the structural similarities
between the various types of beings. If the rites and magical
practices are functioning and are giving tangible results, this
means they have found an echo in a world that is invisible
to us. Prayer is part of this approach: when we beseech the
gods, spirits, or saints to help us overcome our problems, it
is as if we are sending out a radar signal toward the invisible
in the hope of picking up an echo.

In order to establish communication between the different types of being, the rites that are dubbed Tantric use the similarities between the archetypes at the base of our Sexual Body, our genetic code, and the analogous ones that give rise not only to the subtle beings but also to the other forms of life (plants and animals).

We call gods or spirits all those beings that cannot be directly perceived by us, but whose existence and presence we can sense. They are of various types: they are not immortal and differ from us less in their form than in their substance, dimensions, and length of life.

Our efforts to communicate with subtle beings, the spirits or the living creatures of other worlds, presupposes that their concepts of time match ours (and there is no evidence of this) or that they are temporarily to be found at the meeting points between the different worlds. This is why attempts to establish contact are usually unsuccessful. Interaction between beings of different dimensions and time are only possible in certain specific cases. We cannot communicate with extraterrestrials, fairies, or genies unless they are, however temporarily it may be, in conditions of time and space similar to our own. Otherwise, communication can only be by means of that part of our subtle faculties which is not the prisoner of relative space and time.

Beings for whom, according to the theory of cycles, a human day corresponds to a second or to several centuries, can never be perceived by us: this is the cause of the problems of communication between different worlds, for the value that we attach to a given length of time is relative to our physical body. It is determined by the vital rhythms of each species.

One of the characteristics of what we consider to be sightings of celestial beings or extraterrestrials is the speed with which they disappear in relation to what is normal for our vision of time. Their presence in our world, which may last a day for them, takes only a few seconds for us.

The animist intuition and experience of the mystics are

part of the experimental forms of Mîmânsâ. The problem is to discern with which types of beings, with which types of invisible forces, we are establishing contact and with whom we are eventually entering into agreement. A misunderstanding as to their nature or a mistake in the rites might make them harmful. Those who try to make contact with the spirits by making tables turn are taking part in a form of ritual experience similar to those of religious or magical rites.

The second, "higher" Mîmânsâ (Uttarä Mîmânsâ) attempts to define the nature of the subtle beings that we contact through rites, and whose very existence we sense through mystic intuition. Such an intellectual approach, which tries to rationalize and to explain the features of mystical and ritual experience, might be termed theological or metaphysical. The Uttarä Mîmânsâ analyzes the echoes of the invisible so that it can establish a kind of hierarchy for the forces which control the subtle world.

The Gods

THE Absolute, "that indefinable thing which is only Being" (*sattâmâträ*), is outside the world and hence unknowable. It can only be conceived of in negative terms. This is why it can only be said that it is impersonal, formless, inactive, unreachable, inconceivable, without dimension or limit.

The ancient languages never used the world *god* to refer to this timeless, immaterial, and unmoving principle; instead, they had neutral terminology such as *logos, Parä-Brahman* (the immenseness of the beyond), or *Paramä-Shivä* (the transcendent aspect of Shivä).

It is out of the question for living beings, whether men or gods, to reach the Absolute Being by means of rites or prayer. It is quite outside the sphere of religion or mysticism. At the time of the realization of the plan, conglomerations, centers of individualized consciousness imbued with a sense of self, are formed in energetic substance; they will be witnesses observing the apparent structures of the world at different levels. From the point of view of the Conceiving Being, a god, observer of the play of galaxies, is of no more importance than the observer of the beauties of the Earth.

All aspects of creation are based on patterns, formulae, and archetypes which are always the same and which are to be found in all aspects of the world; in combination with each other they form different models and varieties of things. There is no fundamental difference between gods, spirits, men, animals, and insects. They can be compared to spectators seated in the different circles of a theater.

The word *dieu* (Lat. *deus*, Gk. *theos*, Skt. *devä*) derives from the Indo-European root *div*, which means "radiant/radiating," an ephithet of the sun. The gods are thus considered to be active principles. The word *devä* refers to the forms of subtle and active consciousness present at the different levels of creation and thus part of the multiplicity. It is never used to indicate a principle beyond measurement and outside the apparent world. Even before the primordial explosion of energy from which matter resulted, the principle of consciousness known as the Sovereign Principle (Ishvarä) or Supreme Sovereign (Maheshvarä) emerged.

On the threshold between the nonexistent and the existent, Maheshvarä, the principle of consciousness, is double-natured. One side is compact, without component parts (*nishkala*) and indivisible; the other is composite (*sakalâ*) and presents various aspects; it is the composite aspect that is called Universal Man (Puru<u>sh</u>ä), the plan or model of the universe. In the form of Mahat, universal intelligence, Puru<u>sh</u>ä presides over the development of the world. The various aspects of Mahat, called gods or spirits, take part in the organization of the world and rule over the different degrees of the formation of matter and the different types of beings.

The gods are the personification of the forces that rule the universe and control its development, for creation is a living thing which evolves according to a plan contained in its seed.

Creation does not take place in an instant, but is rather a long process of growth and decline.

Each sidereal organism, each type of molecule of matter, each living species forms an entity, a unit corresponding to a pattern evolving through the passage of time. There exists a consciousness, a thinking being that presides over the achievement and development of each species, somewhat as each human "I" presides over the countless cells that make up his body.

It is with these aggregate consciousnesses that we make contact when we try to communicate with the supernatural world. These are the ministers who accept the prayers and feed on the sacrificial incense that we direct to the gods. In the hierarchy of creation, there are parallels and connections between the various levels of existence corresponding to the combinations of analogous archetypes. This is why the conflicts between the subtle powers that are the spirits and gods are reflected in the wars of mankind and in the upheavals of matter that give rise to cataclysms. They often occur together and can easily be described in terms of one another. Storms, earthquakes, and volcanic eruptions go hand in hand with epidemics, invasions, wars, and massacres. They both reflect and express the conflicts that take place in the parallel world of the heavenly powers.

These subtle beings that humans worship as gods are countless. According to the *Lingä Purânä* (1.4.443–444): "There are two hundred and eighty million gods and subtle beings who move about in flying chariots. During the Manvantarä, the cycles of humanity, their number increases to three billion, nine hundred and twenty million." Religious, mystical and magical experience enables us to make contact with them.

Aspects of Maheshvarä

FROM the point of view of religious experience, the universal consciousness (*mahat*), which is the manifest and divisible (*sakalâ*) aspect of Maheshvarä, is present in all aspects of the world. The divine may be reached through the worship of any form of creation, whether it be an object, a symbol, an animal, a tree, a human, or a spirit. This is reflected in the Purânä by the thousand names of Shivä (*Shivä-sahasrä-nâmä*).

Shivä, Tamas

THE three tendencies (*gunä*[s]) of Primordial Nature (*pradhânä*), endowed with consciousness, are to be found in all levels of the hierarchy of beings. Shivä in the aspect of Tamas, the expansive force which causes the birth of the world, is symbolized at the level of the gods by the Nata Râjä, the cosmic dancer who, in the postures and rhythms of his dance, creates the harmonies, modules, plans, and patterns according to which all structures of matter and life are organized.

In his androgynous aspect (*ardhanarîshvarä*), he is the life principle, the origin of the species. As Bhairavä (the Terrible), he is the death principle: the image of the impermanence of transitory beings, on which the existence of species rests in a perpetually transforming universe. Shivä is also depicted as Kâlä, the time principle, who measures the duration of worlds and beings. The Pâshupatä consider Bhairavä, the destructive and terrifying aspect, to be the basis of the other aspects. It is to ward off this aspect that he is called Shivä (the Kindly) or Shambhu (the Peacemaker).

Sattvä, the Goddess, and Vishnu

THE plan becomes reality only when it is realized in matter. Shivä is merely an abstraction until he is united with the energetic principle, Shakti, the substance of the world. Without the "I" which is his energy and the source of his power of creation, Shivä is but a form without life, as inanimate as a corpse (*shavä*).

The creation of the world can thus be seen in terms of two aspects, one masculine, the establisher of laws, and the other feminine, the concretizer of those laws.

In the Shaiva pantheon, each aspect of the plan corresponds to a realization represented by a goddess.

The opposition between male and female appears at every stage of manifestation. All atoms, elements, forms, substances, and beings are an expression of it. These two principles are forever united and inseparable, and can only exist through one another, yet they are at the same time utterly opposed, completely contradictory and irreconcilable.

Sattvä, the second of the Gunä(s), the qualities or tendencies of Prakriti, is the principle of attraction and condensation, the negative pole. Sattvä corresponds to the feminine principle, as represented by the goddess in her various forms, including a masculine aspect called Vishnu. In the form of Mohini, the Enchantress, Vishnu transforms himself into a woman in order to seduce Shivä. The goddess and Vishnu are protective divinities.

The goddess is called Pârvati, the Lady of the Mountain, for mountain peaks, which manifest terrestrial currents of energy, are the negative pole that attracts the celestial currents apparent in lightning.

The goddess is also known as Sati (Faithfulness), for she is inseparable from the god. She is Kâlî, the Power of Time, for she is the incarnation of its destructive power.

She is Sarasvati (Daughter of the Waters), goddess of the sciences and arts. In this aspect, she appears in the form of the ten Mahâ-Vidhyâ(s), the higher levels of knowledge. She is Lakshmi the billionaire, goddess of wealth and material goods, protector of the family, the home, and the family hearth.

The Shaktä(s), who worship the feminine principle, believe that the aspects of the divine that can be reached through rites are part of the realized plan and not part of the abstract one. It is therefore the goddess and not the god who is the object of worship.

Rajas, Prajâpati-Brahmâ

IN the aspect of Rajas, the principle of gravitation, of activity, and of the motion that results from the other two tendencies, Shivä is called Prajâpati, Lord of the Creatures. He is also called Brahmâ, Lord of Spaces. He represents equilibrium, wisdom, and justice. It is to him that the gods appeal to settle their conflicts.

As the creator of the world, he is known as Vishvä-Karmä, architect of the universe.

Many of Prajâpati's aspects, such as the incarnations of the tortoise, the wild boar, and the lion man, were, in later times, attributed to Vishnu. In the *Taïttiriyä Brâhmanä*, it is Prajâpati who takes the form of the boar Emusa in order to raise the earth out of the primordial ocean. Likewise, it is Prajâpati who takes the shape of a fish at the time of the deluge.[1]

In trying to define the nature of the divine, in wishing to reach back to what appears to us to be the first cause of the world, we can stop at any one of the stages of creation. This fact will affect all our religious, moral, social, philosophic, and scientific concepts.

Symbols of the Gods

ALL aspects of creation correspond to basic formulae that can be portrayed by means of geometric or mathematical figures. The formulae of the major gods are portrayed by Yanträ(s), flat geometric figures, or by Mandala(s), designs in space which are used as guides in the building of sanctuaries.

These basic formulae are to be found at all levels of the creational hierarchy. In the field of sound we can trace them in the combinations of sound relationships in music (*râgä*[s]) or in language (*manträ*[s]), which, like the Yanträ(s), evoke the various aspects of divinity. These relationships are also to be found in the patterns that establish the nature of beings. They are the key to the nature of animals and plants and their connections with particular divinities.

Each god is associated with an animal called his "vehicle," which is worshiped as his symbol. In the hierarchy of living beings, Shivä is the bull among animals, and the pipal, or sacred fig, among trees. His image among men is that of the Guru or master, the source of knowledge; among the sages he is Yogeshvarä (the master of Yogä).

Many spirits exist among the lower divinities: the Yak<u>sh</u>ä who watch over the equilibrium of nature reside in springs, grottoes, and trees. They are often hostile to men, who seek to woo them with gifts.

The Cult of the Lingä

THE Lingä, or phallus, is the principal symbol of divinity as worshiped by the Shaivas. Maheshvarä, the Great God, is the personification of Puru<u>sh</u>ä, the universal man of the Sâmkhyä. From him springs forth the abstract models, the archetypes which gradually become incarnate in matter originate with them. The semen, or code, incarnating in the egg, finds its substance in the female body. This is the aspect presented by the symbol of a phallus imprisoned in a vulva. When the plan (Puru<u>sh</u>ä) enters matter (Prak<u>ri</u>ti), the world appears. When consciousness (*cit*) enters substance (*sat*), delight (*ânandä*) appears. *The world is nothing other than voluptuous delight.* Its splendor, its beauty, and its diversity make the most wonderful of spectacles. It is as illusory, ephemeral, and unreal as pleasure. Yet it is the only reality. It is out of voluptuous pleasure that all living creatures are born. The phallic cult is a reminder that each of us is but an ephemeral being of little importance, and that our only role is to better the chain that we represent for a moment in the evolution of the species, and to pass it on. The cult of the phallus is therefore connected to a recognition of the species's permanence in relation to the individual's impermanence; of the principle that establishes the laws out of which we have emerged (and not of their accidental or temporary implementation) of the principle of life, and not of the living beings; of the abstract and not of the concrete. This concept finds its application on all planes, whether ethical, ritual, cosmological, or societal. To renounce the cult of the phallus, in order to worship a person, whether human or divine, is idolatry and an outrage against the creative principle.

The Assimilated Gods

MANY of the ancient divinities from the Shaiva pantheon have been absorbed into Brahminism (which identified Shivä with the Vedic Rudrä). Mayon (the Black God) of Dravidian tradition was somewhat belatedly considered to be an incarnation of Vishnu with the name of Krishnä (the Black One). According to the *Vâyu Purânä*, Krishnä is a hero who was initiated into the Pâshupatä Yogä by the Rishi Upamanyu. In the *Mahâbhâratä*, we can see that Krishnä worships Shivä and the Lingä.

Râmä himself is also a pre-Aryan hero. It was he who installed and worshiped the Lingä of Râmeshvarä (god of Râmä) in the extreme south of India.[2]

Skandä (the spurt of semen), the son of Shivä, was born of the god's semen or Somä, the elixir of immortality, which fell into the sacrificial fire and from there into the Ganges.

The ancient Dravidian Murugan, Skandä is the god of beauty and perpetual youth. He is called Kumârä, the adolescent. Begotten by Shivä alone with no female counterpart, he is hostile to marriage. As head of the celestial cohorts, he has no other spouse than his army (Senä). His cult excludes women. It is he who teaches the sages the bases of knowledge. He rides a peacock.

He is also called Shanmukhan (the six-faced), corresponding to the Sumerian Sanmugan, who possessed the same characteristics (adolescent god, head of the armies, riding a bird).

Ganeshä, the elephant-headed god, is the son of the goddess alone. He represents the seemingly impossible unity between large (elephant) and small (man), between macrocosm and microcosm. Because he is the god of wisdom, he is invoked before anything is undertaken.

Monotheism

THE theologies of the various religions are distinguished by their more or less approximative methods of analyzing and representing the subtle world and of explaining our perceptions of the supernatural. All religions, even those that we term primitive, try to classify and personalize cosmic principles and their relationships with the various levels of creation. The depiction of the gods in anthropomorphic or theriomorphic form is the result of an attempt at classification of animist intuition; this is done by establishing parallels and correspondences between the various hierarchic levels in the visible and invisible worlds.

All religions were originally, and in practice still are, polytheistic; they involve the invocation, through magical rites and prayers, of multiple and specialized entities, whatever the generic name that may be given to them: saints, angels, or spirits.

The ethnological study of religion leads inevitably to the realization that the gods in all religions (or their substitutes: virgins, angels, demons, prophets) have developed from analogous concepts and represent universal principles born of perception of the fundamental structures of the world. This is one of the aspects of knowledge that the simplification of monotheism tends to obliterate.

The principle of self (*aham*), which developed from Mahat (the universal consciousness), is the basis of multiplicity. It is the opposite of unity. It is nonsensical to imagine the existence of a conscious entity being able to act before "I-ness" came into being. There cannot be an entity who says "I" and issues commands, and yet is not part of a multiplicity.

Monotheism is but the divinization of the stage of I-ness, the Aham in the hierarchy of creation. Monotheism presupposes the existence of a personal god who rules the world as he pleases and who is in fact merely the depiction of the divine according to the human model.

By personalizing the word (*logos*), by reducing the transcendent hierarchies to a humanlike individual, the so-called monotheistic religions have simplified and falsified all concepts of the cosmos, of the nature of the world, and of the divine; they have also permanently severed theology from science and from mystical experience. Perception of the supernatural appears in many, very diverse forms. The experience of mystics, visionaries, spiritualists, and occultists is in complete contradiction to monist simplification. *"The number one is at the heart of error,"* say the Tanträ(s) (*Ekä Shabdâtmikâ Mâyâ*). The religions that claim to be monotheistic are in fact always prophetic religions. The abstract god is merely an excuse for the deification of the prophet, whose revelations are presented as the words of God.

Monotheism reduces the celestial hierarchies to a single figure with whom prophets and pontiffs claim to communicate; this figure places upon them the responsibility of enforcing so-called moral and social laws of human invention, just as if man were the center of the universe and the reason for its existence.

Monotheistic religions are, moreover, mutually exclusive, each one receiving contradictory instructions from its god. There is, therefore, in each case, an elected god, which Hinduism calls an Ishtä-devatä. A type of dualism comes into being when the creative principle is personalized and separated from what is created. This leads to contempt for the divine work, which man can then exploit as he pleases, referring to the instructions revealed to him by a fictitious personality, and which in fact are merely the projection of his ambitions, his wish for power, and the subjection of nature to his depredations. "A monistic god paves the way for subsequent productivity and introduces totalitarianism" (Michel Maffesoli, *L'Ombre de Dionysos*, p. 53).

It is this reduction of the subtle active forces to a single divine being which has allowed the monotheistic religions to become instruments of obscuratism and oppression, culminating in the ridiculous behavior of the religious sects characteristic of modern times, from the Inquisition to Khomeinism. The fiction that is monotheism will allow any tyranny.

The shaman and the medium are quite right to believe that they can receive information from the intermediary powers, whereas the high priest who claims to embody the will of a universal principle outside creation can only be a madman, a liar, or a charlatan.

A denial of a single god by no means includes a denial of the supernatural. Monotheism itself is in fact close to atheism; it prepares the way for materialism by replacing with an abstraction the reality of the celestial powers who are the gods.

Curiously, it is thanks to the concepts expressed in the Sâmkhyä (which tends to be thought of as atheistic since it does not recognize the possibility of a single active god) that one can observe among the Hindus the feeling that the invisible is omnipresent, the respect for the mystery and unexpectedness of the work of the creator, *and the principle of tolerance, which is in fact simply respect for multiple paths in the search for the divine.*

NOTES

1. See J. Muir, *Journal of the Royal Asiatic Society* 5.
2. See M. R. Sakhare, *History and Philosophy of Lingayat Religion*, pp. 147–150.

2

The Doctrine of the Pâshupatä

The Teaching of Lakulishä

LAKULISHÄ IS CONSIDERED TO BE THE LAST REPRESEN-
tative of primordial tradition. He is the last of the visionaries/
seers (the Rishi[s]) who brought to mankind yet again a message of wisdom that might bring about a delay in the destruction inherent in the ending of the Kali Yugä. It is not necessarily
the only such message, for, at the same moment in the cycle,
other voices in other places arose in an attempt to curb mankind's madness. Their teaching went astray, just like Lakulishä's did in India. What survives is, however, sufficient,
if we have the courage to reverse the tendencies of the modern
world and to renounce the absurdities of religious, moral,
and social ideologies which conceal reality from us, to allow
part of humanity to survive a little longer and permit a few
to pass through the apocalypse and be part of the birth of a
new world.

The teachings of Lakulishä expose the principles of the
Darshanä (the paths of knowledge) in a simple and popular
form full of imagery, and suggest patterns of behavior suitable
for the final stages of the Kali Yugä.

Texts

THE texts concerning the doctrine of the Pâshupatä(s), as portrayed by Lakulishä, are assembled in a series of essays entitled the *Lakulâgamä Samayä* (Summary of the Tradition of Lakulishä). The adherents of this philosophy are known as Lâkulä(s), Pâshupatä(s), or Kâlâmukhä(s) (Black Faces). Lakulishä takes up the ritual and moral traditions of ancient Shaivism in their entirety and takes into account the materialistic philosophy of the Vaïshes̱hikä and the logic of the Nyâyä.[1]

No available Pâshupatä ritual or philosophical texts date from before Lakulishä's time. There are, however, several later works written by the Pâshupatä(s) which summarize the ancient texts. Most important among them are the following:

The *Pâshupatä Sûträ* and the commentary on it by Kaund̲inya, called the *Panchârthä-Bhas̱hya*

The *Gan̲a Kârikä* of Haradattä and its commentary, the Ratnat̲ikâ by Bhâsarvajñä

The *Ishvarä-Kartr̲i-Vâdä* (the creative power of the divine beings) by Bonteyä Muni, who preached Lakulishä's doctrines in Andhra during the eleventh century

The *S̱haddarshana Samucchayä* (a summary of the six philosophic approaches) by Râjashekharä (1350)

The *S̱haddarshana Samucchayä* by Haribhadrä with a commentary by a Jaïnä author named Gun̲aratnä (c. 1375)

The chapter on the "Nâkulishä-Pâshupatä Darshanä" in the *Sarvä Darshanä-Samgrahä* (History of the Philosophic Systems) of Sâyan̲ä-Mâdhavä (fourteenth century), is one of the best expositions of the doctrine.

Pashupati: Lord of the Animals

IN ancient Shaivism, the creative principle was worshiped in the form of Pashupati, Lord of the Animals. Pati, the herder, is the creator and sovereign of the world. Pashu, the livestock, comprises all the beings of creation: gods, spirits, animals, men. Pâshä, the snare, is the visible world: material, illusory, in which all living beings are imprisoned.

The cult of Pashupati is the aspect of Mîmânsâ that concerns earthly life and the relationships between humans and the supernatural and natural worlds. It enables man to carry out his role harmoniously among the other species.

Pati: The Herder

ACCORDING to the Pâshupatä doctrine, Pati, the master of the herd, is everywhere. He is not restricted in time or space.

The power of action or energy (shakti) is part of the material world of Nature (prakriti). The herder resides in Nature under the form of consciousness. Nature is unable to act separately from this consciousness. Nothing in the world happens by chance or hazard.

Man is created in the image of the divine being, but the divine being is not hemmed in within the five formulae (manträ[s]), which are at the base of the Tanmaträ(s), the five types of interaction in matter, the source of the five elements. The word manträ is used here to mean the formulae, in the mathematical sense of the word, which are at the base of all forms of creation. In Yogä, manträ corresponds to a sound formula which is the verbal expression of an archetype that represents a state of being, ultimately a divinity, and allows that being to be summoned. [Mrigendrä-Âgamä 3.7.5]

Pashu: The Animal

PASHU, the herd animal, includes the subtle beings that we call gods, genies, or demons, as well as the animal species including man. The mission of some of these beings is to direct the development of each of the species. It is with the genies closest to us that we are able to enter into contact by means of animist perception and rites.

The different levels of creation appear to be quite separate and independent of each other, yet they form an indivisible whole.

Each living being perceives a particular aspect of creation. It is evidence of one of the many aspects of the divine plan, one of the mirrors in which the creator views his work. The field (*ksheträ*) of each is limited; this is why the animal (*pashu*) (that is to say, the living being [*jîvä*]) is also known as Kshe-träjñä (he who knows the field, that aspect of the world which he is destined to perceive). He represents one fraction of the universal consciousness, residing in a corporeal prison.

Pâshä: The Snare

THE snare, Pâshä, is the apparent world. Consciousness (*chaitanyä*) is the principle of perception, boundless within Pati, the Master, but restricted in the living beings, the beasts (*pashu*), caught in the snare (*pâshä*).

The snare is formed of four materials:

· An individual's innate tendencies (*pravritti*)

· The limits imposed by the divine plan (Ishä-jâlä)

· The effects of behavior (Karmä)

· The illusory nature (*mâyâ*) of the world [*Mrigendrä-Âgamä* 5.13]

There are three components (*kalâ*) of the snare. These are
the limits of the power of the mind (*vijñânâ-kalâ*), the des-
tructibility of living beings (*pralayä-kalâ*), and the multiplicity
of the levels of the created world (*sakalä-kalâ*). [*Mrigendrä-
Âgamä* 3.7.8]

It is the snare that isolates the individual from the universal
consciousness and is therefore the origin of human individuality. Once the obstacles created by the snare are removed,
the individual consciousness becomes part of, and lost within,
the universal consciousness.

The Creative Power of the Sovereign Being
(*Ishvarä-Kartri-Vâdä*)

THE philosophical doctrine of the Pâshupatä(s) as taught by
Lakulishä is called Ishvarä-Kartri-Vâdä (the creative power
of the sovereign being). It was quoted in the ninth century
by Shankarâchâryä in his commentary on the *Brahmâ-Sûträ(s)*
(3.2.37).

An analysis of it is to be found in one of the main Pâshupatä
texts, the *Ganä-Kârikä* of Haradattä, and its commentary by
Kaundinyä called *Pañcharthä-Bhâshyä* (commentary of the five
subjects). Râmânujä attributed this philosophy to the tradition of the Kâlâmukhä(s), the sect of "Black Faces" to which
Lakulishä belonged.

This doctrine is divided into five parts, known as Kâranä
(cause), Kâryä (work/task), Kalâ (divisibility), Vidhi (method),
Yogä (union), and Dukhântä (the end of suffering).

The Cause (*Kâranä*)

KÂRANÄ (the cause) is the word used for the Sovereign Principle (Ishvarä) which creates, upholds, and destroys the universe. *Shivä* (the Benevolent) and *Pati* (the Master) are the

words designating this causal principle from which the world has resulted. In its destructive aspect, it is called Bhaïravä (the Terrible).

> One of the most distinctive features of the Pâshupatä doctrine as propounded by Kaundinya and the *Ratnatikâ* is the belief in God's absolute independence, (svatantratâ). This . . . means that God acts without regard for human actions (karmâdini-rapekshä). This doctrine is connected to Gosâlä's determinism (Niyati). [Lorenzen, *The Kâpâlikas and Kâlâmukhas*, pp. 190–191]

The creative principle (*kartri*) is independent of all cosmic or moral law (*dharmä*). It cannot be influenced by the actions (*karmä*) of the beings it creates. The reward for merit is a gift from the gods; it is not automatic.

The Work (Kâryä)

KÂRYÄ (the work) represents the world, matter, and life. Kâryä, the substance of creation, has three components called Vidyâ (knowledge), Kalâ (divisibility, multiplicity), and Pashu (the animal, the living being). Vidyâ, in the form of consciousness (Cit, corresponding to the Mahat of Sâmkhyä), is present throughout the work in as much as it is a product of the Creator and inseparable from him. The principles of matter and of life are themselves also in one sense eternal.

Divisibility (Kalâ)

THERE are two aspects to the Sovereign Principle. One is manifest and composite (*sakalâ*); the other is transcendent and indivisible (*nishkalâ*). In his composite form, the divine being is immanent, present in all things, and therefore has many facets or aspects.

In his indivisible form, he is shapeless, unknowable, and beyond thought and words. In these two aspects the Sovereign Principle has limitless powers of knowledge (*jñânä-shakti*) and action (*kriyâ-shakti*).

The qualities of sovereignty (*patitvä*), of existence (*sattvä*), of being the beginning of all things (*adyaträ*) and not being born of something else (*ajatvä*) belong to the composite aspect, corresponding to the Sâmkhyä's Purushä. This is the aspect which is at the base of the "constituent elements of the apparent world" (the Tattvä[s]) envisaged by the Sâmkhyä.

Method (Vidhi)

THE other aspects of Lakulishä's doctrine concern not the nature of the world, but rather the nature of man and the rules of his behavior. Method is divided into four sections called Padä(s) (feet). They are Kriyâ (things needing to be done, meritorious acts), Charyâ (observances), Yogä (union), and Jñânä (knowledge).

Meritorious Deeds (Kriyâ)

THE *Padmä Samhitä* (3.1.6) says that Kriyâ(s) (obligations, meritorious deeds) are mainly the construction of sanctuaries and the creation of images. An important part of the Âgamä(s) concerns the selection of the sites, plans, architecture, sculpture, and installation of images within a sanctuary.

The Temple

THE temple is a Mandalä, a geometric configuration designed according to the archetypes and patterns that are the basis of the structures of the universal and of the human being.

Sacred architecture, based as it is on the symbolism of

numbers, the geometric diagrams of the Yanträ(s), and its orientation in relation to the constellations of the zodiac and other astrological features, plays an essential part in communication between the various states of being, between men and gods. The real presence of the divine being can be invoked, through the power of the Manträ(s) (magical formulae), within the image at the center of the sanctuary.

The Kali Yugä is the age of the worship of idols. Contact between man and the supranatural is most easily achieved through the architecture of the temple and the images of the gods based on magical diagrams. The god Shivä taught mankind music, dance, sculpture, architecture, and the ability to work with bronze and iron at the dawn of the Kali Yugä. In all civilizations, the origins of sacred architecture and the concept of the Great Work can be traced to protohistoric Shaivism, beginning with the megalithic monuments to be found wherever Dravidian influence extended. The "idolatrous" Shaivas have long been criticized for the building of temples and the worship of images. The cult of images was unknown to the nomadic and warrior peoples who survived the Tretä Yugä and who did their best to destroy sanctuaries and idols until at last they adopted them themselves. The iconoclastic Hebrews overthrew the Golden Calf and laid the temples of Baal to ruin. (There is a striking parallel between the biblical Baal and Bala (the adolescent), another name of Skandä (head of the army of the gods, the son and double of Shivä), who is worshiped in the form of a bull.) Later, the Islamic Arabs destroyed temples in India and the Christians broke up the images of the Roman gods before filling their churches with statues of the Virgin and the saints.

There is no mention in the Vedic texts of the building of temples or the worship of idols. Vedic sacrifices were (and still are) carried out under temporary shelters, the Mandapä(s) being built for the occasion and subsequently destroyed. The building of temples and worship of images are by contrast a fundamental part of Shaivism.

The Freemasons and guilds in the West are the remnants

of the ancient associations of temple builders and can provide
us with an idea of the moral and social values of an artisanal
tradition.

Following the destruction of the cities of the Indus by the
Aryans, sacred architecture disappeared from India. Only
small sanctuaries, a few stones surrounding a Lingä, are to
be found in the mountains and other isolated places. It was
the Buddhists, much later, who again took up the construction of stupä(s) (mounds covering relics) derived from the
ancient dolmens.

It was only with the Shaiva renewal that the construction
of temples began again, using the traditions whose secrets
the artisanal associations had preserved. Pâshupatä temples
were built almost everywhere in India, including Kapishä
(Afghani Nuristan), during the time of Harshä (606–647);
the work had, however, begun in the time of the Guptä(s).
The Chinese pilgrim Hsüan Tsang makes mention of them.

An extraordinary number of temples were built in the areas
where the influence of Lakulishä was strongest; from Raj-
putana to Orissa, and in the south of India. Among them
were the temples of Ellora, Elephanta, Bhuvaneshvar, Khajuraho, and, in the south, Badami, Aihole, Chidambaram,
Conjeevaram, Madura, etc. They are among the most beautiful monuments in the world, evidence of a period of religious
exaltation that calls to mind the later golden age of cathedrals
in the West, which was influenced in all likelihood by the
Indian architects who fled the Muslim invasions (see Alain
Daniélou, *Le Temple hindou*).

Union (*Yogä*)

IN the texts of Shaivism, Yogä is defined as "the establishment
of a relationship between the individual being and the universal being through the gateway (dvarä) of the consciousness
(chittä)." According to the *Ratnaṭikä*, "Yogä is the means that
permits the identification of the living being (*jîvä*) with the

total being or Sovereign Principle (Ishvarä)."[2] This relationship is established in the first place by the repetition of Manträ(s), verbal formulae which evoke the archetypes that constitute the nature of certain aspects of the divine being. This initial preparation is followed by mental concentration (Dhyânä) and other observances of Yogä that lead to mastery of the various faculties and energies that make up the human person.

The End of Suffering (Dukhântä)

THE sixth subject with which the doctrine of Lakulishä is concerned is known as Dukhântä (the end of suffering). This involves the destiny of beings after life. According to Kaundiyä, there are two varieties of Dukhântä: the personal (sâtmakä) and the impersonal (anâtmakä). In the personal form achieved by the Siddhi(s), the human being can pass beyond the animal condition and, becoming a subtle being, can unite with Shivä (Rudrä sayujyä). In the impersonal form, the self ceases to exist and the various components of the living being return to the universal principles from which they came.

NOTES

1. See M. R. Sakhare, The History and Philosophy of Lingayat Religion, pp. 212–214.

2. Chittadvârenä Âtmeshvarä sambandhäheturyogah.

3

Communities and Monastic Orders

The Monastic Orders

THE MEMBERS OF THE SHAIVA SECTS ARE REFERRED to in the Vedä(s) by the name Vrâtyä (the Excluded), meaning people living on the fringes of society, practicing ecstatic dances and sexual rites with prostitutes, sacrificing animals and eating the flesh of their victims, drinking intoxicating beverages, and worshiping serpents and trees. They earned their living as roving minstrels, specializing in song, sex, and dance.

The *Rig Vedä* (X.136) describes one of these non-Aryan ascetic-magicians, whom it calls Âjîvikä(s) (beggars), "with long hair (*keshin*), clothed in space (*vâtä-rasanä*), driven mad by austerities and the practice of silence, body smeared with yellowish dust, possessing magical powers and drinking poison (a drug) in the company of Rudrä (Shivä)." It was, however, these Vrâtyä(s), the Excluded, considered outcasts, who little by little introduced Tantric rites and the practices of Yogä into Aryan society, including Ur Yogä or Union by Force, by which the Vîrä (hero), through his power, conquered the heavens, and also Ultâ Sâdhanâ (the inverse method), which utilizes for man's spiritual progress the very elements that are normally the cause of his fall.

The priests, described in the *Atharvä Vedä* as practicing magic rites, were probably the Kâpâlikä(s) (Skull-Bearers). They are also mentioned in the *Maïtrï Upanishad*. These ascetics, who perpetuated the religious practices of the pre-Aryan world and had been able to maintain the ancient traditions with a remarkable continuity for more than two thousand years despite persecutions, invasions, and religious and social changes, came out again at the time of the Shaiva revival. We still meet them today, covered with ashes, in forest hermitages or pilgrimage places. They live completely outside of official Hinduism.

These ascetics are divided into several sects, among which the Âgamä(s) mention principally the Pâshupatä(s), Kâpâlikä(s), Kâlâmukhä(s), Soma-siddhantä(s), and Lakulä(s).

The Shaddarshanä Samucchayä (Summary of the Six Philosophic Systems), a Jaïnä text, considers that the most important sects are the Shaïvä(s) (worshipers of Shivä), the Pâshupatä(s) (who worship Pashupati), the Kâpâlikä(s) (Skull-Bearers), and the Kâlâmukhä(s) (Black Faces). All rub themselves with ashes, wear a sacred thread, and knot their hair on top of their heads. They are differentiated from one another by their rules of life (achara).

The Baul(s), the wandering mystic minstrels of Bengal, are considered to be inheritors of the ancient Vrâtyä.[1]

The different groups of ascetics can be recognized by exterior signs.

The Shaïvä(s) attach Lingä(s) to their arms; the Rudrä(s) (who worship the destructive aspect of Shivä) draw a trident on their foreheads; the Ugrä(s), who worship Durgâ, the terrible aspect of the goddess, draw a Damaru (drum) on their arms; the Bhattä(s), or bards, draw Lingä(s) on their foreheads, both arms, heart, and navel. [Anandä Giri, *Shankarä Vijayä*]

The Kâlâmukhä(s) mark their foreheads with a black line. It is the Kâpâlikä(s) who practice the difficult discipline of the Great Vow (Mahâvratä). The Kâlâmukhä(s) are also skull-bearers, but do not practice the Great Vow.

The Black Faces (Kâlâmukhä)

THE Kâlâmukhä(s) are the adepts of the sect of the Pâshupatä(s) to which Lakulishä belonged. Their practices are less extreme than those of the Kâpâlikä(s). They are divided into two orders according to whether a divinity is worshiped under a masculine or a feminine aspect. These orders are called the Order of the Lion (Simhä Parishad) and the Order of the Goddess (Shakti Parishad). Additional orders consider the divinity as androgynous. These are the Ganapatyä(s), who venerate Ganapati, the elephant-headed god, (son of the Goddess and the Saumyä(s), from Somä, the seed). They have Skandä (the jet of sperm), son of Shivä, as their divinity.

The Kâlâmukhä(s) most important obligation is the construction of sanctuaries and the installation of idols. They practice the rites of Lingä worship and always wear a Lingä about their person. The priests are called Jangamä (moving lingä[s]). Some Kâlâmukhä(s) live in community in monasteries. The Order of the Lion, reorganized by Lakulishä, recommends a tranquil life like that of the forest-ascetics, dedicated to the profound study of the Âgamä(s).

There are numerous girl servants of the gods, Devä-dâsî(s), in their sanctuaries, and during the months of the year when they wander, they are often accompanied by a concubine. Khajuraho was one of the centers of the Kâlâmukhä(s) where many Devä-dâsî(s) resided.

The festivals of the Kâlâmukhä(s) include the receiving of the sacred thread, the passages of the sun from one zodiacal sign (Samkrânti) to another. The month during which the moon is in the fourteenth lunar house (the constellation called

Citrâ (March–April) is for them an important month. On the religious and ritual plane they observe no caste distinction.

The Skull-Bearers (Kâpâlikä)

THE founder of the Kâpâlikä(s) was a mythological sage called Âdinâthä. In the doctrine of the Kâpâlikä(s) the various gods are aspects of Shivä, the supreme ruler of the "multiple" (*sakalâ*), which implies that he appears in various forms. These forms are divided into creative aspects (Sams<u>ri</u>-Kart<u>ri</u>) and destructive aspects (Samharä-Kart<u>ri</u>). The ultimate aspect (Paramâtman) is the destructive aspect called Bhairavä (The Terrible). It is with this aspect that the Kâpâlikä(s) seek, in a sort of mystic communion, to identify themselves. The Shaktä likewise worship the goddess in her destructive form, Kâlî.

In their attempts at such identification, the Kâpâlikä(s) try to make themselves resemble the image of Bhaïravä. This is why, according to the *Tiruvo<u>rr</u>iyer Purâ<u>n</u>am* (written in Tamil):

The Kâpâlikä(s) must wear distinctive signs (*mudrä*[s]) which evoke the image of the god and which are as follows:

· Three lines of ashes are drawn on the forehead.

· The head is shaved except for a lock of hair at the top of the head, attached with a string of bones.

· Large rings are worn in the ears.

· A necklace of bones is worn.

· A black sacred thread made of braided hair is worn.

· He must rub his body with ashes.

· He must have a Rudraksha seed tied to his wrist by a string and carry a strip of cloth to attach his knee in some of the Yogä postures.

The *Âgamä-Prâmanyä*, quoted in the *Shrî-Bhâshyä* of Râ-mânujä, adds the following distinctive ornaments:

- A pendent (*ruchakä*)
- A jewel on the forehead (*shikhâmani*)
- As accessories (*upä-mudrä*), a human skull (kâpâlä), a club (*khatvângä*), and a wand (*laguḍä*) or a trident (*trishûlä*)

The Kâpâlikä(s) use a human skull as a receptacle for their food. They eat meat and drink wine, particularly palm wine (toddy). They utilize wine in their rites. They practice all the prohibited forms of sexual relations.

The Kâpâlikä(s) are considered experts in alchemy (*dhâtuvâdä*); they practice the transmutation of metals and prepare an elixir for long life (*rasâyanä*). This implies a serious responsibility. Even in our days, whoever has acquired the power to make gold incurs a curse if anyone is suffering from hunger within a radius of a half-koshä (1,800 meters) from the place he inhabits.

The goal of the Kâpâlikä(s) is not to obtain a hypothetical liberation after death; they seek, rather, by means of Siddhi(s) or magical powers, to transgress the limits of the material body which imprisons the true being to attain a consubstantiality with the celestial beings by practicing rites of communion or else directly through the favor of a god obtained by austerities and sacrifices.

The keystone of the Kâpâlikä faith was bhakti, a personal devotion to a personal god. This god was usually identified as Shivä in his terrific Bhaïravä incarnation. The rituals were propitiatory and imitative. The aim was an identification or mystical communion of the worshiper and his god. . . . On the mundane plane, the devotee gained suprahuman magical powers (*siddhi*[s]) while on the eschatological plane, he attained final liberation (*mukti*) from transmigratory existence and dwelt in a heaven of perpetual sexual bliss. . . . He becomes homologous with the god and participates in or receives the gift of divine attributes. [Lorenzen, *The Kâpâlikäs and Kâlâmukhäs*, p. 83]

Urban society is always opposed to the practices of the Kâpâlikä(s). The *Lalitavistarä* describes them as madmen who smear their bodies with ashes, wear red garments (*kasâyä*), shave their heads, and carry a trident (*tridandä*), a pot, a skull, and a club (*khâtvangä*).

Râmânujä, in his commentary on the *Brahmä Sûträ* (II.2.35), calls them the "enemies of the Vedä(s)" (Vedäviruddhä) and describes them as rubbing themselves with ashes from the funerary fires and eating ash, using a skull as a receptacle for their food, armed with a club, using palm wine in their rites, carrying a Rudrâkshä (eye of Shivä) rosary made of the seeds of a sacred plant, and also wearing one wrapped around their bun of hair. It was in opposition to these practices that the adepts of Vedic religion in the epoch of Buddhä and Mahâvîrä decided to give up eating meat and drinking alcohol.

According to the doctrine of the Kâpâlikä(s), as presented by Bodholbanä-Nityânandä and quoted in the *Shankarä Vijayä* of Ânandä Giri, Bhaïravä has eight major aspects: Chandä (violent), Krodhä (wrathful), Unmattä (demented), Kâpâlin (skull-bearing), Bhishanä (terrible), and Samhârä (destructive). It identifies these aspects with the Brahmanic gods Vishnu, Brahmâ, Sûryä, Rudrä, Indrä, Chandrä, and Yamä. The eighth, Samhârä, is Bhaïravä.

Practices (*Charyâ*)

AMONG the practices recommended by Lakulishä are found:

1. Yogic exercises for the purpose of acquiring magic powers

2. The six purifications (Shat-Karmä) of Hathä Yogä

3. Sexual practices, considering erotic delight as an experience of the divine state

4. Initiatic or other rites of the Kâlâmukhä(s) and the Kâpâlikä(s)

5. Participation in rites of sacrifices and the eating of the victim's flesh at the sacred banquets

6. The use, during the course of congregations of a mystic character, of an intoxicating beverage made from Indian hemp, which encourages states of trance

The observances recommended for ascetics are seven in number. They must:

1. Live naked and smear their bodies with ashes three times per day, preferably using ashes from funerary fires

2. Sleep on a bed of ashes

3. Shout a particular manträ: *Ahâ, Ahâ*

4. Sing aloud the praises of the god

5. Dance together, either according to the art of dance or in other manners

6. Curve the tip of the tongue backward and bellow like a bull, the sacred animal which is Shivä's vehicle (this bellowing is called *hudukkârä*)

7. Prostrate before holy places and circumambulate them while invoking Shivä

They must avoid practicing these observances in the presence of noninitiates.[2]

The Five M's

THE living being is an image of the universal being. All the body's organs, therefore, have correspondences within the divine being. One can approach divinity through any of the vital functions. In Tantric practice, the less intellectual ones are considered as the most direct. Thus, the alimentary functions, the creators of energy, and the purificatory functions, the functions of rejection, can also be utilized toward the goal of making contact with the supernatural. Tantric rites include practices linked to what the texts call the five *M*'s, for their Sanskrit names each begin with this letter. The five *M*'s are considered sources of pollution in the rites of the right hand, but in the ritual inversion of Tantrism they become the elements of purification. The mystic poems of Kanhapâdä repeatedly state that what is lowest in the world is highest in the domain of spirit.

The five *M*'s are meat (Mansä), wine (Madhyä), copulation (Maïthunä), excrement (Malä), and urine (Muträ). Urine is also called Shivâmbu (water of Shivä) since it issues from the Lingä. Modern commentators have substituted for the last two *M*'s fish (Matsyä) and dried grains (Mudrä).

According to the *Kulârnavä Tanträ* (v. 79–80), "Wine is Shakti, the Goddess; meat is Shivä; erotic delight, the current which unites Shivä and Shakti, is the divine state called liberation (Mok<u>sh</u>ä)."

Malä and Muträ

ALL Hindus ritually absorb each day a small quantity of the five products of the cow, including the dung and the urine. There exist additional practices and rites connected with the functions of rejection which are given in the <u>Damarä</u> Tanträ and revealed to initiates only.

Meat (Mansä) and Sacrifice (Medhä)

THE consumption of meat is tied to the principle of sacrifice. Communion, the consumption of a piece of the victim by the participants, is an essential element of the rite.

Life exists only through perpetual massacre. No being can survive except by devouring other living beings. In order to draw near to the celestial powers, we must associate ourselves with the cosmic sacrifice, coaxing the gods by offering victims and thus avoid hecatombs. The act of killing is a responsible act, which must be accomplished as a rite. The victim must be offered to the gods before being consumed. We then eat only the scraps from the god's table and cease thereby to be murderers. We thus prevent the gods from striking at random.

Human Sacrifice

LIKE the ancient Greeks, Indians believed in the efficacy of human sacrifice. To avoid wars, cataclysms, and hecatombs, men should offer victims to the gods. The necessity of sacrifice is an important element in the Kâpâlikä doctrine. According to the *Kâlîkâ Purânä*, "The goddess Kâmâkhyâ, companion of Bhaïravä, is satisfied by an offering of flesh. The consecrated blood becomes an ambrosia. The head and flesh of the victim must be offered to the goddess. Morsels of flesh are a part of the food offerings."

According to the *Prabodhä-Chandrodayä*:

> The Kâpâlikä who eats human flesh from the skull of an honorable man becomes the image of the Great God (*Mahârâjä parajayä*). He breaks his fast by drinking wine from the skull of a brahmin.
>
> The personal counterpart of human and animal sacrifices is self-sacrifice. This concept subsumes a wide range of activities from . . . suicide to self-mutilation and from physical penance to simple exercises of mental discipline. The chief penance performed by the Kâpâlikäs was of course the Mahâvratä (Great Vow). [Lorenzen, p. 87]

Alimentary communion in ritual is based on the notion that we become what we eat. The identification of ritual foods with the body and bodily products of Shivä and Shakti create a consubstantiality of the communicant with them. He becomes god and participates in divine attributes such as immortality and magical powers.

The ancient rites of human sacrifice (*purushämedhä*) were performed frequently during the medieval period. They are mentioned in various plays of the classical theater. In the *Mâlatî Mâdhavä* by Bhavabhûti (seventh century), a Kâpâlikä seeks to sacrifice the heroine, Mâlatî, with the aim of acquiring a power of incantation (*manträ-siddhi*). In about the same period, Vadirâjasûri, in his *Yashodharä-Kavyä*, describes the saving of two children who had been groomed and bedecked with ornaments prior to being led to the place of sacrifice.

The *Vetâläpanchavishati* tells how King Vikramä, who was in the process of being robed for the sacrifice, was saved by a Vetâlä, a phantom who had incarnated himself in the body of a dead person.

The seventh day of the festivals dedicated to Shivä (Shivä Mahotsavä), still celebrated today at Madura, reenacts the impalement of numerous Jainä(s) ordered by King Tirujanar Sambandhar (seventh century). This event is described in the *Kâranâgamä* in the part concerning the life of this Shaiva saint. [Gopinatha Rao, *Elements of Hindu Iconography*, vol. 1, Introduction]

Again, in the sixteenth century, the king Narä Narâyanä in north Bengal had 150 men sacrificed during the course of a single ceremony.

Intoxicating Liquors (*Madhyä*)

A state of drunkenness, which obliterates material preoccupations, is a useful preparation for ecstatic rites. Dancing is also a means of preparation for magical practices. The wine generally utilized is palm wine, today called toddy. But the intoxicant most commonly employed in Tantric ritual is Vijayä, a drink made out of Indian hemp, today called bhang. It is recommended to drink it an hour and a half before the rites concerning the five *M*'s. According to A. Bharati (*The Tantric Tradition*, p. 252), its effect is considered to be aphrodisiac (*uttejakä*).

Drugs

EACH of the substances which make up matter corresponds to a graph, or an entity expressible by means of a diagram or by a mathematical or chemical formula. As we have seen, there exists a consciousness, or individuality, which governs each formulation, each conglomerate, each aspect of matter. The substances of which living beings are composed correspond to complex formulae. The living being is a biochemical factory, and the phenomena of perception, of sensation, of pleasure and pain, of memory and even of thought, can be regarded as reactions resulting from the activity of chemical components that act on the cells of our nervous system and brain. The intrusion of an excess of one of these components modifies, if only temporarily, our emotional equilibrium, our capacities for pleasure or suffering, for action, lucidity, memory, perception, our joy in life, or our depressive states.

These substances called drugs—stimulants, depressants —are by no means neutral products. Like all the components of the living being, they correspond to entities who come forth from the divine plan and who are endowed with personality, consciousness, and autonomy. The states of our soul are due to the contingencies of a sort of war between armies of molecules corresponding to subtle beings. The aggression of one of these chemical spirits upon the human being is no different from that of a demon or an angel. It is a sort of possession. This is why a drugged person is no longer master of himself. He may detest the drug that imposes itself upon him despite himself. There exists a spirit of tobacco, a spirit of hemp, a spirit of peyote, a spirit of the poppy, a spirit of wine, which, if they are not controlled, lead their victim as they fancy. All religions have recognized the existence of these subtle forces and have sought to cajole them.

There is no religion whose rites do not make use of an intoxicating substance. Something of this always subsists, even if we have lost its meaning. We drink to the success of an enterprise, and wine plays a role in the Christian mass. The Amerindians utilized tobacco to seal an alliance and practiced very elaborate peyote rituals. A ritual exists for opium smokers and for tea ceremonies. The Somä rites, which bring on mystical ecstasy, are an essential element in the Vedic rituals, and the god Somä occupies an important place in the Aryan pantheon. In the West, Dionysos, as god of wine, takes the place of the god Somä. In India today, bhang (a drink made of Indian hemp) is consumed in assemblies of a ritual character.

When the gods wish to destroy a wicked tyrant, they inspire the madness in him which causes him to lose himself. Drugs are among their armaments. Their irrational and immoderate intrusion signals the imminent end of the species at the end of the Kali Yugä.

To control the chemical spirits that wish to take possession of our faculties, we must first of all understand their nature and venerate them. Every drug is both angel and demon. It is by ritualizing their use that we can, as all traditional cultures have done, master them or eliminate their influence.

Sexual Rites (Maithunä)

ACCORDING to the Kâpâlikä Unmattä-Bhaïravä, in his commentary on Madhavä's Shankarä Digvijayä (XV.28):

> The state of ecstasy which manifests in the sexual act is a participation in the very nature of Bhaïrava. What we call liberation (mokshä) is the achievement of a state of ecstacy. Liberation is comparable to a permanent orgasm, an active

state of delight (*anandä*) which is a part of the nature of the gods.

He who venerates the self, established in the vulva (*bhâgâsanä-sthä*) attains liberation. [*Âgamä-Prâmân̠yä*]

The union of the sperm (Shivä) and the menstrual blood (the goddess) in their perpetual copulation forms the Tantric ambrosia (*kulâmr̠itä*). In the yogic practice called Vajroli Mu-drä, drinking the nectar issuing from the sexual union sig-nifies the reabsorption through the penis of the sperm emitted in coitus mixed with the feminine blood.

Love and Death

FOR the Kâpâlikä(s), the relationship of eroticism and death forms part of a theory of "passages," that is, the points at which the visible and the invisible worlds touch one another. It is by means of copulation that the mystery of the living being's "passage" from nonexistence to existence takes place. The sexual act is therefore a magical act. At the moment of this rite, the passage that connects creator and created is opened. Whether or not conception occurs is a secondary matter.

The second place of passage is the one at which the living being dissolves into nonexistence: the funeral pyre. It is only at the moment of cremation that the material structures which form the habitat of the subtle body are destroyed. Apparent death is not the end of the body, since a Yogi or a wandering spirit can, by inserting his psychic energy into a corpse, re-suscitate the dead person and for a time make use of his structure.

The principle of life is not localized only in the brain or the heart. This is evident since organ transfers allow resus-citation. It is difficult to know at what moment the internal organ dissolves, to what part of matter one's consciousness and "I" remain attached. It is only when the body is entirely destroyed that the complete liberation of the subtle energies take place. This is why the place of cremation is also a place of passage between two worlds. It is therefore a magical and sacred place. The Yogi who covers his body with the ash of a dead person gives a human form once more to that person's matter. He becomes in some way his reflection, his living phantom, and as such finds himself in contact with two worlds. He acquires the mysterious powers by appropriating the psychic energy of the deceased. In a play by Bhavabhûti, the *Malatî Mâdhavä*, a Kâpâlikä says: "It is by wandering about the funeral pyres that I have been able to reach beyond the world of appearances (*samsârä*)."

During the practice of the sexual act or equally when he rubs himself with the ashes of the funeral pyre, the ascetic draws near the boundary point (*bindu*) where the divine and the human touch each other, and if he has the force to cross this narrow passage, the living being can go beyond the human state and join the company of higher beings to become the companion of Shivä (*Rudrä-sayujyä*). The Kâpâlikä(s) do not practice cremation. Their bodies are buried directly in mother earth. Those who succeed in the transmutation and abandon their earthy presence in yogic posture are immersed by their brothers in the sacred river (the Ganges), which comes forth from the hair of Shivä, or else a stone structure covered by a tumulus is constructed over them, without touching them. In any case, they consider cremation grounds to be magical places where being and nonbeing meet at the moment when the body is delivered to the flames.

The most varied sorts of funeral rites were, and still are, practiced in India. The *Manimekhalaï* gives this description:

The cemetery was divided into sectors according to the various ways of disposing of the dead. A rather small area was reserved for cremations. There was also an area of wasteland where bodies were simply left in the open, without any burial. The cemeteries are farther along. In one of them, the dead are buried in tombs that are simply dug into the earth, while in the other, the bodies are placed in small chambers hollowed out of the ground, whose openings are then closed. There was also a sector where the bodies were covered by large earthenware pots. The cemeteries were the scene of a constant uproar due to the din of drums being beaten in honor of the dead, mixed with the sound of voices reciting the merits of deceased monks and the cries of those weeping for the dead, to which was added the howling of jackels and owls.

Vâhai trees, the favorite abodes of evil spirits, were planted in certain places along with Vilâ trees, where the vultures perched, who fed on the flesh and fat of cadavers. Groves of Vanni were planted in whose shade the Kâpâlikä(s), the skull-bearers, resided, and groves of Ilandaï, where the mendicant ascetics who make necklaces of skulls camped. There were also other treeless areas where people who eat the flesh of corpses gathered. An enclosure, encircled by a wall pierced by four doors, contained a temple dedicated to Kâlî and monuments of various sizes bearing inscriptions concerning the dead, whose remains they cover. These inscriptions gave the name, caste, mode of life, or status in society and manner of death of those for whom these monuments were erected. There were also columns dedicated to the different gods before which offerings were placed.

Shelters were constructed on stone platforms where the guardians of the cemetery could be protected from wind and rain. There were also covered areas where visitors could rest. [*Manimekhalaï*, Book 6]

The Great Vow (*Mahâvratä*)

THE Great Vow is an extreme form of propitiatory asceticism which purifies the body and is followed by "communion rituals in which the worshiper is united with divinity through food, drink, sex, or mental ecstasy" (Lorenzen, p. 88). "One must prepare oneself for the Great Vow by fasting and the observance of the six rules (*yamä*) and the six prohibitions (*niyamä*) of Yogä and, during this period, one must sleep on bare ground and walk about holding a skull in the right hand and a stick in the other" (*Vishnu Smriti*).

The means of subsistence (*vritti*) are begging (*bhaikshyä*) for table scraps (*utsrishtä*) and whatever comes by chance (*yathâlabdhä*). Initiation to the Great Vow includes severe practices of asceticism, but also ritual humiliations, obscene words, and sexual practices. The Kâpâlikä(s), during the Mahâvratä, practice self-mutilations, cutting pieces of their own flesh to make offerings to the goddess. According to the *Harshächaritä* of Bânä (sixth century), the Kâpâlikä(s) who practice the Great Vow, in order to obtain the favor of the Mâtrikâ(s), the Celestial Mothers, burned themselves with a lamp, offered a skull, put melted resin on their heads, made offerings of their own flesh, and sold human flesh, including that cut from their own bodies.

In the *Kadambari*, Bânä attributed the origin of these practices to tribal customs. He mentions that "the people of the Shabarä tribe offered human flesh to the goddess Chandikâ" and that "they were covered with scars because of their offerings of blood."

According to the *Vishnu Purânä*, "He who practices the Great Vow must construct for himself a leaf hut in the forest and live there. He must bathe three times a day, walk from village to village, sleep on a straw heap, carry on the end of a bamboo pole the skull of a man ritually killed. This must be that of a man of quality (*uttamä purushä kapâlä*) or of a Brahman (*brahmä kapâlä*)." According to the *Yâjñavalkya Smriti* (III.243), he must use a skull as a recipient for begging his food.

Initiation of the Pâshupatä

FROM the Tantric point of view, there are only two castes: that of male beings and that of female beings. Shaiva initiation is open to everyone, without distinction of caste or sex. A Shudrä can thus become the Guru of a Brahman.

The only sacrament held by Shaiva sects is the rite of initiation. Haradattä, in the *Gana-Kârikâ*, explains that Pâshupatä initiation includes five degrees, called Vyaktä (exterior), Avyaktä (secret), Jayä (victory), Chedä (rupture), and Nishthä (realization). The forms of initiation described concern essentially those who intend to take up monastic life in order to become bearers of the occult tradition.

THE FIRST INITIATION

The site of the first (exterior) initiation is the dwelling place of the Guru; the source of its force (*balä*) resides in the devotion of pupil to master (*Guru bhakti*). Its purifying effect (*vishuddhi*) is the elimination of ignorance (*ajñânä-hâni*).

The means (*upâyä*) is the impregnation of doctrine (*vâsä*). The benefit (*lâbhä*) is the access to knowledge (*jñânä*). The stage attained (*diksh̲â-karin*) is that of substance (*dravyä*).

The rules of conduct (Charyâ) of the first stage include the six offerings (S̲hadangä Upahârä), which are dancing, singing, laughing, shouting a good omen (*hadu̲k* or *dumdum*), prostrating oneself, and reciting Manträ(s) (*japyä*) in the company of other Pâshupatä(s). In the first stage, the aspirant adopts the signs of the sect and carries out certain vows. He rubs himself with ashes and sleeps in ashes. He wears garlands of flowers taken from an image of Shivä. He lives in a temple.

THE SECOND INITIATION

The site (*deshä*) of the second (secret) initiation is in the middle of a public place (*janä*). The source of its force (*balä*) is the dedication of one's mind (*mati prasâdä*). The impurity (*malä*) from which it delivers one is the notion of prohibitions (*adharmä*). Its purifying effect (*vishuddhi*) is the elimination of prohibitions (*adharmä-hâni*). The means (*upâyä*) is the observance of rules (*charyâ* or *vidhi*). The benefit (*lâbhä*) is austerity (*tapas*). The stage attained (*dikṣhâ-karin*) is the mastery of time (*kâlä*).

According to the *Pâshupatä Sûträ*, in the second stage the aspirant must, first of all, seek to "break away from society." It is for this reason that he tries to inspire the disdain of the people of the sacerdotal and bourgeois castes. He thus maintains his independence and his integrity. He must appear mad, miserable, his body dirty, with nails, hair, and beard unkempt. *Kauṇdinya* says that in the second stage the aspirant leaves the temple and removes the distinctive signs of his sect. He encourages the public's contempt, particularly by means of the six practices called "doors" (*dvârä*), which are:

Krâthanä, pretending to be asleep and snoring

Spandanä, shaking one's limbs like someone having an epileptic seizure

Mandanä, walking like a lame person

Shṛingâraṇä (exhibitionism), making obscene gestures in the presence of women

Avitatkaraṇä, pretending to be an idiot

Avitatbhâshaṇä, expounding nonsensical discourses

He must wander like a phantom (*pretä*) and practice the vows by which he identifies himself with animals. The *Bauddhâyanä* (II.1.3), a Buddhist text, claims that some of these aspirants wear a donkey's skin, the hair on the outside.

THE THIRD INITIATION

The third stage of initiation is called the Victory (*jayä*) stage. Its site (*deshä*) is a cave (*guhä deshä*) or a secret place. The source of its force (*balä*) is the realization of the illusory character of the contraries (*dvandvä jayä*)—true/false, beautiful/ugly, good/evil, and so on.

The impurity (*malä*) that creates obstacles consists of everything that attracts (*shakti hetu*). Its purifying effect (*vishuddhi*) is to destroy all attachments (*sangakarä häni*). The means (*upâyä*) is the repetition of Manträ(s) (*japä*) and meditation (*dhyânä*). The benefit (*lâbhä*) is to obtain the perennity of the gods (*devä nityatvä*). The stage reached (*diksha karin*) is that of the power to act (*kriyâ*) on all beings and all elements.

THE FOURTH INITIATION

The fourth stage of initiation is called rupture (*chedä*). At this stage, the initiate breaks all his earthly links. The site (*deshä*) is the cremation ground (*smashânä*); the source of its force is self-realization (*dharmä*). The impurity (*malä*) to be vanquished is doubt (*chyuti*). The purifying effect (*vishuddhi*) is faith, the absence of doubt (*chyuti häni*). The means (*upâyä*) is constant meditation on Shivä (*sadâ Rudrä smriti*). The benefit (*lâbhä*) is identification with Shivä (*Rudrä sthiti*). The stage attained (*dikshâ karin*) is that the adept (*sâdhakä*) becomes the image (*murti*) of the god and an object of veneration.

THE FIFTH INITIATION

The fifth stage of initiation is the final realization (*nishtä*). The adept renounces all physical or mental effort, whether religious or secular. The site (*deshä*) is Shivä himself. The origin of its force is the absence of distraction (*apramâdä*). The impurity (*malä*) to overcome is the fact of being a living being (*pashutvä*). The purifying effect (*vishuddhi*) is the elimination of the animal nature (*pashutva häni*). A method does not exist. All depends upon the grace (*prasâdä*) of the god. The benefit (*lâbhä*) is the obtaining of magical powers (*siddhi*). The stage reached is that of Guru.

NOTES

1. See McEvilley, *An Archeology of Yoga*, I, p. 69.
2. See M. R. Sakhare, *History and Philosophy of Lingayat Religion*. p. 223.

4

Preliminary Practices

THE RULES OF MONASTIC INITIATION APPLY ABOVE ALL
to those undertaking the ascetic life of a wandering monk.
For all others, the Shaiva initiation rites are very simple and
are practiced in the forest or on a riverbank. To prepare for
them, the aspirant must in any case observe a few rules of
conduct. This is particularly important for a Mlecchä, someone born outside of the sacred territory that constitutes the
Indian continent.

At the request of a foreign disciple, Sadhu Shambhudâsä
indicated some rules of behavior that prepare the individual
for a reintegration into the Shaiva tradition. This has been
translated from the Hindi in the following section.

Advice to a Mlecchä, by Sadhu Shambhudâsä

"IT is only by a return to the values and practices represented
by the Shaiva tradition that humanity can hope to retard its
end. But a reintegration in the tradition requires a preparation
for which the observance of certain rules of living is important, even if they go against one's habitual modes of thought."

1. YOGÄ

"One should undertake the practice of Hathä Yogä as a physical discipline and as a means of exploring man's inner universe and of controlling the vital energies, without allowing oneself to fall into the vague negative aspirations of transcendental meditation or other similar approaches."

2. RESPECT FOR CREATION

"The man respectful of the plan of creation must oppose the destruction of both animal and vegetal species for commercial ends. He must venerate trees and the spirits that inhabit them. Each person must choose a particular tree and practice every day a rite of veneration (*pujah̲*) near its roots, as the Indian villagers do. The bull is the vehicle, the symbol of Shivä. One must care for and venerate all cattle and seek to live in an atmosphere of trust and friendship with animals."

3. SACRIFICE

"The sacrifice of a bull or other animals must be accomplished following local rites (Mithraïc in Europe). The eating of the victim's flesh must take place at a sacred community meal. It is essential to sanctify the sacrifice. *Man lives only by sacrificing life; whether he is vegetarian or carnivorous, he kills. He must consider this act as a sacred act.*

"In principle, he must himself participate in the act of killing the animal that he eats. He must avoid the hypocrisy that pretends ignorance of the horror of slaughterhouses. He must oppose all torture practiced in the mass raising of animals and never nourish himself with tortured flesh.

"The wise man asks pardon of the spirit of the tree, whose branch he must cut and offer, before eating, the first morsel of food to the gods."

4. SPIRITS

"One must remain attentive to supranatural presences and honor the spirits that reside in springs and forests. When one encounters evil signs, one must, using appropriate gestures, exorcise the bad spell. Sighting monks and priests is a bad omen since they claim to renounce the divine experience of pleasure in the name of dubious moral values."

5. DANCING

"One must practice collective dancing. Rhythm gives rise to a state of trance, which brings the human being nearer to Shivä, the Cosmic Dancer."

6. EROTICISM

"Perception of the divine state, which is existence-consciousness-bliss (*sat-chit-ânandä*), is possible on three planes: Union (Yogä), knowledge (Sâmkhyä), and orgasm (Maithunä). Voluptuousness is the only experience that is immediately accessible. *One must practice erotic acts while remaining aware that sensual delight is an approach to the divine.* One must invoke Shivä at the moment of orgasm. There exist no taboos or restrictions concerning the variants of eroticism."

7. PROCREATION

"It is imperative to respect the lineage of one's ancestors and avoid the mixing of races through procreation. This alters the divine order and provokes regression of the species. Marriage rites or procreation rites must be accomplished with awareness of the responsibility of the transmission of life, having solely in mind the quality of the product, the child, according to the rules of genetic selection defined by the texts of the Âgamä(s)."

8. THE COUPLE

"The rules of life are different for men and for women. Avoid the life of the couple and seek to maintain the extended family group."

9. UNTOUCHABILITY

"One must avoid accidental physical contact with the people of another race or of another clan.

"Men must avoid contact with women during their menstrual periods.

"Women must isolate themselves during their entire period—during which time the goddess, Shakti, manifests in the form of the menstrual blood—and must purify themselves afterward. Men must also practice purification following an emission of sperm. All persons must practice purification after a contact with death."

10. PURIFICATION

"Purification consists of a bath in running water, in a river, in a shower, or under a tap (but never in a bathtub), followed by the veneration of the image of a divinity and the application to the forehead of sandal paste used in the rite. One must wash one's hands carefully seven times after the natural functions."

11. ABLUTIONS

"Before taking food or speaking or performing rites, one must practice daily morning ablutions while invoking the sun, source of life and light, then get dressed in clean clothes."

12. VENERATION OF THE MASTERS

"Every person must respect the work that has fallen to him, perform it with love, and venerate his tools and his masters.

One must honor his master once each year at the time of
Guru Pûjâ<u>h</u> and venerate the tools used for work on the day
indicated for the feast of Sarasvati, goddess of the sciences
and arts. One's tools are not to be used on this day."

13. THE FEEDING OF WANDERERS

"Wanderers are beloved of Shivä. Everyone ought to have a
period of wandering, visiting sacred places, if possible. (The
practice of wandering is difficult in the modern world, although this tendency is very evident among present-day youth.)
Every well-off person must honor and feed wanderers, whether
hitchhikers or beggars, monks or fugitives.

"The merit is in the gift. The quality of the recipient—
whether he be sage or vagabond—is of no importance."

14. SACRED BEVERAGES

"The use of certain hypnotic beverages, such as bhang, the
infusion of Indian hemp, is advised to facilitate the perception
of the subtle world and for mental concentration. Most other
drugs are injurious, particularly the opiates. Bhang should
be sipped in a tranquil place, preferably in the company of
several friends, and followed by a period of discussion, reflection, and games. One must never consume bhang in moments of physical activity and if one is not observing the other
rules of conduct. Neither must one smoke hashish."

15. THE VENERATION OF THE LINGÄ

"Everyone, man and woman, must venerate the phallus, image of Shivä, have a Lingä installed in the household, and
practice a Puja<u>h</u>, a daily rite of veneration, with flowers,
incense, offerings, and Manträ(s). One must wear a Lingä
on one's person, and also a rosary of 108 Rudrâkshä seeds
used for the reciting of Manträ(s). Alternatively, one can
venerate the Yoni, the female organ, or the Shâlagrâmä in

[153]

the form of an egg, or invoke the goddess, the Shakti, under the form of the Shrî Yanträ. The shakta rites, addressing Prak<u>r</u>iti, the principle of matter, require sacrifices and demand a particular initiation.

"The goddess is present in numerous forms; her main aspect is Kâlî, the principle of time and of death. It is under the aspect of the mother, and not of the partner, that one invokes the goddess."

16. FUNERAL RITES

"One must observe funeral rites, and not seek to imprison the spirit of the deceased; one must neither remove any organs nor freeze the body. One must dispose of the body at the last possible minute, either by placing it directly in the earth or by incinerating it. Avoid coffins and sepulchers."

"By observing these rules of conduct, the being of flesh finds again his place in creation and can live in harmony with the world. Gradually, he becomes qualified to be a receptacle for the teachings of the possessors of knowledge. It is then that initiation (*dikshâ*) becomes possible.

"It is neither in the pious and puritan Vai<u>sh</u>navism of the commercial and political classes, nor in the ashrams, nor with the Brahmans, that one can encounter the joyful and relaxed atmosphere of the Shaiva people, so gay and tolerant. The ash-covered ascetics who live in brotherhood with trees and animals have remained close to the mysterious world of spirits and gods and know the rules of life that can delay the fearful events that will destroy mankind at the end of the Kali Yugä."

PART FOUR

SOCIAL MAN

❀❀❀❀

1

The Individual and the Species

THE LIVING BEING IS A PREDATOR THAT SURVIVES ONLY by devouring other living beings, to become, in its turn, food. "The living 'I' is that which devours and which is devoured," says the *Chhândogyä Upanishad*. This destructive/destructible function, being synonymous with impermanence, can only take place in relative time. The living being might seem to be merely a digestive system, but it is also the bearer of a message or plan, issuing from Purushä, which it can transmit either through cellular division or through the sexual act.

The individual is but a transitory moment of the species, which is a permanent reality. It is the species that represents one aspect of the divine game (lîlâ) *of creation.* Although insignificant as an individual, the living being is necessary as a link, as one ring in the chain that continues through the generations from the birth of a species until its extinction. *Each species evolves as a living entity*: it passes through childhood, the prime of life, and the decline of old age.

The individual is similar to one of the relay runners carrying the Olympic torch. He is the conveyor of a model, of a permanent code that is carried on from individual to individual. It is the ability to reproduce and to perpetuate and transmit oneself that is the characteristic of life. The complex

[157]

of forms and abilities characteristic of the individual is given continued life through procreation. A species evolves through thousands of generations. Man is called Lingä-dharä, the "bearer of his penis." His individuality is of no importance except inasmuch as it adds something to the code received by him at birth and which he must pass on within the framework of the species to which he belongs.[1]

The duration of our species depends on the way in which we behave as links in one of the varieties of that species with respect to the law governing our *raison d'être* on the physical, social, and moral levels.

The progress of the human species rests on the increasing usefulness of each of its elements and varieties; a man progresses by carrying out the role that nature has given him; he degrades himself if he abandons that role. The perfect man, the harmonious man, the useful man, is the man who, like an actor, plays to perfection the role assigned to him.

The Clan (*Jâti*)

ALL living species, so long as they are not drawn from their assigned role, observe a set of innate behavioral laws. They reproduce only within their own group. The same is true of the human races that are not debased. This is why mankind is divided into tribes or clans (Jâti), which correspond to genetic models, within which marriage is acceptable. Each type of person has a role to fulfill in a complex society, just as each type of cell in a living body has a different function. A cancer is the result of cells developing the urge to proliferate freely and breaking free of the organic role assigned to them. The same is true of society. In the plan of a species, each individual has aptitudes that correspond to a predetermined role. If he ceases to perform this function, he becomes a social cancer.

The beauty and richness of creation rests in the variety of species, in their purity, their diversity, and their perfection.

This is why the problem of the transmission of life must be resolved carefully. There is no transmigratory body that is not linked to a particular type of man and a lineage that personifies it. The transmission of the Lingä-Sharirä, the genetic code inherited from the ancestors; its planting in carefully chosen ground; and the transfer to a new being of the ancestral heritage comprising the archetypes issuing from divine thought constitute the most important act in the physical being. It must be carried out in a ritual form that takes various factors, including astrological ones, into account in such a way that the new bearer of the flame is perfectly adapted to its role, and in such a way that the species fashioned through the long ancestral line is not degraded or extinguished.

The child, the receiver of the code, must as far as possible be the image of his father, and his continuator in the evolutionary scale.

When the genetic code is transplanted into unsuitable ground, as is the case of the intermingling of castes or races, it becomes confused, and the resulting offspring do not have the necessary qualities to transmit the ancestral heritage of knowledge. It is in this way that civilizations die.

The modern idea that genetic mingling improves a species is only true on a superficial level, taking no account of the psychological facts or the hereditary abilities of the harmony between the physical and intellectual aspects of a being. Moral characteristics become disconnected from physical ones and in time come into conflict. Progress rests on the accentuation of diversity; *in any domain a leveling is the prelude to death*. A mingling of races or species leads to regression in the evolutionary plane. The more the sexual partners belong to the same stock, the more the race that they represent is refined, is improved, and progresses. We are well aware that this is the case for animals; we tend to forget that it applies to humans just as much.

In intermingling societies, the son no longer resembles his father; he is no longer the continuation of his father. The ties that bind them are loosened, and the family dissolves. In hybrid societies, the roles are poorly distributed: warriors lack courage, intellectuals are irresponsible, merchants are thieves, and artisans have no love for their work. Deprived of their proper function and place in society, heroes become gang or guerilla leaders, intellectuals disseminate aberrant doctrines, merchants seize economic power and enter into conflict with the artisans who detest their work. This state of affairs, which is due to the mixing of races, must take place at the end of the Kali Yugä.

Physical illnesses bring about physical degeneration and can cause a break in and destruction of a genealogical chain. But illness of the mind—the deformation or incorrect usage of inherited knowledge—deprives the human being of his essential role.

In animals, sexual energy emerges at precise moments for the purposes of reproduction, each within its own species. Cross-breeds never occur in the natural order of things.

Mankind's double nature, however, has led elsewhere. The being of flesh will use this energy in order to reproduce; the being of knowledge will cultivate it as a fuel to develop his intellectual and magical powers. The most varied sexual stimulations will therefore be useful to him in the development of his mental and spiritual self. Moreover, he must control, and indeed limit, the use of his semen when he is engaged in reproduction.

Marriage is not simply a license that legalizes sexual relations, as it tends to become for the frustrated in puritanical societies. It is a responsible, ritualized act whose purpose is the creation of a new link in the line representing one particular human type, that is, one of the variants of the divine thought. Marriage between individuals belonging to different ethnic or racial groups is seen as an outrage against the Creator's plan and harmony of the world. If sexual encounters take place between partners belonging to different groups, it is considered essential to ensure that they remain unproductive, whether through contraception or abortion.[2]

Procreation

THE rites of procreation are described in the Tanträ(s) and in several works related to the Yogä. They include the veneration of the sexual organs, the images of the divine principles, which will join together to bring about the miracle of life. There is a fundamental difference between, on the one hand, sexual play, which is part of the art of living, of the divine experience of pleasure which concerns the individual alone, and, on the other hand, the ritual union whose purpose is procreation and which therefore concerns the species. The problems are different for man and woman, for the one who provides the plan and for the one who brings it to fruition. There cannot be identical rules for these two functions.

The procreative act is the most important of the rites; it represents participation in the process of creation. All the other rites are the symbolic reflection of this union. Agni, the god of fire, the male principle, appears in the Kunda, the hearth on the altar, image of the feminine organ. The Upanishad(s) explain all the aspects of the ritual of sacrifice in terms of the different stages of the act of love.

Woman is the hearth, the male organ is the fire; the caresses are the smoke, the vulva is the flame, penetration is the brand, and pleasure is the spark. In this fire, the gods receive the offering of semen, and a child is born. [*Chhândogyä Upanishad*, 5, 4–8]

The summons is the invocation of the deity; the request is the first hymn of praise. The act of lying next to the woman is the hymn of glory; meeting her face to face is the chorus; the height of passion is the consecration; and the separation is the final hymn. He who knows that the hymn to Vâmadevä (the god of the left hand who represents the Tantric aspect of Shivä) is woven upon the act of love, re-creates himself in each act of union. His life will be long; his descendants and his livestock will be numerous; his fame widespread. [*Chhândogyä Upanishad*, 2, 13–1]

On the fifth day after a woman's period, copulation leads to the birth of a child through the union of the woman's lunar (left) subtle breath and the man's solar (right) breath. Once the necessary purifications following her period are completed, the woman should drink the juice of a plant called Shankhavalli (in the shape of a conch) and then accept the gift of man's sperm at a moment when elements of earth and water are flowing in her veins. . . . If earth predominates, a daughter will result; if water dominates, a son will be born; if, however, the element of fire prevails, the pregnancy will end in miscarriage; and if the element of ether is dominant, the child will be a homosexual. [*Shiva Svarodayä*, trans. Alain Daniélou (Milan: Arche, 1982), pp. 44–65]

In the course of the sexual act, the Sâdhakä (the adept) should recite to himself a special Manträ, a formula that evokes the nature of Shivä in order that the sexual act might be identified with the union of Shivä and Shakti. Orgasm is thus assimilated into a sacrificial rite.

According to Bharati (*The Tantric Tradition*, p. 264), the formula would be: "AUM. Light and ether are my two hands, Dharmä and Adharmä are the ingredients. With the sacrificial ladle I pour this oblation into the sacred fire. Svâhâ!" Other formulae exist, however. The Shaktä should chant mentally the goddess's Manträ.

The Castes (Varnä)[3]

MAN is a social animal, which is to say that the human species forms a whole, an organism, whose various cells have their own distinct functions. This is why the different lineages of mankind exist. The qualities and abilities of each improve over the generations so as to form an efficient, harmonious society that is capable of carrying out the role assigned to the human species in the plan of creation.

In the same way that the different organs of the body have different functions, even though they originate in similar cells, so in the plan laid out for the species there exist particular lineages that are more adapted to certain functions and whose abilities, once they are recognized, encouraged, and developed, become hereditary. Each human grouping, each race, each family, must seek to uphold its integrity, to improve its particular speciality, and to play the social role corresponding to its nature, and above all else to preserve and transmit its own special genetic and cultural heritage.

Our virtues are to a great extent transmissible, being connected to aspects of character that can be inherited. This is why they must be cultivated and improved so that we may play our role to the full in the brief span of our existence.

There is thus for everyone a "natural law" (Dharmä) that regulates the use and development of mental and physical characteristics, inherited at birth, together with the gift of life itself, so that we may play to the full our part in the evolution of our lineage.

Ancestor worship involves above all else the respect and transmission of our double heritage, genetic and cultural.[4]

Each being is born unique. In the almost infinite number of possible combinations of the elements that constitute the living being, it is beyond belief that the same arrangement could be repeated, that two beings could be absolutely identical, with the same nature, appearance, function, and station; nevertheless, the human types defined by heredity can be classified. In order to achieve his physical and spiritual destiny, each individual must establish his basis; determine the class to which he belongs, the duties and qualities inherent in that class, and its unique characteristics so that he may make them productive; and, eventually, go beyond them. Everyone must achieve the perfection of a social or exterior role before he can perfect his personal or interior role. The two roles can be vastly different and even contradictory; thus, we see that men from the artisan castes can earn their living in their humble professions and yet can at the same time be philosophers, holy men, and artists before whom kings and Brahmans bow with respect.

The circumstances of our birth correspond to the level of development of our own lineage and to the conditions in which we can best progress. Each of the links in the lineage is found at a particular stage of the evolution of that species—in its youth, maturity, or decline. This is why individuals of different races are not at the same level in their evolution.

There is no advantage to anyone in wanting to change one's situation or function, nor in wanting to perform the duties of another. Thus, except in very rare cases, one does not change one's sex, species, race, or caste during one's life. The external hierarchy of beings and things is often the opposite of the interior order. This is the reason why, during the Kali Yugä (the present world age), it is most desirable to be either woman or worker (Shudrä), for through mere humility and devotion to their role or work, these people can attain exterior perfection, which in turn permits the interior development that frees them from the weighty chains of life and leads them effortlessly toward the higher spheres of knowledge. The state of prince, or Brahman, noble and magnificent though it may seem, is disastrous in the dark age, for the discipline that they demand is so severe and the virtues so difficult that failure is almost certain.

It is not at all by chance that for nearly the last thousand years, almost all the great mystic poets and holy men of India have been men of humble birth who could so easily free themselves from their social and ritual responsibilities and devote themselves to their inner life.

An organic society can only exist on the basis of a division of powers and functions.

With the appearance of urban societies at the dawn of the Kali Yugä, a system developed in India whereby the different groups were able to intermingle and collaborate; each group was able to maintain its own identity, traditions, and knowledge, while at the same time cooperating in the development of a common civilization.

Ancient cities were divided into four parts, separated by avenues in the shape of a cross; each part was reserved for one of the four functions: priest, soldier, merchant, and artisan. The word *quarter* is the remnant of this division.

The Lineage (Goträ)

THE development of the different genealogical lines adapted to essential functions is linked to the cycle of the four Yugä(s), the four ages that mark the development and decline of the human species. They represent the peoples of the Golden Age, living like animals on nature's bounty; the nomadic warriors of the tribal period; the peasants and sedentary merchants of the agricultural age; and the artisans of the industrial era. A lineage (*goträ*) is thus a group of individuals transmitting a special genetic code that evolves as it passes through innumerable carriers. Each lineage is an organ of the social body, and it is the social body as a whole that maintains the culture or civilization, which, in turn, allows the development and transmission of knowledge.

The functional hierarchy that assures the transmission of knowledge and rites has been maintained in the framework of Shaivism and Tantrism among non-Aryan populations, even though reduced, without distinction of rank, to the position of slaves by the Aryans. Even today, "in the Marhatta lands the Aryan Brahmans do not officiate in temples where the Lingä is worshiped. There is a separate caste for that, called Guravä, of Shudrä origins" (P. Banerjee, *Early Indian Religions*, p. 41). In the temples of Orissa, such as the Lingäräjä of Bhuvaneshvar, the Brahman and non-Brahman priests alternate in the performance of services.

The institution of royalty appeared in the Tretâ Yugä, the second age of mankind. There are certain sciences and arts that are distinctively royal and warlike. The *Râmâyanä* describes the education of Râmä and his brothers, typical of pre-Aryan warrior princes. The anointing of kings and their power of healing are the remnants of the initiatory traditions of the Kshatriyä, the warriors' traditions as distinct from those of the priests. It was a legendary hero, Parashu-Râmä (Râmä the battle-ax wielder), later thought to be an Avatârä of Vishnu, who rooted out the order of the Kshatriyä (i.e., the warrior tribes of the Tretâ Yugä) from India, to the benefit of the sedentary populations of the Dvâparä Yugä.

The lineages of farmers and merchants first appeared during this third age. They are the ones who produce and accumulate food and wealth, and who thereby provide the financial resources for cultural and religious institutions, and indeed the resources for the power of states. It was not only urban civilization and seaborne commerce that developed thanks to them, but also the organized urban religions, which, being ritualistic, moralistic, puritanical, and restrictive, will henceforth enter into conflict with the unfettered Dionysiac Shaivism.

Jainism, the atheistic religion of the commercial classes, first appeared in the Dvâparä Yugä, the Age of Doubt. Sentimental religiousness and puritanism would remain characteristic of the merchant caste, and these tendencies are for that matter clearly present in modern Vaishnavism.

The Popular Framework

THE popular and artisanal classes often formed a protective shell that allowed the occult tradition to be maintained. The common people remain attached to those external aspects of the tradition which are regarded as superstitions; they believe in spirits, magic, fate, and spells, in pilgrimages, idols, sacred places, and the seasonal festivals, thereby forming a defense against the intellectualism and tyranny of the urban religions.

A part of the occult tradition is transmitted within the framework of the ritual festivals and through the worship of objects, images, and holy places that never change no matter what name or justification is given them, and through the orgiastic, ecstatic, magical, and mystical practices which make up popular religion and which remain untouched by the ambitions of urban society.

It is in these popular arenas, those of the artisans and peasants, always in reaction against bourgeois civilization, that the traditions of sacred knowledge were able to find refuge in India in periods of crisis. These traditions are carried on by the wandering initiatory orders, the mysterious Sannyâsi, who, even in modern Hinduism, transmit the highest levels of initiation, closely connected to Shaivism, Tantrism, and Yogä. The word *pagan* (*paganus*) in fact means "peasant," for it was in the popular classes, Western as well as Indian, that these traditions, patterns of thought, and millennarian beliefs were sustained while the bourgeoisie lost touch with the ancient knowledge and rites.

Coexistence

EVERY society must make way for invaders and migrants. In this way, linguistic, religious, and professional groupings develop. These must be recognized and linked to the four principal groups, even while maintaining their separate identity, solidarity, and the means of defending their cultural uniqueness.

Besides a few exceptional individuals, who are mutants and therefore tend to associate together in a kind of parallel society, the problems of individual freedom in relation to social order are the concern of groups rather than of individuals. Every caste or ethnic, religious, or professional grouping tends to establish rules appropriate for itself, building up codes of behavior that cannot be generalized.

Rules of morality that imply codes of honor regulate the activities of each group. If these rules are not followed, the groups self-destruct. *Immigrants belonging to a foreign culture will alter the social order if their autonomy is denied and they are forced to assimilate.*

The hierarchy of the caste system allows for the coexistence and collaboration of human groups even though they belong to different levels of evolution. Attempts to bring about equality are destructive of the individuality of the person and of the group. *Coexistence demands respect for all the differences and varieties in human beings.* In this sense, traditional Hindu society is fundamentally antiracist. It rejects the colonialization through assimilation that the current Indian government, infected by Western ideas, is using to assassinate the primitive tribes left over from the Satyä Yugä and totally unable to adapt to the ways of life of the modern world. The government claims that these groups are the backward elements of a single population; but one cannot respect and protect the various human societies by refusing to acknowledge their very existence, autonomy, importance, rights, and uniqueness. Every group has its usefulness, a role to play in the balance of nature and society. The caste system tries to determine this role, stabilize it, and make it easier. The abilities, duties, virtues, and rules of each group are different: it is impossible to establish behavioral laws that would apply to all.

A division into castes, whatever may be its defects, is essential to the smooth running of every society. If, as a consequence of ill-considered intermingling, a society no longer has these distinct categories, they will tend to re-form, slowly but inevitably, just as a wound heals over: the social framework is its own healer. According to the *Manu Smriti*, the codified laws of Manu, abilities and talents should then be the basis on which to reestablish castes. There is a similar idea behind the modern I.Q. tests. However, we do not have the established corporate bodies that could make these abilities productive and provide a way of life, security, and a social family for those oriented toward a particular vocation. All this is crucial for the well-being of any society. The Western world's vanity (the implicit belief by which Westerners consider themselves a superior species) is revealed in its determination to impose upon all peoples its languages, beliefs, and social and moral concepts, in the belief that these represent progress.

Those attached to Indian culture liken themselves to the Aryan Brahmans, whose rites they pretend to practice and whose codes of behavior they claim to follow. This has cut them off from the other brands of Indian tradition.

The study of Shaiva tradition has been neglected to the point that most of the Westerners who claim to study India and its rites, customs, and knowledge have not even the slightest idea that there are other strands besides Vedic Brahmanism, even though it is these strands which are most suited to their own needs. Why does a Westerner who, at home, would study architecture, medicine, music, or perhaps astrology, alchemy, or magic, ignore the related fields which in India carry on similar traditions, with their particular initiations and rites, and which continue to teach the related religious and philosophic concepts?

The few Westerners who have really been able to enter the Hindu world are those who have taken an interest in the study of the crafts (music in particular) and have been accepted into an artisanal group. Others, in investigating religious or magical practices, have been able to find a place for themselves in the Tantric world that has opened before them. Such was the case of Sir John Woodroffe for Tantrism or Verrier Elwyn for the Munda tribes.

There are no exclusions in Shaivism and Tantrism concerning religious and ritual practices.

Tiruvallur, the author of the *Kural*, the most venerated work in Tamil literature, was of very humble origins. He wrote: "All men are equal. The differences between them come about through their occupations. . . . Even today, a pariah who has undergone the Shaiva initiation (Shivädik<u>sh</u>â) can transmit it to a Brahman and thus become his Guru" (Sakhare, *History and Philosophy of Lingayat Religion*, p. 175).

From the point of view of the social framework, the abilities and moral qualities of individuals are part of the genetic heritage of their lineage, and are generally related to the family's occupation. Just as there are game dogs and sheep dogs, each genetic code is adapted to particular functions.

Woman

THE division of the sexes implies separate functions as well as different natures. Since they have distinctly different abilities and roles, men and women form a double caste. They are closely interlinked and interdependent; they are different but complementary except where one or the other develops androgynous characteristics. It is only when they follow their separate behavioral patterns that these two halves of humanity achieve their purpose and are equal.

The masculine nature's principle is characterized by odd numbers; the female's is characterized by even numbers. This is why the nature and the function of woman is twofold: she is at the same time humble yet exalted, slave and goddess, submissive lover and all-powerful mother.

As lover she represents the creative power; without her the male principle is sterile. She is the image of Shakti, the power of the gods who without her have no reality.

It is in the mother's womb that the transition from non-existence to existence takes place. It is the place where the Creator does his creative work; it is the point where divinity and humanity meet, and is therefore the most sacred of sanctuaries. The mother goddess is the source and principle of life itself. It is thus in her role as mother that woman gains divinity and is worshiped. The mother is without artifice, without makeup (*nirañjanä*). She is the comfort of man wandering in the deserts of the world. She is forgiveness, charity, and limitless compassion. As the image of Prak<u>ri</u>ti, woman is the incarnation of the nutritive principle, which is the basis of material reality.

She is the guardian of the hearth, the priestess of Agni, god of fire. It is she who maintains the home, the center of family life. She is the axis of society, the center of each of society's cells, and hence is at the center of the social unit's stability. The original Shaiva society was matriarchal: women ruled in the home, the interior and concealed social cell, the sanctuary, of which she was the goddess. The father may have performed the rites of initiation for his sons, but it was the mother's blessing which was needed before he could enter the secret path of Sannyâsä, or renunciation.

In India, as elsewhere, the nomadic, patriarchal invaders (Aryans, Parthians, Scythians, Mongols, Semites, and finally Europeans) tried to overturn these ancient social institutions. In the artisanal castes, which remained faithful to Shaivism, the female predominates in the realm of the esoteric. In the public corporative rites, however, in the dances, ceremonies, symbols and invocations, the male aspect of divinity is to the fore: the symbolism is phallic.

The Family (Kulä)

IN India, the family group is under normal circumstances an extended one, stretching out over several generations. The women and children form the central, closed, cell. The pubescent males join the external cell, open to the outside world.

Although the choice of sexual partners is in principle exclusive for genetic reasons, man and wife do not formally live as a couple. The idea that the couple is the basis of social stability is a pernicious concept bearing no connection with the nature of man, and makes of the family a kind of prison.

It is the familial grouping (kulä) that forms the family. It includes brothers, uncles and their wives. The sexes live apart.

Hindu marriage is arranged in childhood according to very precise genetic rules concerning caste (varnä), clan (jâti), and lineage (goträ), which are similar to those we use for breeding animals or flowers.

Infidelity within a clan is not regarded as serious: a certain tolerance exists in fact, if not in theory. A married woman who has sexual relations with other men of her husband's family, stepbrothers, or cousins is not necessarily turned out, for the genetic code is not affected.

The Servants of the Gods

A woman who has had relations with several men of varied origins is no longer a suitable channel for the perpetuation of a genetic code. She is removed from the family, to become part of a new social grouping called the "servants of the gods" (*devä-dâsï*[s]), whose task it is to perform the arts of love, music, and dance. These servants of the gods have an essential part to play in the transmission of part of the cultural heritage.

The prostitution of women allows men to have sensual fulfillment while preserving the family's integrity; it also allows those who have devoted themselves to study and spiritual concerns to maintain their balance without taking on the social obligations and limitations that are part and parcel of marriage. The woman who devotes herself to the arts, to pleasure, or to a spiritual quest finds herself in a similar position to the servant of the gods: her work is incompatible with the reproductive function and therefore with marriage itself. There is always a connection between the erotic pursuits and mystic ecstasy: the paths of love are no obstacle to intellectual or spiritual achievement. The Dharmä, the ethics of these women, is described in the *Matsyä Purâṇä* (see Alain Daniélou, *La Sculpture erotique hindoue*, pp. 71–33).

Her obligations include making herself available without payment to wandering ascetics and feeding them. Once the great temples housed these women, who devoted themselves to dance, music, and the erotic arts, often in connection with mystical experience. Even today, the greatest singers, musicians, and dancers belong to this much-honored group, now considerably reduced in numbers by Anglo-Saxon prudishness: the very institution of Devä-dâsï was prohibited as immoral, to the very great detriment of the arts. It is not only in India that the theatrical and dancing professions were closely connected to that of the courtesan.

Women who follow the ascetic path, or that of pleasures

of the flesh, cannot achieve success unless they renounce procreation.

The quest for knowledge, the experience of Yogä, attracts many women; yet the path of detachment and personal fulfillment is compatible only with difficulty with the role of mother, wife, and manager of the home. Thus, women choose the solitary, monastic path, the path of the wanderer. Indian mystic history mentions many Yogini(s), female Yogi(s), who practiced unbelievable austerities, and holy women who wandered from temple to temple singing the praises of a god.

Miräbaï, a great poetess of the Hindi language, was a Rajput princess who abandoned palace, honor, and wealth in order to lead the life of a mystic wanderer, singing her marvelous poems in the villages as she begged for her food.

Ânandä Maï, who recently died, was very well known. She had many disciples and had a most beneficial influence. Extremely beautiful, she abandoned while still young her profession (as a teacher), husband, family, and children, in order to follow her destiny.

There are also women who have been exceptional by their wisdom and their knowledge, while other have been great warriors: for example, the famous Rani of Jhansi was a great military chief.

The modern woman who wishes to be simultaneously an object of pleasure, a mother, and one who takes part in man's futile activities is a destructive anomaly in society. For men, the home ceases to be a welcoming refuge where the mother is the protective goddess. Delinquency, violence, and social disorder often result from the lack of this refuge, the protective hearth over which women reign supreme.

The Third Nature (Tritîya Prakriti)

THE three Gunä(s), the three fundamental tendencies of Prakriti, are to be found in all that exists. All aspects of the divine are reflected in creation. The primordial impulses are

expressed in the masculine aspect (Purushä-Shivä), substance in the female aspect (Prakriti-Vishnu). The resulting
principle is neutral. It is represented by Brahmâ, the world's
artisan, or by Shivä in the aspect of the primordial androgyne.
Once a certain level of androgyneity develops in living beings,
it is called the Third Nature (Tritîya Prakriti) or the nonmale
(*napunsakä*).

Everything that lies between the poles of absolute masculinity and femininity derives from both. Everything is imbued to some extent with this double nature and is thus both
male and female. The differentiation between things and
beings arises from the degree of masculinity and femininity
of their composing elements, with the result that in the complex relationships of the formal world, each aspect or being
is male or female in relation to another aspect or state of
being. When applied to human society, this principle means
that each hierarchical level is masculine with regard to the
superior or inferior levels. Thus the king is feminine in relation to a priest and is therefore subservient to him; the
merchant is feminine in relation to the king and owes him
obedience; the artisan is feminine in relation to the merchant
and serves him as a slave. All living beings, stemming from
Prakriti, are basically feminine. The adolescent male is feminine in relation to an adult man and only achieves stability
as a male when he realizes his identity with the mature man.

It is the degree of femininity or masculinity in each person
in relation to others that determines his role and function.
In order to achieve his potential, everyone must establish his
position in relation to those with whom he comes into contact,
and thus realize his nature (his *Dharmä*, a word that basically
means "conformity with that which one is"). The task of the
man eager to free himself from the slavery of existence is
thus, first of all, to know himself and conform to his own
nature in order eventually to liberate himself from it.

The ascetics and wise men who saw the god-hero Ramä in
the forest obtained from him as a reward for their sacrifices
the right to be reborn as *gopis* (female cattle-herders) so that

they could be his lovers when he returned to earth in the form of Krishnä, the incarnation of love.

Men and women who are marked by sexual ambivalence have a role other than the transmission of the genetic code, and also have special functions within society. It is largely from among this class of people that shamans, magicians, wandering monks, initiates, holy virgins, priestesses, and also creative artists are recruited. To turn this androgynous aspect to full account, the shaman will dress as a woman and will eventually take a husband. The priests of Cybele dressed as women; some underwent castration, the better to identify themselves with the goddess. Etruscan priestesses wore phalluses.

In modern times, Râmäkrishnä (founder of the monastic order that bears his name), a worshiper of the goddess Durgâ, wore feminine clothes for many years as part of his *Sâdhanä* (his method of spiritual fulfillment). The adoption of female dress by male shamans and priests is a worldwide phenomenon.

Some Chukchee shamans wear women's clothing and even marry other men; the Akkadian priests of Ishtar wore female attire. The Tantric term *Vamachara*, the "left-hand way," literally means "the woman practice." According to the *Achârabhedä Tanträ*, "The ultimate female force is to be propitiated by becoming a woman" (McEvilley, *An Archeology of Yogä*, pp. 71–72).

Intersexuals, in whom certain male and female aspects are combined, are considered holy because they evoke the primordial androgyneity, the wholeness of principles. Corresponding to the neuter principle represented by the god Brahmâ, the creator in the cosmic trinity, they are particularly adapted to artisanal or artistic creation. In all societies intersexuals play an important part in literature, poetry, and the arts.

In their sections on fertility, the practical works on Yogä, such as the *Shivä Svarodayä*,[5] explain the psychological, physical, and astrological circumstances that give rise to intersexuals. They speak of fourteen nonreproductive categories (*napunsakä*), outlined by V. S. Apte in his Sanskrit dictionary. Castration, impotence, continence, and homosexuality are various forms of exclusion from genetic continuity which affect man as an individual, but even more as a link in the genetic chain, for these traits break the continuity of that chain and destroy one of the prime functions of the being of flesh. Nevertheless, this break in the chain is also part of the plan.

The Greek word corresponding to *napunsakä* is *eunychos*, meaning "he who guards the marriage bed"; that is, he who protects the virtue of women while the menfolk, the warriors, are absent. There is no implication here of the emasculation involved in the modern term *eunuch*. It was thus a misrepresentation of the Evangelist's words (Matthew 19:10–12) to use the word *eunuch* (in place of *homosexual*) when Jesus said, "There are those who have been born eunuchs, others who have been made eunuchs, and others who have chosen the path in their wish for the solitary life, and who are not suited for marriage."

The early Christian Gnostics attached great value to non-reproductive eroticism. It was only in the fifth century that these practices began to be condemned.

> The common rule of all the Gnostics was the refusal of procreation; those who advocated continence or the abolition of marriage did so with that in mind; those who did engage in sexual relations made them infertile through contraception or abortion. . . . The ritual orgy was an ostentatious means of collectively reinforcing this rejection. [Alexandrian, *Histoire de la philosophie occulte*, p. 63]

Epiphanius, Bishop of Constantia (Cyprus), relates in his *Panarion* (written c. 370) his experiences in Gnostic orgies (see Alexandrian, ibid).

Since they are not involved in reproduction, and since this breaks the genetic chain, homosexuals fall outside the castes. One of their functions is to establish links between the different castes and races, and also between men, spirits, and the gods. They play a key part in magical practices.

As it has no genetic consequences, homosexuality should be considered a harmless erotic and sentimental pastime: the *Kâma Suträ* and other works on the arts of love all include it.

Male prostitutes (*shand*) and transvestites (*kanchukin*), nowadays called Hijrâ or Laundâ, have a recognized place and enjoy a similar status to the Devä-dâsï in traditional society. They are a separate social group under the direction of a Guru who enjoys certain privileges, particularly in the field of holy spectacles. Even today, the presence of a male prostitute in female dress, the last vestige of the androgynous shaman, is a good omen in a marriage ceremony.

The influence of Anglo-Saxon puritanism has meant that the anglicized groups in modern India pretend that they do not know of the sacred aspect of the Third Nature and homosexual practices.

The absence of a third, neutral gender—the essential complement of the masculine and feminine—in a language such as French indicates a mental limitation with psychological and social consequences.

NOTES

1. According to Mendel: "The genes are at the root of it all. It is they that determine completely what we are. They reproduce in identical form from generation to generation without the environment having the slightest influence on them. Occasionally, however, it happens that one of these genes mutates spontaneously; this mutation is perpetuated just as is the normal gene."

2. According to a report by the FAO of November 1983, in recent years high-yield food plants have been developed through hybridization; research has led to the development of plants that are all genetically similar. Should disease strike them, the contagion might destroy the entire species if the original variety of species no longer survives. Such "genetic erosion" is spreading around the world as quickly as fire on a prairie. There remain no more than 80 vegetal species in Peru out of

more than 1,500 before the Incas. Things are no different for the animal species, including mankind.

3. See Alain Daniélou, *The Four Aims of Life: Social Structures of Traditional India.*

4. "The castes are not distinct entities, as classes in the Western tradition may be. . . . Castes are above all contrasting elements which may eventually be in harmony with each other, but which are in all events necessary to each other. The hierarchical unity of the caste system is a combination of various distinct sets of relationships. What Western Monism has persistently stifled and rejected flourishes in such a system in all its richness. In place of one-dimensionalism, which entails isolation, we find polytheism, which rests on interdependence. Instead of gregarious solitude, we find the richness of a harmonious solidarity. Thus, rather than a denial of the reality of contrasting elements, with the risk of seeing them reemerge later in multiple forms of bloody violence, the acceptance of an organized plurality will lead to an integrated, dynamic society. . . . The family, the mafia, the group, the village, and the district of a city are so many channels for community life" (Michel Maffesoli, *L'Ombre de Dionysos*, pp. 87 and 501).

5. *Shivä Svarodayä*, translated from the Sanskrit by Alain Daniélou.

2

The Transmission of Knowledge

The Master (Guru)

THE FIRST GURU, OR MASTER, IS THE MOTHER. FROM her the child learns the basics of language, the tool of communicaton and knowledge. The father and masculine society become involved only later. It is to the father that the duty falls of teaching the civic virtues and techniques that will allow the child to enter a social grouping.

Once the child reaches the age for study, following his first entrance into masculine society and his separation from the women, he is placed in the hands of a master who teaches him the sciences, rites, and technical aspects of the knowledge that he must acquire to fulfill the role of his lineage and caste.

While his studies are in course, the child enters his master's household. He will, if necessary, beg in order to contribute to the household's meals. If he belongs to a scholarly family, he will become familiar during this period with philosophical, theological, and scientific literature. He is also introduced to the oral tradition of which his master is the custodian. He will learn by heart a considerable number of texts, which are for that reason largely in verse form. In

[179]

India, these texts include grammar rules, etymologies, dictionaries, ritual and philosophic texts, all of which are the grounding for his later work. The written word is but a supplement to the memory, which allows an expansion of certain aspects and ensures their survival.

If the student belongs to lineages that are not literate, then his studies take a different form. If he comes from a warrior or princely family, he will study the arts of government and warfare, archery, the care of horses and elephants, the use of spies, and the astrological and magical factors that will ensure victory. Today, he would learn to drive tanks and use explosives.

In the artisanal castes, the student is an apprentice who gradually learns the secrets and techniques of his craft. This is true also of the visual arts and of architecture and music. The apprentice takes part in the work of his master, who remains his tutor until he has mastered his craft. In India, just as in Italy until the Renaissance, painting, sculpture, and architecture were workshop concerns. The students collaborated in their master's work. A pupil does not pay his master, for knowledge cannot be sold; but once a year, at the time of the Guru Pûjâ*h*, the rite of veneration of one's master, the student offers him, if at all possible, gold coins on a silver platter, in addition to the symbolic offerings of flowers, fruits, and incense. At the end of his studies, he will give his master a gift according to his means. Besides the ritual elements, this gift can be land, cattle, books, or gold.

The Guru's Responsibilities

THE Guru's responsibilities are manifold. He is the bearer of an ancestral heritage of knowledge that he must pass on. Just as the marriage codes ensure the survival of the genetic heritage, and the maintenance of the abilities, physical beauty, and moral virtues of the child, so the handing down of knowledge involves a heavy responsibility, for knowledge, when placed in the hands of those who are not worthy of it, can become a dangerous weapon.

He who is the bearer of a tradition of knowledge is under an obligation to pass it on. The master's major problem is to find a suitable candidate on whom he can rely. This is the reason why a Guru takes extreme precautions before accepting a disciple. The Western "trendies" who pass around the names of good Gurus as if they were restaurants have been dealing solely with charlatans.

From the Hindu point of view, a modern Western democratic education is completely immoral. Scholars accept payment to deliver to anyone at all the secrets of the most dangerous sciences. Some atomic scientists have realized this too late and are now terrified by the awesome responsibilities they took upon themselves.

The Limits of Knowledge

THE development of creation proceeds from darkness toward light, from childhood toward maturity, from ignorance toward knowledge, until at length a regression sets in and the darkness returns.

Among the species on the earth today, man represents a culmination in this evolutionary pattern. The more he understands the hidden nature of the world, the more he understands the Creator's art, the more he fulfills his role.

Yet, there are limits to this role. It is not for mankind to master the hidden forces of nature; that is the role of the subtle beings whose perception of the play of creation and responsibilities are to be found on a different level. It is not for mankind to encroach on the domain of higher beings. This is the reason why "it does not please the gods to allow mankind to attain a state of knowledge."

Just as there are limits to sensory perception, so there are barriers on the path of knowledge which man cannot pass without abandoning his role, thereby running the risk of bringing the wrath of the gods to bear in the destruction of his species.

Man is therefore in a contradictory position: his *raison d'être* is to seek knowledge, but there are limits to his search that he must not overstep.

The Choice of a Disciple

THE pupil, the Shi*sh*yä, is the receptacle (*patra*) of the teachings of his master or masters, who impart to him those elements of knowledge that he seems to deserve. A pupil has no right to publicize the name of his Guru in case his errors and faults rebound on his master. Only if the master wishes it, and if the pupil has undergone a final initiation ceremony, which is in fact virtually an adoption ceremony, can he make himself known as his master's heir and provide a provenance for his learning by naming his master.

There are several factors that disqualify (*viparyayä*) an individual from the transmission of some aspects of knowledge. The texts list some as an aid to the Guru in the choice of candidates suitable (*adhikâri*) for the task of passing on the hidden aspects of knowledge. According to the *Sâmkhyä-Kârikâ(s)* (47–50) and their commentary, the disqualifications are of four types. The first category includes mental or psychological unfitness, of which there are five types:

Stupidity (*tamas*) (eight sorts)

Lack of judgment (*mohä*) (eight sorts), which makes one mistake one thing for another

A perversity of spirit (*mahâmohä*) (ten types), which deforms basic data

Despondency (*tâmisrä*) (eighteen types), such as doubt and lack of persistence)

Despair (*andhä tâmisrä*) (eighteen types), which leads to the belief that knowledge cannot be attained

The second category is that of physical disabilities (*ashakti*), twenty-eight in number, which are connected with defaults in the organs and with physical and mental deficiencies (blindness, deafness, paralysis, timidity, the lack of a sense of smell, dumbness, deformity, lameness, castration, madness, etc.).

The third category concerns self-satisfaction (*tushti*), of which there are nine forms: four interior (*adhyâtmikä*) and five exterior (*bâhyä*). The four interior varieties are:

· Of nature (*prâkritä*): to be satisfied with a superficial knowledge of things

· Of means (*upâdânä*): to consider the means as an end in themselves; for example, the belief that dressing as a monk will enable one to achieve detachment from the world

· Of time (*kâlä*): to believe that the passage of time will cure all wrongs

· Of chance (*bhâgyä*): to believe that chance will provide a cure to all wrongs

The five exterior forms are connected with the five senses (hearing, touch, sight, taste, and smell), because of the worries to which they give rise. They are:

· The acquisition of material possessions (*arjanä*), the work entailed in the care of cattle, and the guarding of wealth

· The preservation of wealth (*rakshanä*) and the anxieties it causes

· Extravagance (*kshayä*), which results in the loss of that material security which is vital to the quest for knowledge

· Dependency (*sangä*): the inability to do without certain things

· Violence (*himsâ*): anything obtained to the detriment of anyone else is a form of violence and is therefore a source of instability. [Gaudpadä, Commentary on the *Sâmkhyä-Kârikâ*, 50]

There are, for the pupil once he is accepted, eight "paths to progress" which enable him to benefit fully from the teachings of his master.

The first is reflection (*ûhä*). Knowledge is achieved through meditation about the basic questions. The pupil should ask himself questions such as the following: What is truth? What is the beyond? Is Puru*sh*ä different from Pradhânä? Is intelligence a separate entity from self? What differentiates the Tanmaträ(s), the senses, the various elements, etc.?

The second is language (*shabdä*). Language is the channel for the transmission of knowledge. One should therefore increase one's vocabulary and know the precise meaning of words, etc.

The third is study (*adhyâyanä*), a knowledge of the learning of the ancients.

The fourth, fifth, and sixth concern internal peace, through the elimination of the three forms of physical, mental, and spiritual suffering (*dukhä-vidhâtâ-trayam*).

The seventh is friendship (*suhrit prâpti*). The emotional relationships between friends, the conversations and discussions, are a source of intellectual enrichment.

The eighth is generosity (*dânä*). The egotist who cannot share his belongings and his learning is isolated from the traditions of thought and becomes intellectually sterile. [*Sâmkhyä Kârikâ* 51]

The Wanderers of the Path of Knowledge (*Brahmächârî*)

IN the caste system the transmission of techniques and rites is tied to the transmission of life. The true tradition of knowledge, however, does not operate in the same way. The transmission of knowledge is carried out through the chain of initiations, quite independently of the genetic chain. Its adherents may be born in any social group, and must live on the fringes of society. It is their task to maintain in secret the highest forms of the tradition of knowledge regardless of religious, social, or linguistic changes in the outside world. He who wishes to achieve the higher destiny of man (that is, to be not a link in the transmission of life, but rather a link in the handing down of hidden knowledge) must leave his family and seek out a Guru. As he wanders from village to village begging for food, he devotes himself to the "quest for knowledge" (Brahmācharyä). He becomes a Brahmāchārî, one of the "wanderers of the path of knowledge" (from *chârî*, to move, and *brahmä*, knowledge). He is also known as a Sannyasi (from *nyâsä*, renunciation, and *sat*, material possessions). He must find a representative of this esoteric tradition who considers him a worthy candidate able in his turn to pass on the heritage.

It is this master who is the true Guru. The Brahmächârî must follow a long initiatory process to show that he is in fact suitable (*adhikâri*). He must live at his master's side, serve him, and obey him in all matters. It is this chain of initiations that has allowed Shaivism and the highest forms of ancient learning to survive periods of persecution in order to reemerge at the appropriate moment. It is still true today. The occult traditions continue parallel to the official education system.

In today's puritan world the word *Brahmächârî* has come to mean "chaste." Originally the word meant "the search for knowledge"; it is only recently that it has acquired the meaning of sexual continence. There is nothing to justify this interpretation. What is important as far as the Brahmächârî is concerned is not the renunciation of pleasure, but rather the renunciation of marriage and the social ties it creates. The state of Brahmächârî might be compared with what in Celtic tradition is represented by the quest for the Grail. In truth, the Brahmächârî has a role to play in the hierogamies, the ritual sexual couplings of Tantrism. Some of these wanderers have a female companion or a favored pupil and engage in erotic activities that may or may not be connected with

Yogä. Massages of the spine which lead to ejaculation are popularly known as "monk's massages."

Those who have studied the professional techniques of their own social group can, once their studies are finished, return to the family and become a link in the transmission of the lineage and social function. Those, however, who adventure into the parallel discipline of the quest for knowledge must remain aloof from the religious or political establishment and must also sever all ties with the family and society into which they are born. When man renounces the world, his station, and his social duties in order to devote himself to spiritual realization, he loses his caste and name. He sets out naked or dressed only in a seamless piece of material in the color of mourning, orange, which signifies that as far as he is concerned, the distinctions caused by castes and social hierarchy are ended, and that he is in a manner of speaking dead to the world. Whatever an individual's place in the human hierarchy may have been, the path of Sannyâsä allows no materialistic activities and no role in social life.

An essential part of this quest for knowledge is the wandering: the complete absence of social ties, marriage, and material obligations during the time of study and, for those who gain initiation, for the whole of life. This entails the establishment of a system of holy begging, which is a basic part of Hindu social organization. "There is a need for wandering which does not fit in at all with the sedentary nature of the productive principle" (Michel Maffesoli, *L'Ombre de Dionysos*, p. 39).

In order that the esoteric tradition may continue, Hindu society imposes a moral obligation on all households to provide food to all wanderers who may appear at their door (whether they be students, monks, travelers, or vagrants). Before meals, the children sit in front of the door to signal the approach of the unknown guest who is to be served first. The holy beggar will not ask for anything: he stays standing before the door for a short period of time. According to the rules of the various monastic orders, the number of households he may approach with his begging bowl is limited to three, four, or five. The households are enjoined not to ask questions or to vary their treatment of the wanderers according to their appearance. This allows the initiates to remain indistinguishable among the innumerable false ascetics and vagrants.

Wandering is a means, for those who do not wish to take up the family profession, to escape from the caste system. By renouncing its advantages, they are freed from its obligations, prohibitions, and restrictions.

PART FIVE

THE
THEORY
OF
CYCLES

1

The Duration of the Universe

ACCORDING TO A THEORY THAT SHAIVA PHILOSOPHY calls Determinism (*niyati*), the development of the world and the galaxies, like species or individuals, is governed by cycles. Civilizations are born and die according to certain inescapable rhythms. For this reason, we can only understand human history in relation to the duration of the cycles that regulate life on earth.

The first stage of creation is that of space, of the receptacle in which the world will develop and which, at the outset, has neither boundary nor dimension. Time at this stage exists only in a latent form that we can call eternity, as it has no measure, no duration, no before or after. A moment is not intrinsically longer or shorter than a century, except in relation to an element of consciousness by which it is possible to establish its direction and measure its duration. It is energy, by producing vibratory waves having direction and length, that will give birth to the rhythms whose perception will create the dimension of time, the measure of space, and at the same time the structures of matter. This is why the formation of the world is symbolized by the beat of the drum and the dance of Shivä (principle of expansion). For man, the perception of the dimension of time is determined by his

[191]

vital rhythms—his heartbeat—as well as the movements of the sun, the moon, and the earth, which determine the duration of the cycles, the years, the nights, and the days in this cell that we call the solar system. Time as perceived by man corresponds to a completely relative duration, revolving around a center of perception (the living being) in a specific world which is the earthly one. It is not an absolute value of time. Yet human time is the only unit of measure that we can understand. In relation to it, we can estimate the duration of the universe, which, from the viewpoint of the creative principle, is only a day's dream, just as the life span of certain atomic worlds is in our view infinitesimal. The laws that govern the development and deterioration of the universe as a whole are the same as those which govern that of each of its parts. For this reason, one can compare the duration of the body of the universe, of Cosmic Man, Puru_sh_ä, with that of a human being, who is his image, a small-scale model of him, or even with a tree, an animal, or a species. Man's life is neither shorter nor longer than the life of a god or a universe. Its duration differs only in relative terms, for the value of time exists only in relation to a specific system of perception.[1]

The time scale of the creative principle, the duration of a day of Brahmâ, which sees the world appear, evolve, withdraw, and disappear, is called a Kalpä. Its night lasts another Kalpä. [*Lingä Purâ_nä_* 1.4.6]

The duration of the material or visible world (Prä_kr_itä) is called the day of Brahmâ. The night of Brahmâ is a period of time of equal length during which the world ceases to exist. In reality, it is not a matter of night and day; these terms are used symbolically. [*Lingä Purâ_nä_* 1.4.3–6]

In the course of the day of Brahmâ the cells that make up the universe (the galaxies, the solar systems) are formed, destroyed, and renewed, just as the basic molecules of the human body are continually destroyed and renewed.[2]

Precise calculations of the cycles of time, which go from the blink of an eye (Kaṣḥtä, approximately one-fifth of a second) to the duration of the universe, are given in many works, in particular, the Purâṇä(s).

The life of Brahmâ (or the duration of the universe) is divided into a thousand cycles called Mahâ-Yugä(s), or Great Years (corresponding for the earthly world to the cycles of the precession of the equinoxes). The Mahâ-Yugä, during which the human race appears and disappears, is divided into a little more than seventy-one cycles of fourteen Manvantarä(s). [*Lingä Purâṇä* 1.4.7]

The Manvantarä is the cycle of a Manu, the forefather of a human epoch. (These last figures are, in reality, an expression of the figure 1,000 (that is, $14 \times 71.42 = 1,000$), this figure being considered symbolic).

Before the appearance of living species, beings appear who then preside over the development of various aspects of creation. The forms of consciousness that rule over the organization of matter are called the Elemental Gods (Vishvädevä[s]). Those which govern the life of living creatures, regarded as entities that develop in time and of which individual beings are the cells, are the Lords of the Species (Prajâpati). The beings that have charge of the development of knowledge, in parallel with that of life, and who are the conscious witnesses of the secret nature of the world, are called the Seers (Rishi[s]). The Rishi(s) appear from time to time in human form.

During what is called the day of Brahmâ, everything which "evolves" (*vikriti*) including the Elemental Gods (Vishvädevä[s]) and those which preside over the evolution of the species (Prajâpati), as well as the subtle or incarnate beings who govern the evolution of knowledge, that is, the witnesses or seers (Rishi[s]), are present. They disappear during the cosmic night and arise again at the break of day. [*Lingä Purâṇä* 1.4.1–4]

According to the calculations of the Purânä(s), the duration of the universe is 34 billion, 560 million years. The Mahâ-Yugä or Great Year lasts 4,320,000 years. According to modern data (Reeves), the age of the universe is around 15 billion years, and of the earth 4.5 billion years. The universe is therefore still young and would only be halfway through its life. Its expansion should last another 2 billion years before its period of retraction starts.[3]

"The duration of the demi-Kalpä, according to the calendar of the gods, is 2,867,000,000 years. Eight thousand years of Brahmâ form its Yugä. One thousand Yugä(s) of Brahmâ are a Savanä, and nine thousand Savanä(s) are a day of Rudrä" (*Lingä Purânä* 1.4.37–40). The interpretation of these data poses a few problems as they concern in some cases lunar years (or human years) or ancestral years (years of the various races) or even the years of the gods. We will follow here the interpretation of the astrologers, who attach a great deal of importance to the duration of the cycles.

The Cycles of the Yugä

The cycles, in conjunction with astronomical phases, determine the life span of the species. The duration of a human species is included in a cycle called Manvantarä (the length of the reign of a Manu, the forefather-lawmaker of the human race). Each Manvantarä is divided into four ages or Yugä(s), producing a gradual decline in spiritual values at the same time as material advances. "The relative duration of the four ages is respectively 4, 3, 2, 1. Each age is preceded by a period of dawn and followed by a period of twilight. These transition periods (*amshä*) at the beginning and end of each Yugä last a tenth of the duration of the Yugä. [*Lingä Purânä* 1.4.3–6]

The duration of time viewed at different levels in the hierarchy of creation presents a harmonious relationship.

On earth a human year forms a day and a night of the ancestors (that is, of a lineage, a model, from its appearance to its end). The period of the year (from the winter solstice to the summer solstice) when the sun rises toward the north (*uttarâyanä*) is equivalent in length to the day of the ancestors; the period when the sun goes down toward the south (*dakshinâyanä*) (from the summer solstice to the winter solstice) is their night.

With regard to the year of the gods, thirty human years correspond to a month of the gods, one hundred human years make three months and ten days of the gods, 360 years of man make one year of the gods, 3,030 years of man make one year of the Seers (Rishi[s]) (that is, of a tradition of knowledge passed on through initiation). Nine thousand and ninety years of men comprise one year of the cycle of the North Star (Dhruvä). [According to modern astrological data, the cycle of the eccentricity of the earth's orbit which determines the position of the North Star is in reality around 92,000 years.] Thirty-six hundred human years are a century of the gods; 360,000 human years make a thousand years of the gods. [*Lingä Purânä* 1.4.16–23]

The night and the day (of humans) are each divided into fifteen periods (*muhurtä*) of twenty minutes. A lunar month corresponds to a day of the ancestors (*pitri*). Thirty human months constitute a month of the ancestors; 360 human months (thirty years) constitute a year of the ancestors, that is, one generation. One hundred human years are three ancestral years. Twelve earthly months make up one human year, twelve ancestral months, one ancestral year. [*Lingä Purânä* 1.4.7–14]

The duration of the lineage of the ancestors corresponds to the evolution and predominance of a particular race. One hundred and twenty ancestral years, that is, the life of a race, corresponds to approximately four thousand human years.

The number of days in a year is not constant. The rhythm of the earth's rotation varies over very long periods. A figure of 360 is considered to be the average. The figures and dates calculated on this basis are therefore approximate since they are based on the circle and its division into 360 degrees (Kalâ), giving an approximate picture of the cycles. The circle is an illusion, for the cosmic mechanism is in reality always formed of spirals. Nothing ever returns to its point of departure. However, the circle does give us a simplified image. With regard to the Kali Yugä, the world age in which we now find ourselves, the difference between the cycle of 360 days and the actual duration of a year results in a difference of approximately fifty years over the five thousand that constitute the Yugä.

"The absolute maximum life span for man is 120 terrestrial years, for gods it is 12,000 celestial years. [Because one celestial year equals 360 human years] the life span of the gods is therefore 360 × 12,000 = 4,320,000 human years" (*Lingä Purânä* 1.4.4 and 1.4.24–36). We have seen that 71.42 Manvantarä(s) form one year of the gods. Each cycle of four Yugä(s) therefore lasts 60,487 years (being 4,320,000 divided by 71.42) as astrological treatises see it. Similarly, the normal human life span is 43,200 days (360 days × 120 years).

The cycle of 4,320,000 years, the Mahâ-Yugä, which corresponds to the life of the gods, is divided, according to the *Lingä Purânä*, into "a little more than seventy-one periods" (71.42 × 14 = 1,000), each divided into four Yugä(s) whose duration relative to each other is 4:3:2:1.

$$\frac{4,320,000}{71.42} = 60,487.25 \text{ human years}$$

The duration of the four Yugä(s) with their dawns and twilights is therefore:

Dawn of Kritä Yugä:	2,016.24	
Kritä	20,162.40	
Twilight	2,016.24	Total: 24,195
Dawn of Tretâ	1,512.10	
Tretâ	15,121.80	
Twilight	1,512.10	Total: 18,146
Dawn of Dvâparä	1,008.10	

Dvâparä	10,081.20	
Twilight	1,008.10	Total: 12,097
Dawn of Kali	504.06	
Kali	5,040.60	
Twilight	504.06	Total: 6,048.72

Total of the four Yugä(s): 60,487 human years

According to the traditional Indian calendar, which is still in use, the Kali Yugä commenced in 3012 B.C. If we accept this date for the beginning of Kali Yugä, the following calendar results:

Dawn of Kritä Yugä	58,042 B.C.
Beginning of Kritä Yugä	56,026 B.C.
Beginning of Twilight	35,864 B.C.
Dawn of Tretâ Yugä	33,848 B.C.
Beginning of Tretâ Yugä	32,336 B.C.
Beginning of Twilight	17,215 B.C.
Dawn of Dvâparä Yugä	15,703 B.C.
Beginning of Dvâparä Yugä	14,695 B.C.
Beginning of Twilight	4,614 B.C.
Dawn of Kali Yugä	3,606 B.C.
Kali Yugä	3,102 B.C.
Middle of Kali Yugä	582 B.C.
Beginning of Twilight	A.D. 1,939
End of Twilight of Kali Yugä	A.D. 2,442

The twilight of the Kali Yugä therefore would have started in 1939, in the month of May. The final catastrophe will take place during this twilight. The last traces of this present humankind will have disappeared in 2442. The figures, as we have seen, are accurate to within fifty years. Using these dates as a starting point and going back, we find that the first manifestation of humanity came forth in 419,964 B.C., the second in 359,477 B.C., the third in 298,990 B.C., the fourth in 238,503 B.C., the fifth in 178,016 B.C., the sixth in 118,529 B.C., and the seventh in 58,042 B.C.

The beginning of the present human cycle, the seventh,

in 58,042 B.C., seems to correspond to the appearance of
what we call *Homo sapiens* or Cro-Magnon man. The species
that preceded this is probably that to which we give the name
Neanderthal, whose brain capacity (1400 cm³) was markedly
superior to ours, which varies between 1,200 cm³ (Nordic
males) and 650 cm³ (Polynesian females); according to an-
thropological treatises, Neanderthal man probably dates back
to 118,000 B.C.

The first period, the Krïtä Yugä, is the age of accomplishment and wisdom (corresponding to the Golden Age of Hesiod).
Including its dawn and twilight, it lasts 24,195 years. Next
comes the Tretâ Yugä, "the age of the three ritual fires," the
age of rites but also of the hearth, that is, of sedentary,
agricultural, and urban civilization. Its duration, counting
the dawn and twilight, is 18,146 years in all.

The third age, the Dvâparä Yugä or "age of doubt" sees
the birth of the anti-establishment religions and philosophies.
Man loses the sense of the divine reality of the world and
grows away from natural law. The Dvâparä Yugä lasts 10,081
years, and its dawn and twilight last 1,008 years each, a total
of 12,097 years.

Finally comes the fourth age or "age of conflict," the Kali
Yugä. It lasts 5,040 years, and its dawn and twilight each
last 504 years, totaling 6,048 years. It will end with the nearly
total destruction of the present humanity.

The word *Tretâ*, "triad," refers to the three ritual fires.
Dvâparä can mean "after the two," but more especially "doubt"
or "uncertainty." *Kali* (two short syllables), which means
"quarrel" or "conflict," bears no relationship to *Kâlï* (long
syllables), which is the name of the goddess, of the power of
time and of death.

The Flood

THE present phase of mankind commences with a great flood,
which is recorded by all civilizations, which probably took

place around 60,200 B.C. A lesser flood, dated in Sumerian writings at around 3000 B.C., heralds the beginning of the Kali Yugä. The Sumerian dynasties are classified as antediluvian and postdiluvian. The Purânä(s) mention the change in men's moral behavior from the dawn of the Kali Yugä.

Vaivasvatä Manu (the Noah of the Bible), survivor of a previous human cycle, was saved by Vishnu who, in the form of a fish, pulled the ark to dry land.[4] The decendants of Manu's companions, intermingled with the new races then still in semi-animal form (the Nephilim of Genesis), constitute the present humanity.

NOTES

1. We could perhaps, in modern terms, consider that the unity of cosmic time, linked to the initial explosion of the energetic principle, is the speed of expansion of the universe, which seems to be constant within the period of the evolution of the universe, during which time living species are born and die. According to Hindu cosmology, we are a third of the way through the expansion of the universe. This speed should gradually diminish to zero, then inverse itself when the universe is reabsorbed.

2. According to modern data, "the number of cells which make up the human body is 3×10^{28} or thirty billion billion billion" (Hubert Reeves, *Patience dans l'azur*, p. 122). According to Indian theory, this figure should be similar to the number of cosmic cells or galaxies that constitute Cosmic Man.

3. Until relatively recently, the data of Hindu cosmology were considered absurd and were often ridiculed by the West, which maintained that the world was created in seven days, concluding, according to Johannes Kepler, on Sunday, 27 April, in the year 3877 B.C. This date, of biblical origin, derived from Sumerian data, corresponds approximately to the beginning of the Kali Yugä, the fourth and current age of mankind, and not to the creation of the world.

4. According to a theory suggested by the Commentaries of the Purânä(s), the ark may have been a space vessel in which some survivors of the previous human cycle had taken refuge. It would have been they who gave birth to the new humanity and its Golden Age.

2

The Three Cities

The Ages (Yugä)

ACCORDING TO SHAIVA TRADITION, SINCE THE WORLD has been inhabitable, several manifestations of humanity have existed. Each had its period of glory, of technological development, of knowledge, then of decline, and has reached its end in a cataclysm. We are part of the seventh "humanity." The earth has therefore already known six successive appearances of mankind, each of which have disappeared,[1] leaving to the following "humanity" some traces of their knowledge and sometimes a reminder of their glory. After the termination of the present humankind, the earth will know human or similar species seven more times before becoming uninhabitable. All living species evolve as entities, as individuals. They have their gestation, childhood, adolescence, maturity, and decline.

In the Purânä(s) we find the account, passed down over millennia, of the circumstances that surrounded the end of the cycle of the human species preceding ours. However, details of two catastrophes are intertwined in this account: on the one hand, that which caused the end of the civilization of the Assurs, more than 60,000 years ago, and, on the other hand, the destruction of the cities of the Indus by Aryan invaders, which, two thousand years before Christ, marks the beginning of the Kali Yugä, the period of the decline of the present human race. This account gives us a clear picture of the conditions that lead to the destruction of the species at the end of each of the cycles that punctuate life on earth. The history of the Assurs is at the same time an account of the past and a prediction of the future.

There is an obvious parallel between the events, the religious concepts, the ideologies, and the social and moral theories that caused the destruction of the Assurs and those which, since the beginning of the Kali Yugä, characterize the present human cycle and the "self-induced catastrophe" (*naimittikä pralayä*) that eventually awaits us.

The history of the Assurs also teaches us how, by our actions and especially by our moral and religious concepts, we can delay the final day for the whole or a part of the human race. This would enable some to survive the cataclysm and take part in the Golden Age of the future mankind.

The Destruction of the Assurs

THE Assurs, who had attained a tremendously high standard of civilization, are depicted as fervent worshipers of the god Shivä. They practiced the cult of the Lingä, the divine phallus. With the help of Mayä, the architect of the spirits, they had built three impregnable cities. One, on the ground, was of copper; another, floating above the ground, was of silver; and the third, high in the heavens, was gold.

According to the *Shivä Purânä*:[2]

The Assur princes were moderate men, well mannered, disciplined, decent, courageous, persevering. They were the enemies of the Aryan gods. They could control the sunlight and had a great variety of uses for this energy. They distributed food to the hungry. . . . Dressed in silky-looking clothing [underwater suits], they could even survive below the ocean without any trouble. . . .

In the three cities of the Assur, there were many trees of plenty [supermarkets?] where it was possible to get whatever one desired. There were also a great many elephants and horses, and palaces decorated with rare gems. Flying chariots, dazzling as the sun and adorned with rubies [red lights?], were traveling in all directions. Some, like moons, lit up the cities. There were many trees and idyllic gardens, vast reservoirs, ponds, wells, rivers. There were machines to tell the time, playing fields, places of study. All sorts of people, good and bad, populated the cities. Chivalrous and courageous noblemen and learned scholars could be found there.

The Assurs had broad chests and shoulders like bulls. Their hair was black and wavy. They were strong, heroic in battle, skillful in the art of war. Indifferent to the rest of the world, they lived in their cities, faithful to the worship of Shivä. [*Shivä Purâṉä, Rudrä Samhitâ* 5.1.10–78]

Shivä, the principle of time, which is the measurement of space, is the only god who has the power to destroy. It was therefore to him that the other gods went when they wanted to conquer and annihilate the Assurs and their magnificent cities.

The gods of the Aryans (the barbarian invaders who were trying to take over the territory of the civilized peoples and who had found in the Assurs a formidable enemy) tried to gain Shivä's favor in order to be able to destroy their fortresses. But the god of justice, who is the god of all living beings, could not enter into this quarrel.

"The Assurs," he said, "have done no wrong and are my humble worshipers. I could only destroy them if they forsook me." The Aryan gods then turned to Vishnu (the god who governs civic virtues). Vishnu said to them, "You will not succeed in destroying the three cities without the help of Shivä, the lord of sacrifices." The Aryan gods therefore organized a great sacrifice in Shivä's honor. Thousands of evil spirits (*bhûtä*[s]), armed with all kinds of weapons, came out of the ritual fire. Some weapons made use of a destructive fire similar to the sun's energy. However, when they attacked the cities of the Assurs, their efforts were futile. Vishnu explained to the gods: "Because they worship Shivä and his emblem, the phallus [the symbol of life], all the desires of the Assurs are realized. It is not possible to conquer them and the Vedic religion is threatened. You must get them to renounce the god who protects them and who alone can reduce them to ashes" (5.3.30–50).

In order to put an end to the virtuous activities of the Assurs, Vishnu devised a plan. He created a strange individual, a perverse being who promulgated a puritan religion. His head was shaved, his clothing dirty. He carried a basket to collect alms and a fly whisk made of a roll of cotton, which he shook continuously. His hands were frail, his face pale and sickly (5.4.1–3).

Unlike all the other ascetics known before this time, who were naked, with unkempt hair and flashing eyes that suggested astonishing magical powers, "this one's head was shaven and he wore a long robe. His eyes had no fire." The bogus sage approached the god and asked him, "What is my name? What must I do?" Vishnu said, "Your name will be Arihat [destroyer of pious people]. You must write a (pseudo-)holy book of 1,600 verses, in everyday language, condemning the castes and the duties of the various ages of life (*âshramä*[s]). You will be given the power to work a few miracles. . . . The basis of your teaching will be: heaven and hell exist only in this life; and you will teach this doctrine to the Assurs, so they can be destroyed."

The character then recruited four disciples. Shaven-headed, they proclaimed the heretic cult. They all carried a basket in their hand and covered their mouth with a piece of cloth to prevent them from swallowing insects. Their clothes were unkempt. They spoke little but repeated continuously: "The law that we proclaim is the only truth, the essence of all things." They carried a small broom to sweep the ground in front of them for fear of crushing living creatures, and they walked cautiously. They were known as the Venerables (*pûjyä*) (5.4.8–33).

They started to expound the most absurd doctrines. In a world born of sacrifice, where nothing can survive without taking life, they declared: "You must not kill any living creatures." They rejected all the worldly pleasures that draw us close to the gods and claimed that the worship of the phallus, the source of life, was an abomination. They asserted that the individual being does not continue his existence through his progeny but survives death by transferring himself from one body to another by transmigration. The son was therefore no longer the continuation of his father but a stranger incarnated by chance. For this reason the son no longer respected his father nor the father his son.

"These ascetics wandered, begging for their food and murmuring platitudes such as 'Abstinence leads to paradise,' 'Chastity and nonviolence are the highest of the virtues,' and other precepts. Under Vishnu's instructions, the treacherous sage Nâradä had himself initiated into the new cult and took the monks to the gate of the city of the Assurs" (5.4.34).

There they settled down under a tree not far from the town. Nâradä then sought an audience with the king, who welcomed him graciously. Nâradä said to the king, "I have come to inform you of the presence, on the outskirts of town, of a great sage who brings the message of a new religion, superior to any the world has known up until now. You must listen to his teachings and be converted to this doctrine. You must renounce all the ancient rites and the horrors of sacrifices."

The king, inspired by Vishnu and deceived by Nâradä, agreed to follow this advice. He listened to the sermons of the false prophet. He had himself initiated and pledged obedience to the false sage. Most of the valorous Assurs adopted the new religion, (5.4.35–36). They abandoned the rites, sacrifices, and worship of the phallus.

Once he had initiated the king of the Assurs into the rites and obtained the vow of obedience from him, the false sage Arihat taught him his doctine: The universe is eternal. It has no Creator. Creation has no purpose. It evolves, then destroys itself. Every living thing, even a blade of grass, is a god in itself. There are no other gods. The ones we call by the names Brahmâ, Vishnu, and Shivä were only men like us who have been deified. All beings are destroyed when their time comes, whether they are gods or mosquitoes. No body is superior to any other. All eat, make love, sleep, and fear death. It is the same for everyone. All beings are equal; no harm should be done to any living creature. The only virtue is to show the same kindness to all creatures. Nonviolence is the only real virtue.

Heaven and hell are here on earth, nowhere else. Pleasure is heaven, suffering is hell. Sacred texts that recommend sacrifices to the gods are apocryphal.

Therefore, life should be enjoyed for as long as the body is strong; then it should be destroyed (by committing suicide). There is no point in dividing mankind into different castes. They are all men. No one is superior or inferior.

He denied the difference between the virtues of women and the manly virtues. He forbade the revering of gods and rejected the power of rites. All the ancient rites were therefore abandoned in the three cities.

It was thus that the power of the Assurs declined. [5.5.1–60]

It was then that Shivä gave the new gods his word to destroy the cities of the Assurs, who had renounced his worship. But before abandoning his reprobate servants, Shivä demanded that the Aryan gods acknowledge his suzerainty. In this way, the Aryan world acquired in part the heritage of the wisdom of the Assurs.

Shivä demanded that all the gods, like all other living creatures, consider themselves part of a flock of animals of which he was the shepherd. It was as Lord of the Animals (Pashupati), Supreme Lord of the heavenly, human, animal, or vegetable beings, that he agreed to undertake the task of destroying the Assurs. [5.9.13–14]

The god mounted his chariot, drew back his bow, and waited until the three cities lined up close to each other, as happened periodically. [5.10.15]

When the three cities were in line, Shivä launched his most terrible weapon on them, a fiery weapon which in an instant burnt everything, destroying all life. At the time appointed by fate (*abhilâsä*) he fired his weapon, which shone like a thousand suns and made a horrifying sound. The three cities were reduced to ashes and collapsed into the middle of the four oceans. [5.10.25–28]

The brave Assurs were completely destroyed. Trying to escape, they fell like flies. Some had started a meal, which they never finished. Others died in the arms of their spouses in the act of love. Terror-stricken women ran here and there trying to protect their children who were already dead. The king of the Assurs lamented abandoning Shivä. Everyone cried out before dying: Shivä, why have you forsaken us?

The children and the aged were reduced to ashes. Women were caught off guard in the arms of their lovers, others in their sleep, others while drunk, others in the middle of the sexual act. All were burnt. On waking, some tried to flee amid the confusion, but soon collapsed. Not even the smallest creature, animate or inanimate, escaped the terrible fire which enveloped the three cities. [5.10.28–40]

Nothing remained of the three cities, and the noble Assur race was completely destroyed.

Seeing this destructive fire as brilliant as many suns, similar to the one which will cause the end of the world, the gods themselves were terrified. [5.11.8]

The only people saved were a few faithful followers of Shivä who had escaped to the region inhabited by the Ganä [Shivä's

companions; that is, the Mahar, or extraplanetary realm].
[5.10.40–44]

These survivors were responsible for preserving in secret certain elements of the knowledge of the Assurs for future civilizations.

> The false sage then came and bowed down before Vishnu and said to him: "I corrupted the Assurs as you commanded and stripped them of their power and of Shivä's protection. I have performed an abominable deed. What must I do now?" Vishnu said to him: "Withdraw to the desert and await the arrival of the Kali Yugä (the Age of Conflicts, which will precede a new end of the world). When the age of Kali arrives, you will again spread your message with the help of your disciples, and the disciples of your disciples. So you will spread your teachings among the vain and stupid men of these times and bring them to their downfall, until the final explosion which will bring an end to the human race." [5.11.28–32]

The practice of the new religion had stripped the Assurs of their virtues, virility, courage, and power. Puritanism had made them liars and neurotics. Vegetarianism had reduced their strength. Nonviolence had made them faint-hearted and had extinguished their courage.

In addition they had renounced the cult of Shivä and the phallus, the source of life, as well as Dharmä, the law that governs creation and assigns each person duties according to his nature.

In the meantime, the new gods had been forced to recognize the preeminence of Shivä and accept the legacy of the knowledge of the Assurs. But they did this reluctantly, as it hurt their pride.

Shivä, among the Aryans of India, like his counterpart among the Greek Aryans, Dionysos, was always to remain the supreme god, and yet be cursed.

Aryan peoples have everywhere adopted the moralistic religions, born of Arihat, which mark the end of the Kali Yugä.

The wisdom of the Assurs, linked with Shaivism, has survived, however, like the Shivä cult itself, but secretly, in an esoteric and initiatory tradition. The history of the three cities represents the end, with the aid of extremely powerful weapons, of a highly technologically advanced civilization. Is it the recollection of a distant past or a premonition of the future? Perhaps both. What is important and concerns us about this story is what it teaches us: that is, that it was a change in religious, social, and moral concepts which caused the decline of the Assurs. The worship of the phallus, symbol of the principle of life, the practice of Tantric Yogä, and the quest for an understanding of cosmic realities and the natural order were replaced by sentimental and negative notions, abstinence, puritanism, nonviolence, equality, and the like. The present times give us a disturbing image of this. *It is a strange pride that motivates man to try to replace the divine order, the natural order, with a human order*, which opposes so-called moral virtues to the magic of rites and sacrifices, and disregards the power obtainable through the practice of Yogä. This attitude, which leads to a negation of the order of the world, can only result in disaster. We can see that in almost all the problems that affect today's society, facing reality is avoided. Even scientific works, impartial in principle, do not dare to mention realities that conflict with the ideologies born of Arihat's teachings.

NOTES

1. The idea that we find in the Bible of the creation of the world in seven days is perhaps an evocation of the birth of the seven cycles of humanity. Similarly, the mention of seven wise men in various traditions, in particular in the Epic of Gilgamesh, ties up with the seven "Manus" who have reorganized human society at the beginning of the golden age of each of the seven cycles.

2. The parts of the account that are not extracted or in quotation marks are résumés of chapters or excerpts taken from commentaries.

PART SIX

FORESTALLING
THE END

1

Predictions

Precursory Signs

THE PERIOD PRECEDING THE CATACLYSM THAT MUST destroy the present species of humans is marked by disorders that are portents of the end. As was the case with the Assurs, Shivä can only destroy societies that have deviated from their role, that have transgressed the natural law. According to the theory of cycles that governs the evolution of the world, we are today drawing near to the end of the Kali Yugä, the age of conflicts, wars, genocides, corruption, abnormal social and philosophical systems, and the pernicious development of knowledge which falls into irresponsible hands. Races and castes mix. Everything is tending toward a leveling, and this equalizing, in every sphere, is the prelude to death. At the end of the Kali Yugä this process accelerates. The phenomenon of acceleration is one of the signs of the approaching catastrophe. The Purânä(s) describe the signs that characterize the last period, the twilight of the Kali Yugä.

According to the *Lingä Purânä*:

It is the lowest instincts that spur the men of the Kali Yugä on. They prefer to choose false ideas. They do not hesitate to persecute sages. Desire torments them. Slovenliness, illness, hunger, and fear spread. There will be severe droughts. The different regions of countries will be in conflict with each other.

The sacred books are no longer respected. Men will be without morals, irritable and sectarian. In the age of Kali false doctrines and misleading writings spread. People are afraid because they neglect the rules taught by the sages and no longer carry out the rites correctly.

Many will perish. The number of princes and farmers gradually declines. The working classes want to claim regal power and share the knowledge, meals, and beds of the ancient princes. Most of the new leaders are of working-class origin. They will hunt down the priests and upholders of knowledge.

Fetuses will be killed in the stomachs of their mothers and heroes will be assassinated. The Shudrä will claim to behave like Brahmans and the priests like laborers.

Thieves will become kings, and kings will be the thieves.

Women who have relationships with several men will be numerous.

Everywhere the stability and balance of the four classes of society and the four ages of life will disappear. The earth will produce plenty in some places and too little in others.

Rulers will confiscate property and use it badly. They will cease to protect the people.

Base men who have gained a certain amount of learning (without having the virtues necessary for its use) will be esteemed as sages.

Men who do not possess the virtues of warriors will become kings. Scholars will be in the service of mediocre, conceited, and malevolent men.

Priests will degrade themselves by selling the sacraments.

There will be many displaced persons, wandering from one country to another.

The number of men will decrease, while that of women will increase.

Predatory animals will be more violent. The number of cows will diminish. Men of integrity will cease to play an active role.

Ready-cooked food will be on sale.

The sacred books will be sold on street corners. Young girls will do trade in their virginity. The god of the clouds will be inconsistent in the distribution of the rains. Shopkeepers will run dishonest businesses. They will be surrounded by pretentious, false philosophers. There will be many beggars and unemployed people. Everyone will use hard and vulgar language. No one will be able to trust anyone else. People will be envious. No one will want to return a favor. The degredation of virtues and the censorship of hypocritical and moralizing puritans characterize the period of the end of the Kali Yugä. There will no longer be any kings. Wealth and harvests will decrease. Groups of bandits will organize in towns and in the country. Water will be lacking and fruit scarce. Thieves will be numerous. Rapes will be frequent. Many people will be treacherous, lustful, base, and foolhardy. They will have disheveled hair. There will be many children born whose life expectancy is no more than sixteen years. Adventurers will take on the appearance of monks with shaven heads, orange clothing, and rosary beads around their necks. Wheat supplies will be stolen. Thieves will steal from thieves. People will become inactive, lethargic, and purposeless. Illness, rats, and noxious substances will plague them. People suffering from hunger and fear will take refuge in "underground shelters" (*kaushikä*).

People who live for a hundred years will be few. The sacred texts will be adulterated. Rites will be neglected. Vagabonds will be numerous in every country.

Heretics will rebel against the principle of the four castes and the four periods of life. Unqualified people will pass as experts in matters of morals and religion.

People will massacre women, children, cows, and one another. [*Lingä Purânä*, chap. 40]

According to the *Vishnu Purânä*:

The people of the Kali Yugä will claim to be unaware of the differences between the races and of the sacred nature of marriage (which ensures the continuity of a race), the relationship between teacher and pupil, and the importance of rites. During the Kali Yugä, people of all origins will marry girls from any race. Women will become independent and seek handsome males. They will adorn themselves with extravagant hairstyles and will leave a husband with no money for a rich man.

They will be thin, greedy, and slaves of pleasure. They will produce too many children but will be given little respect. Taking an interest only in themselves, they will be egotistical. Their words will be false and deceitful.

Women of good birth will abandon themselves to the desires of the basest of men and perform obscene acts.

Men will devote themselves to earning money; the richest will hold power. Those who own many elephants, horses, and chariots will be kings. People without assets will be their slaves.

The state leaders will no longer protect the people but, through taxes, will appropriate all wealth. Farmers will give up their work of plowing and harvesting to become unskilled workers (*kârû-karmä*) and adopt the customs of outcastes. Many will be dressed in rags, unemployed, sleeping on the ground, living like paupers.

Through the fault of the public authorities, many children will die. Some will have white hair by the time they are twelve.

In these times the path marked out by the sacred writings will become obliterated. People will believe in illusory theories. There will no longer be any morality, and as a result life expectancy will be shortened.

People will accept theories promulgated by anyone as articles of faith. False gods will be worshiped in false ashrams in which fasts, pilgrimages, penances, donation of possessions, and austerities in the name of the would-be religion will be arbitrarily decreed. People of low birth will put on religious costumes and, by their deceptive behavior, will make themselves respected.

People will eat their food without washing. They will respect neither the household fire nor the hosts.

They will not perform funerary rites.

Students will not observe the rules of their state.

Successful men will no longer make offerings to the gods, nor will they make gifts to deserving people.

Hermits (*vanaprasthä*[s]) will eat the food of the middle class, and monks (*sannyâsî*[s]) will have amorous relationships (*snehä-sambandhä*) with their friends.

The workers (*shudrä*[s]) will call for equality with the scholars. Cows will be kept only for their milk.

The poor will pride themselves in their poverty and women in the beauty of their hair.

Water will be lacking, and in many regions people will watch the sky, hoping for rain.

There will be no rain; the fields will become barren; fruit will no longer have any flavor. Rice will be scarce. People will drink goat's milk.

People suffering in the drought will eat bulbs and roots.

They will be without joys and pleasures. Many will commit suicide. Suffering from famine and poverty, unhappy and driven to despair, many will migrate toward countries where wheat and rye are growing.

Men of little intelligence, influenced by absurd theories, will live under a delusion. They will ask: What use are these gods, priests, holy books, and ablutions? The ancestral lines will no longer be respected. The young husband will go and live with his parents-in-law. He will say: What is the significance of a father or a mother? Everyone is born and dies according to his actions, his Karmä. (Family, clan, and race therefore have no meaning.)

In the Kali Yugä men will be without virtues, purity, or a sense of decency, and will know great hardship. [*Vishnu Purânä* 6.1]

According to the *Lingä Purânä*:

During the period of twilight that ends the Yugä, the dispenser of justice will come and kill the wicked people. He will be born of the moon's dynasty. His name is War (Samiti). He will wander all over the earth with a great army. He will destroy the Mlecchä (the barbarians of the West) by the thousands. He will destroy the people of low caste who seized regal power and will exterminate the false philosophers, criminals, and people of mixed blood. He will start his campaign in his thirty-second year and will continue for twenty years. He will kill millions of men; the earth will be razed. People will kill each other furiously. At the end, groups of people remaining here and there will murder each other in order to steal from each other. Troubled and confused, they will leave their wives and homes.

They will be without education, laws, shame, love. They will abandon their fields to migrate across the borders of their countries.

They will live on wine, meat, roots, and fruit. They will be clothed in bark, leaves, and animal skins. They will no longer use money.

They will be hungry and sick and will know despair. It is then that some will start to ponder over fundamental values. [*Lingä Purânä*, chap. 40]

The End of the World

There are three kinds of what we call the "end of the world" (*pralayä*): the first induced (*naïmittikä*); the second natural (*prâkritä*); the third immediate (*atyantikä*). Induced destruction (which concerns all living beings on earth) takes place at the end of each Kalpä [cycle of the Yugä(s)]. It is called either accidental or induced (*naïmittikä*).

Natural destruction (*prâkritikä*) is that which concerns the whole universe. It takes place when the divine dream which is the world ends. Matter, space, and time then cease to exist. It takes place at the end of time (*parardhä*). [*Vishnu Purânä* 1.3.1–3]

The third destruction, called immediate (*atyantikä*), refers to the liberation (*mokshä*) of the individual for whom the visible world ceases to exist.

Immediate destruction therefore concerns the individual, induced destruction all living species on earth, and natural destruction the end of the universe.

Accidental or Induced Destruction
(Naïmittikä Pralayä)

What is called accidental or provoked destruction (of living species) (*naïmittikä*) takes place at the end of the Manvantarä (the period of a Manu), the cycle of the Yugä(s). Therefore, it concerns the human species. It takes place when the creator can no longer find any remedy apart from a total destruction of the world to put an end to the disastrous and unplanned increase in the number of living beings. [*Mahâbhâratä* 12.248.13–17]

This destruction will start with an underwater explosion called Vadavâ, the mare, which will take place in the southern ocean.

It will be preceded by a hundred-year drought during which the people who are not robust will perish. Seven explosions of light will dry up all the waters. The seas, the rivers, the mountain streams, and the underground springs will be drained.

Twelve suns will cause the seas to evaporate. Fed by this water, seven suns will form which will reduce the three worlds to ashes; the earth will become hard like a turtle's shell.

A fire from the mouth of an underground serpent will burn the lower worlds, then the surface of the earth, and will set the atmosphere ablaze. This mass of fire will burn with a great noise. Surrounded by these circles of fire, all animate and inanimate beings will be destroyed.

The destroyer god will breathe enormous clouds, which will make a terrible noise.

A mass of clouds charged with energy, destroyer-of-all (*sarvantaka*), will appear in the sky like a herd of elephants. [*Vishnu Purânä* 1.8.18–31]

When the moon is in the constellation of Pushyä (Aquarius), invisible clouds called Pushkarä (cloud of death) and Avartä (cloud without water, *nirjalä*) will cover the earth. [*Shivä Purânä* 5.1.48–50]

[217]

Some of these clouds will be black, others white like jasmine, others bronzed, others gray like donkeys, others red, others blue like lapis or sapphire, others speckled, orangish, indigo. They will resemble towns or mountains. They will cover all the earth. These immense clouds, making a terrible noise, will darken the sky and will shower the earth in a rain of dust which will extinguish the terrible fire.[1]

Then, by means of interminable downpour, they will flood the whole earth with water. This torrential rain will swamp the earth for twelve years, and humanity will be destroyed. The whole world will be in darkness. The flood will last seven years. The earth will seem like an immense ocean. [*Vishnu Purânä* 1.7.24–40]

The world where the human species live is formed by four spheres called Bhûr, Bhuvar, Svar, and Mahar. Bhûr is the earth, Bhuvar the atmosphere, Svar the planetary world, and Mahar an extraplanetary world, perhaps the one we attribute these days to the extraterrestrials. Its duration is longer than that of the terrestrial world. It is there that some men will find refuge at the time of the catastrophe that will destroy the entire species at the end of the Kali Yugä.

When the dissolution of the world seems imminent, some people abandon the earth during the last days of the Kalpä and take refuge in the world of Mahar [the extraplanetary world] and from there will return to the "world of life" (*janä-lokä*). [*Lingä Purânä* 1.4.39–40]

These few humans who survive the holocaust will be the progenitors of the future humanity.

Seven humanities must again succeed each other on earth, and, when the Golden Age reappears, seven sages will emerge to again teach the divine law to the few survivors of the four castes. [*Shivä Purânä* 5.4.40–70]

The Revelation of John presents a vision similar to that of the Purânä(s), the tradition of which was certainly not unknown in his time.

It was only in A.D. 304 that the patriarch Gregory had destroyed, among others, the two Hindu temples built in Armenia during the reign of the monarch Arsacide, in 149 and 127 B.C.

We are approaching the end of the era of the constellation of Pisces. According to the Revelation of John, "the era of Christ will finish with the era of Pisces; then comes Aquarius." We are entering the age of Aquarius, which involves significant transformations. In the description of John (Revelation 8ff):

The earth starts to tremble. . . . The stars fall to earth. . . . A great fiery star falls from the sky.

The sun is darkened by smoke. . . . The day loses a third of its brightness. It hails a mixture of fire and blood. Men are burnt by a great heat and suffer from ulcers. . . . A pain similar to the sting of a scorpion tortures them.

The great men and military leaders take refuge in caves. The merchants, who had become the powerful people on earth, bemoan their destroyed stock. All living beings who were in the sea die.

John also sees "an armor-plated weapon with tails [tanks with canons?] which had a mouth through which they did damage," and says, "The Savior dressed in white then appears on a white horse."

The Disappearance or Natural Death (Prâkritä Pralayä) of the World

The destruction of the world is implied in the very event of the creation and follows a reverse process in the thoughts of the Creator. When the force of expansion (*tamas*) and that of concentration (*sattva*) equalize, the tension (*rajas*), which is the primary cause, the substance (*pradhânä*) of the universe, ceases to exist and the world dissolves into the imperceptible.

All vestiges of creation are destroyed; Pradhâna and Purushä become idle. The earth, the atmosphere, the planetary and the extraplanetary worlds disappear. Everything that exists is united in one single liquid mass, an ocean of fire in which the world dissolves. It is in this immense cosmic ocean (*ekarnavä*) that the organizing principle, Brahmâ, sleeps until, at the end of the night, he awakens and, taking the form of a wild boar, raises a new world out of the waves. [*Lingä Purânä* 1.4.36–61]

The duration of the universe is expressed by a number having eighteen figures. When the end of time has come, the principle of smell (*gandhä tanmâträ*) disappears and, with it, solid matter. Everything becomes liquid.

Then the principle of taste (*rasa tanmâträ*) disappears and with it the liquid element. Everything becomes gaseous. Then the principle of touch (*sparshä tanmâträ*) disappears and with it the gaseous element. Everything becomes fire. Then the principle of visibility, the *rupa tanmâträ* (form and light), is obliterated. When visibility disappears, all that remains is the vibration of space, which in its turn fades.

All that remains is space like a void of spherical shape where only the vibratory principle exists. This vibration is reabsorbed in the "Principle of the Elements" (*bhûtâdi*), that is, the principle of identification or of individuality (*ahamkarä*). The five elements and the five senses having disappeared, all that remains is the principle of individuality (*ahamkarä*), which is part of the force of expansion (*tamas*), which itself dissolves into a great principle (*mahat tattvä*), which is the principle of consciousness (*buddhi*).

The plan (*purushä*), indestructible, omnipresent, which is emanation of Being, returns to its origin. [*Vishnu Purânä* 1.8, 9]

The game (*lîlâ*) of the birth and the disappearance of the worlds is an act of power of the Being who is beyond substance (*pradhânä*) and beyond the plan (*purushä*), beyond the manifest (*vyaktä*) and the unmanifest (*avyakta*), and beyond time (*kâlä*). The time of the Being has neither beginning nor end. That is why the birth, duration, and disappearance of the worlds never stops.

At the time of the destruction neither day nor night, space nor earth, darkness nor light, nor anything else exists any longer, apart from Being, beyond the perceptions of the senses or thought. [*Vishnu Purânä* 1.1.18–23]

NOTES

1. We have already seen in relation to the Assurs the description of the destruction of the world by means of terrifying weapons that destroy all life forms. The modern descriptions of an atomic war are almost identical to the vision of the Purânä. According to Jonathan Schell: "In the first moments of an attack . . . dazzling fire balls would appear out over metropolises, towns, and suburbs, like so many suns even more blinding than the star itself; simultaneously most of the inhabitants would be irradiated, crushed, burnt alive. The thermal radiation would subject more than 1,500,000 square kilometers to a heat of 40 calories per square centimeter—the temperature at which human flesh is carbonized."

❀❀❀❀

2

Forestalling the Final Day

The Return to Shaivism

HUMANKIND IS DESTROYED ONLY AFTER IT HAS OUT-
lived its reason for existence; from the point of view of both
carnal and spiritual beings, this occurs when the lineage is
debased by racial mixing and when the tradition of occult
knowledge can no longer find any receptacle to receive and
pass on its heritage.

The extent to which certain men will be able to reverse
the tendencies of the modern world, and rediscover ways of
life and thought in keeping with their true nature, will determine for how long the final day can be forestalled, or at
least allow some groups of individuals to escape the cataclysm
and participate in the formation of the future humanity and
of the new Golden Age, which should appear after the next
flood. Therefore, it is not a pointless exercise for human
beings to try to cut themselves off from the modern world
and rediscover the values and virtues whose rules and principles have been preserved by esoteric teachings.

According to the Âgamä(s), the survival, short- or long-
lived, of the present humanity depends on a return to the
religious, moral, and social values that have been preserved

in Shaivism. Its teachings constitute the seed of the Golden Age of the future humankind. Mahâyânä Buddhism, from Tibet, has managed to reincorporate numerous philosophical, ritual, and erotic aspects of Shaivism and has, as it were, reinstated itself in the ancestral tradition. It thus offers an alternative course. On the other hand, during the first centuries after Christ, at the same time that in India we see Vaishnavism, which stemmed from Arihat, once again being substituted for Shaivism, we also see the mystical and liberating Christianity of the Gnostics of the earliest times changing into a dogmatic, moralistic, and puritanical religion no longer bearing any relation to the teachings of Jesus.

The recent reappearance of numerous texts of the Gnosis, which are very close to the ideas of Shaivism, and of gospels that the Church had rejected and declared apocryphal, is a good omen for the future.

The present period shows some signs of a return to Shaiva and Dionysian values, which may herald a reprieve from the brutal end of the Kali Yugä. One of the most important phenomena of the present era is the reestablishment of a cohesion between scientific research and cosmological speculation, an effort to understand the nature of the world which shows a continuity between physics, metaphysics, and eventually spirituality, in contrast with the dogmatism of the religions coming from Arihat.

The "new alliance" of philosophy and science may lead us back to Dionysian wisdom. . . . Today, we again encounter a multitude of erotic practices that may be signaling what could be a resurgence of the Dionysian mystery.

Often the liberation from convention has been the guarantee of a great cultural development. . . . The myth of bisexuality is one way of expressing the divine totality (cosmic, societal). . . .

It is this mythical and primordial androgyny that sociologists can detect in many of the behavioral patterns of today's youth. [Michael Maffesoli, *L'Ombre de Dionysos*, pp. 29, 40, 129, and 187]

The end of the Kali Yugä is a particularly favorable period to pursue true knowledge.

Some will attain wisdom in a short time, for the merits acquired in one year during the Tretâ Yugä can be obtained in one day in the age of Kali. [*Shivä Purânä* 5.1.40]

At the end of the Kali Yugä, the god Shivä will appear to reestablish the right path in a secret and hidden form. [*Lingä Purânä* 1.40.12]

3

Conclusions

SOME CONTEMPORARY ASTROPHYSICISTS AND BIOLO-
gists, in the course of their most audacious speculations, are
beginning to become aware of a strict coexistence and interdependence between consciousness and matter. There exists
no matter without consciousness and no consciousness without matter. One of the fundamental conceptions of Shaiva
philosophy is that each form of existence, animated or inert,
each living species, has a role to fulfill in the play of creation
and that this determines its physical appearance and the development of its mental capacities at its level of consciousness.

The tendency in the highest spheres of contemporary thought
to propose hypotheses that resemble aspects of the knowledge
of the Golden Age of humanity at the very moment when all
the premonitory signs of its decline and death are manifesting
is significant. Is it a question of a culmination, of a final
attempt to avoid the catastrophe, or simply a precursory sign
of the humanity that must succeed our own? The question
remains open.

The level of knowledge proper to each of the species is the
key to its reason for being. Physical and mental characteristics
are inseparable in the plan of creation. The development of
our brain is not a result of chance. It is the instrument of a

[225]

perception of the world that varies according to genetic group, and each group plays a different witnessing role, such that a hunting dog has aptitudes different from those of a sheep dog. In the immense display represented by the multitude of the forms of life, the development of intelligence has as its goal the perception of a particular aspect of creation. It is sufficient, in certain cases, that rare individuals or even a single individual reaches a certain level of knowledge such that the Creator can contemplate his work through the beings that He has created, not at all in his image, but as mirrors in which he contemplates himself. The mastery of the secrets that permit the destruction of the atom and the manipulation of genes causes the species "man" to draw near to Purushä, Universal Man, the computer of the created. Men encroach upon the domain of the gods, and the yogic texts warn us of this transgression beyond the domain which is allowed us. "The gods do not like men to reach knowledge," say the Upanishad(s).

In mastering the forces of matter and the arrangement of genes, has humanity accomplished the termination of its own role? And in this case has it only to disappear, or to direct itself toward a new Golden Age? This is a question that future events alone will answer. In the meantime, in the hope of survival, or in order to prepare ourselves to disappear and pass the torch to the supermen who will succeed us, what must our behavior be?

In response to this question, Tradition provides an ethic, a minimal code of behavior, which, if it cannot save us, can at least retard the day of reckoning.

The door that leads to the way of wisdom is opening slightly. Will men have the discernment and courage to enter in and thus forestall the final day? In any case, few will be chosen.

Appendix I

Language: Instrument for the Transmission of Knowledge

The Nature of Language

THE SIMPLEST FORM OF VIBRATION THAT OUR SENSES can perceive is the vibration of air, which, within certain limits, we sense as a sound. We can use sound vibration as a departure point and means of comparison for an understanding of the other, more complex vibratory states—whether they concern the structures of matter or of life, or the phenomena of perception and thought. We have seen that, because of his double nature, man has two roles to play: one concerns the continuation and development of the species; the other concerns the transmission and evolution of knowledge.

There are parallels between the transmission of life and the transmission of knowledge, between the Being of Flesh and the Being of Knowledge. The elements that form the genetic code are, like those which form language, similar and limited in number. They are called the Aksharä(s) (constants).

As far as language is concerned, the Aksharä(s) are the various elements of articulation that the vocal cords can emit and the ear can recognize. There are fifty-four of them. In

[227]

addition, there are the fifty-four intervals of the musical language that can be distinguished by the ear and that have psychological effects. An analysis of musical intervals will allow the establishment of numerical factors that act as a kind of mathematical key to the diagrams and graphs at the base of the structures of life; it will also give us an insight into the mechanisms of perception, sensation and thought.

The Manifestation of Thought

THE basic instrument for the formulation of knowledge is language, whose limits establish the possibilities for analysis and the transmission of thought.

What is language? How can the variations in articulated sounds be used to define, express, and transmit ideas? Indian grammarians and semanticists tried to define the nature, possibilities, and limits of language, as well as its relationships with the structures of the world and the mechanisms of thought. Thought exists outside language; the various languages are merely collections of signs (sound or otherwise) that are used to delineate thought and transmit its approximate outlines. It is therefore essential that the vocabulary and the structures of language not be confused with ideas. Nevertheless, according to the Hindu grammarians, there must be some relation among thought, perception, and language; without it, language could not act as a vehicle for the others. In this area, as in the others, they have therefore sought out archetypes that are common to the mechanisms of perception and thought, and to the structures of language, music, and the other modes of communication.

An idea is an inner vision that we try to formulate with the help of those symbolic elements which are the words or gestures we use. The crudeness of such a formulation may be greater or lesser, depending on the richness of our vocabulary, but it is always a mere approximation. An idea is not in itself connected to language. We seek words to express it, and often hesitate between different alternatives. An idea first appears in an indivisible form called Sphota. It can be compared to a landscape lit up by a flash of lightning. Some notions, some experiences and sensations, often the deepest and the most violent, remain inexpressible. Mystics cannot describe their experiences. We ourselves cannot communicate the nuances of pleasure or sorrow with any precision. Language can therefore be a barrier. It is, according to the theories of Yogä, necessary to remove the barrier of language and to "reduce the mind's activity to silence" in order to achieve a perception of the suprasensory world.

The idea is born in the substratum of consciousness called Parâ (the Beyond), where it appears as a kind of vision (Pashyantî). Dreams form part of this Pashyantî. In order to transform an idea into an instrument of action or communication, we attempt to define and formulate it mentally, using the symbols of language. This stage is known as Madhyamâ (intermediary). It is clear that such a formulation is approximate, for we have at our disposal only a limited number of tokens or words with which to form its outlines. At length we exteriorize it in a sound form called Vaikharî (exteriorized). These last two stages are particularly developed in mankind, although they vary according to the intellectual capabilities and the vocabulary of individuals. They are extremely rudimentary in animals.

Through the practice of Yogä we perceive the four stages in the manifestation of thought as being localized within four of the main centers of the subtle body, which is the inverse of the physical body. Parâ is situated at the base of the vertebral column; Pashyantî is close to the navel; Madhyamâ is in the area of the heart; and Vaikharî is in the throat. As always with Yogä, brain centers are involved which can only be localized and controlled through the parts of the body, the corresponding nervous centers, which they command. The theory of the Creative Word is based on an analogy between the processes involved in the transformation of thought into word and sound vibration, and the processes of divine thought, which becomes the substance of the world in the shape of energy vibrations. This analogy enables the Yogi to start from the word and work his way backward, thereby reaching, without going outside himself, the birthplace of the manifested, the limits of the "beyond" (Parâ), the "Principle of the Word" (Shabdä Brahman). It is through this experience that we can have an idea of the process by which the universe is exteriorized by Divine Being.

> At the beginning, like a wind that is blowing, I cry out the worlds in space," says the Divine Being of the _Rig Vedä_. Divisible being emanates from the Being which is indivisible Existence-Consciousness-Joy; From _Sat_ (existence) springs forth Energy, which manifests itself in the form of an elementary vibration that can be compared to a primordial sound (_nâdä_). It is from this vibration that the boundary point (_bindu_) issues, separating what is manifest from what has not been manifested. [_Sharadâtilakä_ 1.7]

An echo of this concept is to be found in all traditions: "_In principium erat Verbum ante omnia facta sunt. . . ._"

According to the Sâmkhyä, the universe has developed from elementary formulae that are mathematical in nature, or at least able to be expressed in mathematical or geometric terms (in this case called Yanträ[s]) and which are common to all aspects of creation. There is no difference of nature between the formulae at the base of the structures of the atoms of matter, the movement of the stars, the principles of life, the mechanisms of perception and thought, which are, all of them, parallel and interdependent manifestations of energy, resulting from common patterns. Language, by means of which we exteriorize and materialize thought and describe the apparent world as it is perceived by our senses, must therefore present to us characteristics analogous to those of the process by which the universe develops. A study of the bases of language, its limits and constituents, should provide us with an idea of the nature of the world; by delving back to the sources of language, we should gain an understanding of the process by which thought is transformed into speech and should be able to uncover something of the way in which the Creative Principle that is the divine "Word" is manifested in Creation. The same result can be achieved starting from visual elements, such as the language of gestures, or biochemical elements, which are the formulae of matter and life, since all aspects of the world are based on a limited number of patterns and formulae.

A distinction must be made in all linguistic theories between words and their meanings. In the aspect of Mahat, Universal Consciousness, Shivä is identified with the meaning of words. The word itself, the instrument of sound with which we express meaning, is a form of energy and is therefore part of the realm of Pak<u>ri</u>ti (matter), regarded as feminine. "Shivä is the meaning; the word is his wife" (*Lingä Purä<u>n</u>ä* 3.11.47).

A study of the formation of words and the roots of language reveals that they always start from abstract notions and move toward the concrete; they start from the general and progress toward the particular. In order to understand a word, its root must be studied. The processes involved in the formation of language appear analogous to the processes of creation.

Provision is made for the birth, possibilities, and limits of language in the very structures of the human animal. The five places of articulation that allow the formulation of the means of communication which we call language are no more accidental than the fact that humans possess five senses, five fingers, and five forms of perception, and that five apparent states of matter exist for us. Man only invents that which he is predisposed—but not predestined—to invent. The organ of language precedes the manifestation of language, and not the other way around. It is thus implicitly part of the plan from the outset.

The Mîmânsâ(s) and the Tanträ(s) study the ritual and magical formulae, that is, the use of language as a means of communication between different states of being. The Vyâkaraṇä, moreover, studies the structures, the limits, and the contents of language. Its application to Sanskrit is but one example among many. The study of the symbolic meaning of the phonemes, whose use is to be found in Manträ(s), the formulae used to evoke the various aspects of the supranatural world, belong not to the Sanskrit language, but to a general theory of the symbolism of sounds.

The error of wanting to reduce a study of the symbolic bases of language to the elements of a particular language considered to be sacred has often turned the approach to this problem off course, as has sometimes been the case with regard to the Greek, Hebrew, or Arabic alphabets, or for Sanskrit itself.

Texts

THERE are many texts about Creation, conceived as the manifestation of the Principle of the Word (the Shabdä Brahman) and also about the transmission by sound of concepts and the semantic contents of the musical or articulated sound. These texts also study the manifestation of thought through the intermediary of the word, and the parallels that this manifestation can provide with the birth of the world viewed as an apparent materialization of the thought of its creator. Among the most important surviving works on the subject are the Vedic Pratishâkhyä(s), the Kâshikâ, and the Rudrä Damaru of Nandikeshvarä (prior to Pâṇini), Pâṇini's Ashtâdhyayi (fourth century B.C.) and its major Commentary, Patañjali's Mahâbhâsyä (second century B.C.), and Kalâpa's Vyâkaraṇä (first century). To these must be added the ancient Shaiva grammars, of which the one by Râvaṇä is legendary, and to which Bhartṛihari refers in his Vâkyapadîyä (seventh century A.D.). This matter is also treated in several Upaniṣhad(s) and treatises on Yogä.

For this study on the nature of language, I have relied on a long article by Swâmî Karpâtrî, published in the Hindi-language journal *Siddhantä* with the title "Shabdä aur arthä" (Words and Their Meaning).

In mythology the origins of the theory of language is attributed to Shanmukhä, the son of Shivä, and the pre-Aryan Dionysos.

The invocations with which the *Vâkyapadiyä* (Bhartrihari's great treatise on the nature of language) begins appeal to the goddess of the mountains (Pârvatî), to the eternal Shivä (Sadâshivä), to Shivä as the god of the South (Dakshinamûrti); they refer to the Tanträ(s), the Âgamä(s), and to the ancient Shaiva grammar by Râvanä. There is no mention of the Vedä or the Vedic gods. Bhartrihari also makes reference to the Jaïnä tradition, the other great current of protohistoric thought in India.

We have already seen with respect to the Tanmâträ(s) that a form of communication exists which corresponds to each state of matter or element. Thus there is a language of smell (the element of earth), a language of taste (the element of water), and a language of touch (the element of air). (The tactile language is extremely rudimentary in mankind. A shaking of hands, the pressure of feet under the table, not to mention the caresses of love, are all part of the language of touch.) There is also a language of sight (the element of fire), which is used by man in gesture, mime, and ideograms.

The language of sound, corresponding to ether, is divided into a musical language and an articulated language. The musical language is based on the numerical relationships of frequencies and on the rhythmic division of time. Spoken language is formed from articulated sounds, to which certain tonal elements of music are added. The various forms of language can combine with each other. Gesture, mime, intonation, and rhythm work in combination with the word and allow the expression of what words alone cannot transmit. All living beings have a language; yet it would seem that man is the only one in possession of an elaborate language, even though some animals have a significant number of "words" or "signs." The *Shatapathä Brâhmanä* (4.1.3.17) says: "Only one quarter of language is articulated and used by men. Of the remainder, which is inarticulate, one quarter is used by mammals, one quarter by the birds, and one quarter by reptiles."

These languages use various means of transmission, which are not necessarily perceived by us. It is sometimes a question of ultrasonic transmission or along the lines of radio or radar, permitting direct intuitive communication (the reading of thoughts, etc.). Gesture, mime, and the emission of certain waves play an important part in the language of animals, insects, and even plants, although with plants, for which time has a different value, the slowness of movement makes changes imperceptible to us. In the same way, bird language, which is too fast for us, appears to us like a recording played at the wrong speed. Insects communicate over very long distances by means of extremely delicate odors.

Man finds that some sounds have a direct relationship with some emotions, but on the whole we tend to believe that the use of phonemes to represent ideas is conventional. This raises a fundamental question. For the Indian grammarians, sounds must have originally a meaning and a logic of their own. This is what allows them to be the image of material or abstract realities. It was the grammarians' belief that language was originally entirely monosyllabic and tonal. By this theory, Chinese is closer to the primitive languages than the Semitic, Aryan, or Dravidian languages. A monosyllabic language functions by the juxtaposition of substantive elements (*nâmä*), elements of form (*rupä*), and elements of action (*kriyâ*), and therefore lends itself to a parallel representation by means of graphic symbols, ideograms or by gestures (*mudrä*).

The phonemes, which originally have a precise meaning (indeed a natural meaning), form the material from which the basic roots of language are formed; these roots will combine to constitute words whose meaning is a combination of the constituent parts. It would seem that in no language can any new roots ever be invented. These could, in any case, be nothing but a transposition or displacement of the original meaning, since there can be no new elements of articulation. In order to define ideas, all languages therefore use the fifty-four possible articulated sounds. This is very limited material, which means that words can only be approximations allowing a vague outline of the thought they express.

The organ of speech is constituted as a Yanträ, a symbolic diagram. The palatal vault (like the celestial vault) forms a hemisphere with five points of articulation allowing the emission of five groups of consonants, five main vowels, two mixed vowels, and two secondary vowels, assimilated to the planets.

Likewise in the musical scale, there are five main notes, two secondary ones, and two alternative notes, which are not arbitrary but correspond to fundamental numerical relationships between the sound vibrations that we can find at the base of all musical systems. Our perception of colors has analogous characteristics. We cannot in any case invent new vowels, new places of articulation, or new fundamental colors. The possibilities of our vocal organ and the powers of discrimination of our perception are severely limited, coordinated, and preestablished according to criteria to be found in all aspects of creation.

The Maheshvarä Sûträ

THE material of language (that is, the set of articulated sounds that will permit the definition and transmission of thought) is classified in a mysterious formula that is considered to be the source and summation of all language. This formula is known as the *Maheshvarä Sûträ* and is symbolically described as issuing from the Damaru, the god Shivä's little drum, whose rhythm accompanies the dance by which he gives birth to a world which "is nothing but movement" (*jagat*). The *Maheshvarä Sûträ* attempts to establish the relative significance of the phonemes, the basic sound-tokens that form the material of language, and their relationship with the fundamental laws that rule the material, subtle, and transcendent worlds.

The analysis provided here of the *Maheshvarä Sûträ* is based upon the two short treatises attributed to Nandikeshvarä and the commentaries on them. Nandikeshvarä attributes a basic meaning to the various linguistic elements according to the placement and movements of the vocal organs that produce the different sounds of the spoken language. The commentators explain how the sounds produced by the various efforts of the vocal organs can be used to materialize concepts, and how such inflections, which can seem to be minimal even on the microcosmic scale, can, when multiplied to the scale of the universal being, reflect prodigious energies.

Already in mankind the power of language is out of all proportion to the minimal movements of the throat and lips that produce the sounds.

The use of a few vowels and consonants which did not originally exist in Sanskrit seems to indicate that Sanskrit is not at the base of the phonetic system even though it became closely linked with it. The phonetic system is independent of the diversity of languages and of the various systems of writing, through phonemes or ideograms. Alphabets differ only in their imprecision and their deficiencies. The twenty or so alphabets used in India are for the most part merely different ways of transcribing the same phonetic system. The Semitic alphabets (Aramaic, Hebrew, Arabic), as well as the Phoenician and Greco-Roman alphabets, are particularly deficient, being very imprecise. The alphabet of classical Sanskrit, called Devanâgarî, is by far the most suitable for the transcription of the fifty-four elements of articulation at the base of all languages. The limits of the possibilities of language are tied to the limits of our possibilities for collective and transmittable knowledge, that is, to the role that has devolved upon the human species as a whole in the play of creation. We can only surpass these limits if we are able to pass the limits of language and of the mental mechanisms to which it is tied; such experiments are, however, difficult to communicate.

The seeds of all human knowledge, the sciences and all that language can contain and express, can be derived from the *Maheshvarä Sûträ*, which means "Sacred Formula of the Great God." The *Maheshvarä Sûträ* is as follows:

A-I-U-<u>N</u>; Ë-Ü-K; É-Ó-Ñ; È-Ò-CH; Ha-Ya-Va-Ra-T; La-<u>N</u>; Ña-Ma-Ña-<u>Na</u>-Na-M; Jha-Bha-Ñ; Gha-<u>Dha</u>-Dha-<u>Sh</u>; Ja-Ba-Ga-<u>Da</u>-Da-Sh; Kha-Pha-Cha-<u>Tha</u>-Tha-Chha-<u>Ta</u>-Ta-V; Ka-Pa-Y; Sha-<u>Sha</u>-Sa-R; Ha-L.

U is pronounced like *ou* in *you*; *I* like the *i* in *bit*; *Ë* and *Ü* like the French *e* and *u*; *CH* like *tch*; *J* as in *dj* (*z* is considered to be a variant of *j*). The cerebrals, indicated by underlining, are obtained by touching the palate with the tip of the tongue. *Ñ* is guttural. *Sh* is pronounced like the French *ch*, *Ñ* as in Spanish. The half consonants at the end of each group are called "it". Their meaning refers to the whole of the group that they bring to a close. They allow the sets of groups to be established. A–Ch represents the group of vowels.

According to Nandikeshvarä's interpretation, the groups of letters represent, following a given order and hierarchy, the sound symbols that allow the transmission of concepts, starting from the most abstract, just as the series of numbers and their relationships can be the basis for a mathematical expression of the manifestation of the elementary principles that make up the substance of the world. These two series form the base of the sciences and all forms of knowledge. The *Maheshvarä Sûträ* attempts to bring out the relationship between the sounds and the meanings of the various basic elements of language. The roots as well as the grammatical structures of all languages can, in principle, be derived from these data. Pâ<u>n</u>ini provides an explanation of this relationship for the Sanskrit language, but it would be possible to analyze the structures of any other language using the same method. What is important is to establish the connection between sounds and fundamental notions, allowing one to express the other, which is the primary problem of language. The structures of language, formed from elementary meaningful units, appear parallel to those of the elementary cells that give birth to matter and life.

The Nine Vowels

A-I-U-N̲

A represents Purus̲h̲ä, Universal Man, the plan, the first stage in the manifestation of the world. In the first group, A-I-U-N̲, the first letter, A (pronounced as in *father*), is the least articulated sound. It is produced when all the organs of articulation are at rest. All the other sounds are but its modifications. "The totality of speech is contained within the A," says the *Aitareyä Âranyakä;* while the god of the *Bhagavat Gîtâ* also declares: "I am the A among letters." "This is why A, the first of the letters, represents the form (*rûpä*) which the undifferentiated, unqualified, informal principle, the Nirgunä Brahman, takes on when he creates the world. Omnipresent throughout his work, he is the universal ego (Aham) in which the beginning and end are united" (*Nandikeshvarä Kâshikâ* 3–4). The notion of individual person, whether divine or human, exists only within the limits of the apparent world. A is thus the symbol of the first stage of existence, of the passage from a nonexistent, indivisible, and impersonal absolute to a totality of personified existence, represented as the Universal Man, Purus̲h̲ä, whose form is the universe.

I evokes Shakti, the energy and substance of the world. "*I* represents the conscious part (*cit kalâ*) of organized matter" (*Nandikeshvarä Kâshikâ* 3). It is the closest vowel to A, and to produce it, it is necessary only to add an intention or a tendency toward the exterior without moving the lips. Nandikeshvarä explains that "when, in the undifferentiated Principle, the desire to create a world which does not yet exist appears, this corresponds to an *I*. *I* (pronounced as in *bit*) is termed the 'seed of desire' (*kâmä-bîjä*)" (*Kâshikâ* 8). "Without the *I*, which represents his energy, the eternal Shivä remains as inanimate as a corpse (*shavä*). It is only when united with his energy that he can act. From man's point of view, the letter A represents the object of knowledge, while *I* is the instrument of knowledge—consciousness (*cit*)" (*Kâshikâ*, 9).

U (pronounced as in *rule*) represents the accomplished plan, the materialized desire—that is, the universe. If our organs of articulation combine the positions for A and *I*, and the result is exteriorized through the lips, the sound *U* is obtained. *U* is A + *I* exteriorized, that is, the plan exteriorized in matter. "*U* represents the sovereign principle (Ishvarä) of which the universe is the expression" (*Kâshikâ* 3). For the Sâmkhyä, the sovereign principle is Universal Consciousness (Mahat). "*U* represents the consciousness (Mahat) which is present in all things and which we call Vishnu, the Omnipresent" (*Kâshikâ* 9). The first group of letters in the *Maheshvarä Sûträ* thus evokes the eternal Trinity of the ideating principle, the active principle, and their result, the manifested principle (the world). The sounds that are the symbols of these three principles constitute the roots which, in the primordial language, evoke these notions. This is why, in all languages, the sound A expresses the void, the nonexistent, the nonmanifest, and is therefore negative, privative, and passive. It is predominant in the words that represent these ideas, whereas the sound of *I* is an indication of action. *I* predominates in words expressing life, activity, desire, etc. "The letter A, by making vibration perceptible, is the image of the creative principle of the world. *I*, representing Shakti, suggests the energy which is at the origin of [all the aspects of the apparent world represented by] the other letters" (*Kâshikâ* 7). We shall see that the causal aspect of the *I* influences the classification on the consonants. *U* represents localization, the apparent world.

Ë-Ü-κ

A is pronounced with the throat, I with the palate, U with the lips. The two vowels of the following group are pronounced in the intermediate spaces corresponding to a cerebral and a dental. The cerebral Ë corresponds to the French e, according to its definition by the ancient grammarians. Modern Indians, who cannot pronounce it precisely, call it _ri_ which is clearly wrong since a vowel is defined as a prolonged, sustained sound.

The following vowel is a dental Ü, corresponding to the French u. It is pronounced as _lri_ by modern Indians because l is the consonant pronounced at the same place. These vowels are still used in some Indian languages. In these cases one refers to the god Keu<u>shn</u>ä rather than <u>Krishn</u>ä.

"Ë and Ü symbolize movement, the activity (_vrittä_) of thought, an activity which can be compared to that with which the Divine Being engenders through his power of illusion a universe which is pure movement" (_Kâshikâ_ 10).

In the order of manifestation Ë (_ri_) represents the first and absolute reality (_ëtä_ or _ritä_), which is to say the Creative Principle, the Sovereign God personified (Parameshvarä).

Ü (_lri_) represents Mâyâ, the power of illusion by which the universe seems to exist. Ë and Ü thus correspond on the manifest plane to what A and I evoke on the plane of the preexistent. The Sovereign God, by means of his powers of illusion, makes the world appear. Yet the Divine Being cannot be separated from his power of action. This is why

> Ë and Ü are not truly distinct from one another. There is no real difference between the tendency itself and the one in whom that tendency exists; the relationship is the same as that between the moon and its light, or between a word and the meaning it expresses. [_Kâshikâ_ 11]
>
> It is through his own "power to conceive" (_cit_) it that the Sovereign God is able to make the world appear at his whim (God and the world are neither opposite nor complementary principles). Existence is not truly separate from the Being

which it reflects; yet a reflection does not have the ability to act autonomously. This is why the verbal symbols Ë and Ü are ter..ed impotent, neutral, or androgynous (*klïbä*). [*Kâshikâ* 12]

All creatures issue from an androgynous principle, which is subsequently divided, only in appearance.

The fifth vowel is the last of the pure vowels, for we have only five distinct places of articulation. The obstruction or explosion of the vowels in these very five places constitutes the five groups of consonants: the gutturals, the palatals, the cerebrals, the dentals, and the labials.

É-Ó-Ñ

The two vowels of this group are hybrids and not consequential ones like *U*. They are $A + I = É$ and $A + U = Ó$.

É represents the nonmanifested principle (A) when it is combined with its energy (*I*). A is the immovable and indestructible principle (*ak*s*harä*). *I* is illusion, active intelligence, stemming from indivisible, inactive intelligence. "In É [that is, A in *I*] the motionless principle becomes identified with its energy; the nonmanifest is present in its powers of action. We meet this fundamental identity of the creative principle and its powers of illusion in everything that exists" (*Kâshikâ* 13).

Ó represents the principle A present in its work *U*. "Having created the universe, he resides in it." O (A in *U*), the vowel from which the syllable of adoration, *AUM*, is formed, represents the unity of macrocosm and microcosm, of the divine being and the living being; the iconographic form of this symbol is the god Ganeshä, who is both man and elephant. Ó thus declares the "unity of opposites" (*nirâsä*) and reminds us that the total and the individual, the Sovereign Principle (Ishvarä) and his power of illusion (Mâyâ), are one. It is the Sovereign Principle which is consciousness (Mahat), which "like a witness or spectator is the principle of unity present in the [multiplicity] of beings and elements (*bhûta*[s])" (*Kâshikâ* 13).

È-Ò-CH

This group presents open vowels which are almost diphthongs (AÉ, AÓ) and which comprise three elements: $A + É = È$, and $A + Ó = Ò$. È is formed by adding a new A in front of É, which is already $A + I$. È is the retroactive effect of E (the power of manifestation) on A (the nonmanifest principle). E is therefore an image of the relationship between the Supreme Being and the universe contained within him. It is the nonmanifest principle marked by its power of illusion.

In the same way, Ò, which is $A + Ó$—that is, $A + (A + U)$—represents the nonmanifest principle in which the manifest world exists like an embryo within the womb. "The world is but an apparent form stemming from a formless principle in which it resides and which develops it or reabsorbs it as it chooses" (*Kâshikâ* 14).

This completes the series of vowels, which thus comprises nine sounds (seven principal and two subsidiary), like the musical scale but also like the astral molecule which forms the solar system. The musical scale is also based on frequency relationships, which can be expressed in numbers. There are thus arithmetic parallels to the sounds of language; these are also to be found in the geometric diagrams (Yanträ[s]) which are at the base of the structures of matter and the principles of life.

Various elements, when added to the pronunciation of vowels, modify their meaning and allow the expression of multiple concepts. Each of the vowels can in effect be pronounced eighteen different ways, which are differentiated by the pitch of the sound (by raising or lowering the voice of a tone, or by keeping it level), or by its duration (short, long, or prolonged), or finally by exteriorizing or interiorizing it, that is, by making it natural or nasal. (We express a question by raising the voice on, for example, the word "Yes," and express assent by lowering the sound of the same syllable).

All these details are indicated in the system of writing used by the Indian grammarians, thus forming a total of 162 distinct vowel sounds. In a classical example, a mistake in accentuation in a magic rite of the incantation "Indrä shatru<u>h</u>" changed its meaning from "Indra the enemy" to "the enemy of Indra," and the utterer of the rite provoked his own destruction.

The Consonants

CONSONANTS are obstructions placed in the path of the utterance of vowels. Their differences depend upon the place of articulation together with the nature of the explosion and the effort, which can be directed either inwardly or outwardly. There are four categories of inner-directed effort: a strong touch, a light touch, open, or contracted. There are eleven sorts of outer-directed effort: expansion, contraction, and breath, to which are added (for syllables formed of a consonant and a vowel) the volume of the sound, its resonance or nonresonance, light aspiration or strong aspiration, and the tone, which can be high, low, or medium.

The Five Groups (Vargä)

THE various efforts to throw out, interrupt, or modify the vowel sounds in the five places of articulation form the consonants. These are grouped, like the vowels, into gutturals, palatals, cerebrals, dentals, and labials. In each place of articulation there exists an outward effort (*K*, *C* [*tch*], <u>*T*</u>, *T*, *P*) and an inward effort (hard *G*), *J* (*dj*), <u>*D*</u>, *D*, *F*, etc.). Both can be either voiceless or aspirated.

The basic consonants are twelve in number: the gutturals

K and G (hard); the palatals C (*tch*) and J (*dj*); the cerebrals T̲ and D̲; the dentals T and D; the labials P and F; the fricative *Sh* (the French *ch*); and the semivowel L.

Mixed with the aspirates or in combination, these twelve types of consonants produce thirty-three distinct articulations. Their meaning is determined by the meaning of the vowels, the place from which they are articulated, combined with the effort of articulation. The complete alphabet comprises five groups of consonants, called Vargä(s):

1. Five gutturals: K, Kh, G (hard), Gh, and Ñ (guttural-nasal); and also a guttural fricative H̄ (as in Arabic) and an exhaled final H̲ (Visarga).

2. Five palatals: C (*tch*), Chh, J, Jh, and Ñ (nasal-palatal); and also a semivowel Y and a fricative *Sh* (French *ch*).

3. Five cerebrals (where the point of the tongue touches the palate): T̲, T̲h, D̲, D̲h, and N̲ (nasal-cerebral); and also the semivowel R and the fricative S̲h̲.

4. Five dentals: T, Th, D, Dh, N (dental-nasal); and also the semivowel L and the sibillant S.

5. Five labials: P, Ph, B, Bh, M; and the semivowel V and an exhaled final W (Upadmaniyä).

There are thus five groups, each comprising seven consonants (five principal and two supplementary). Two exhalations, the final Visargä and Upadmaniyä, must be kept aside, since they cannot exist in the middle of words. This leaves thirty-three consonants, which, combined with the vowels, form, with very slight variations in pronunciation, the roots and further the words of all languages.

THE FIVE VARGÄ(S)

Gutturals:	K, Kh, G, Gh, N̄, (H̄, H̲)	Vowel A
Palatals:	C, Ch, J, Jh, Ñ (Y, Sh)	Vowel I
Cerebrals:	T̲, T̲h, D̲, D̲h, N̲ (R, S̲h̲)	Vowel Ë (r̲i̲)
Dentals:	T, Th, D, Dh, N (L, S)	Vowel Ü (l̲r̲i̲)
Labials:	P, Ph, B, Bh, M (V, W)	Vowel U

In the *Maheshvarä Sûträ*, the consonants are not presented in alphabetical order. We meet first of all the semivowels, followed by the nasals, which are the fifth letter in each group of consonants. Only then follow the fourth, third, second, and finally the first letter of each group. We shall see how Nandikeshvarä and his commentators explain this order.

In the logic of creation, once the elements and the "spheres of perception" are defined, we arrive at perception and the individual consciousness on which all perception rests. It is perception which, because of its very limitations, gives the world an apparent reality.

The Tattvä

THE Tattvä(s), all that which in the constituent elements of the world can be called "something" (*tat*), will find their expression, the means of pointing them out, in the constituent elements of language.

HA-YA-VA-RA-T AND LA-<u>N</u>: THE ELEMENTS (BHÛTÄ)

Following the vowels in the *Maheshvarä Sûträ* comes the semivowels, or slightly touched (*îshsprishtä*) consonants, in the production of which the tongue comes close to the places of articulation but barely touches them. They are merely lightly articulated modifications of the corresponding vowels. They indicate the spheres of manifestation of the principles that the vowels represent; they correspond, in the order of appearance, to the five elements or degrees of manifestation of matter which are the spheres of perception of the five senses.

The first four elements are considered to be part of the plan (Puru<u>sh</u>ä, the male principle); the fifth, the solid or earth element, stemming from Prakriti, is considered to be feminine. "The five elements (*bhûtä*[s]) stem from the Sovereign Principle (Maheshvarä). Ether, air, water, and fire are known as *Ha*, *Ya*, *Va*, and *Ra*. In the creation by the Word (*vâk*), *H* is the name of ether, air is called *Y*, *R* is fire, and *V* is water" (*Kâshikâ* 15–16).

First among the semivowels appears the guttural *H*, deriving from *A*, the formless, undifferentiated principle. *H* corresponds to the element ether, whose properties are space and time. The first stage in the manifestation is the creation of space and its corollary, time. Once the universe is reabsorbed, space and time cease to exist. Ether is the primordial element on which depends the possibility (*avakâshä*) for the manifestation of the other elements, which are vibratory modulations of it, in the same way that all articulated sounds are modifications of the nonparticularized sound *A*.

The palatal *Y*, which derives from *I*, introduces the first form for the organization of matter; the gaseous state of air.

The labial *V*, deriving from *U*, corresponds to the liquid state of water. The cerebral *R*, from *Ë* (*ri*), corresponds to the state of fire.

LA-N̲

Lastly, the solid state of matter, called earth, supports the other elements. This solid element corresponds to the dental *L*, (from *Ü*, *lri*), and hence to Mâyâ identified with the Earth goddess and the feminine principle (Prakriti). "Earth is the basic element: it supports the others. It is the earth which provides food; from food comes the seed, and from the seed comes life" (*Kârikâ* 17).

ÑA-MA-ÑA-N̲A-NA-M (NASALS): THE SENSES OF PERCEPTION

The successive states of the condensation of energy, which appear to us as gaseous incandescent, liquid, or solid, are all formed from tiny (*sukshmä*) entities, or atoms (*anu*). They resemble dispersed solar systems but are in fact no more than gravitational formations of ether. The states of matter are organized along different means of communication and are only differentiated as far as we are concerned by the perceptions we have of them; and our perceptions are linked to the duration of apparent time and to the relative dimension of space. Their appearance results from the limitations of our five senses. There is a hierarchy of the senses, connected to the order in which the different stages in the formation of matter appear. The ears perceive only the characteristic vibratory forms of space or ether; the sense of touch recognizes the gaseous state; the eyes perceive the igneous state; taste recognizes liquid; and the nose recognizes the solid state. These forms of perception are represented, according to Nandikeshvarä, by the five nasals, which are to be found in the same places of articulation as the semivowels. (In practice, three of these nasals do not appear in the French or English alphabet; they can only be represented approximately.)

"The five nasals are connected with the 'perceptible qualities' (*gunä*[s]): hearing, touch, sight, taste and smell, corresponding to the five states of matter present in all things" (*Kâshikâ* 18). Nandikeshvarä reminds us that from the point of view of experience or perceptibility, the world begins from the materialized energetic aspect represented by *I* and not from the theoretical aspect (A) of the plan. "*I*, representing energy (Shakti), is thus deemed to be the principle of all the other letters" (*Kâshikâ* 7). The nasals thus start with the palatal Ñ, corresponding to an *I*, in other words, to Prak<u>r</u>iti, the plan realized in substance.

The nasals, which appear as the fifth consonant in each group, are as follows: the guttural-nasal N̄ (now placed in the center), representing hearing (ether); the palatal nasal Ñ (as in Spanish), representing touch (air); the labial nasal *M*, representing taste (water); the cerebral nasal <u>N</u>, representing sight (fire); and the dental nasal N, representing smell (earth).

The hierarchy of the senses reflects the hierarchy of the successive appearance of the different elements. Ether or pure vibration is perceived only by hearing or its analogous senses. The others follow in order: the gaseous state of air, perceived by hearing and touch; the state of fire, perceived by sight, touch, and hearing; the liquid state, perceived by sight, touch, hearing, and taste; and finally the solid element of earth, perceived by smell and all the other senses.

JHA-BHA-Ñ AND GHA-<u>DH</u>A-DHA-<u>SH</u>: THE ORGANS OF ACTION

The fourth letter (*varnä*) of each group (*vargä*) represents one of the senses of action which allows the formation of the body of the universe (*virât*) inhabited by consciousness (*cit*). They are present in all beings but are not perceptible in inanimate matter. [*Kâshikâ* 19]

Jh and *Bh* represent the organs of speech and touch. The tongue, organ of speech, corresponds to the element of ether and is represented by the letter *Jh*. The hand (*pânî*), the organ of touch which perceives the gaseous element or air, is represented by the letter *Bh*. [*Kâshikâ* 19–20]

Gh, <u>*Dh*</u>, and *Dh* introduce forms of action which correspond to the elements of fire, water, and earth and which are present in all living beings in the feet, the anus, and the sexual organs. [*Kâshikâ* 20]

The third degree of the manifestation of matter is the state of fire corresponding from the point of view of perception to sight, and to the senses of direction, of which the organ of perception is the eye and the organ of action is the foot.

The earth derives from the sun, which is for man the center of his universe. This is why it is represented by the guttural *Gh* (born of A, the principle). Then comes the liquid element, of which the organ of action in man is the genitals. It is represented by the cerebral <u>*Dh*</u>.

The solid state represented by the dental *Dh* corresponds to smell and to the function of rejection, whose organ of action is the anus. In Nandikeshvarä's text, the inversion of anus–sexual organs (Pâyu-Upasthä) for sexual organs–anus seems to have come about for metrical reasons, although some have chosen to see an allusion to Tantric practices; the sexual organ was viewed as the producer of semen, connected with the sense of smell and a means for sexual communication, while the anus was seen as the residence of Ku<u>n</u>dalini (coiled energy).

JA-BA-GA-<u>DA</u>-DA-SH: THE ORGANS OF PERCEPTION

"In all living creatures the ear, the skin, the eyes, the nose, and the tongue are the five organs of perception. [They are oriented] toward the exterior and correspond to J-G-B-<u>D</u>-D" (*Kâshikâ* 21).

KHA-PHA-CHA-<u>TH</u>A-THA-CHHA-<u>T</u>A-TA-V: THE VITAL ENERGIES

"The five vital energies (prâ<u>n</u>ä[s]) correspond to the second (aspirated) letters of each group: *Kh, Ph, Ch, <u>Th</u>, Th. Kh* is combustion (*prâ<u>n</u>ä*, respiration-digestion); *Ph* is elimination (*apânä*); *Ch* (*samânä*, distribution-circulation); <u>*Th*</u> (*udânä*, re-action, force); *Th* (*vyânä*, planning and specialization)."

CHHA-<u>T</u>A-TA: THE INTERNAL FACULTIES

"*Ch-<u>T</u>-T* follows. These are the first consonants of the three middle groups of the Vargä series; and it is these which symbolize the internal faculties (*antahkara<u>n</u>ä*)" (*Nandikesh-varä Kâshikâ* 22–23).

There are three of these faculties: the mind (*manas*), which discusses; the intellect (*buddhi*, including the memory), which decides; and the Ego (*ahamkarä*), which acts. The fourth of these internal faculties, the consciousness (*cit*), is treated separately, for it is an omnipresent principle. The palatal C represents the mind, the cerebral <u>T</u> the intellect, and the dental T the feeling of autonomy, the Ego.

There is a connection between *Chh* (*sâmanä*, circulation) and C (*manas*, the mind); between *<u>TH</u>* (*udânä*, force) and <u>T</u> (*buddhi*, the intellect); and between *<u>Th</u>* (*vyânä*, specialization) and T (*ahamkarä*, the Ego).

KA-PA-Y: PRAKRITI-PURUSHÄ

"Universal Nature (Prakriti) and Universal Man (Purushä) are represented by the initial consonants of the first and last group: *K* and *P*" (*Kâshikâ* 24).

Now that we have defined in man (the microcosm) the elements that correspond to the constituents of the universe in the creative principle, we shall return to the First Cause, to the origin of all forms of existence; to the fundamental dualism.

> *K* (the first letter of the first group) evokes nature, Prakriti, the substance of the universe, which is considered to be a feminine principle; *P* (the first letter of the last group) represents Purushä, the plan of the universe, considered to be a masculine principle. [*Kâshikâ* 24]

SHA-SHA-SA-R: THE THREE GUNÄ

"Sattvä, Rajas, and Tamas are the three fundamental tendencies that form the nature of the world. They are represented by *Sh*, *Sh*, and *S*. The Great God (Maheshvarä) can act (create the world) by becoming incarnate in these three tendencies" (*Kâshikâ* 24).

The palatal *Sh* represents Rajas, the tendency toward gravitation (and toward equilibrium between the contrary forces which permit the formation of atoms and worlds). The cerebral *Sh* is Tamas, the centrifugal force (which animates and creates but also disperses and destroys). The dental *S* is Sattvä, the centripetal force of attraction (which concentrates, conserves, and protects). These three tendencies are characterized by the colors red, black, and white. They are personified in the three divine aspects of Brahmâ, Shivä, and Vishnu. Shivä is the ultimate principle: the principle of expansion, from which all else stems and to which everything returns at the end.

HA-L

The last formula of the *Maheshvarä Sûträ* represents a return to the principle, the beginning and end of all existence, to the Being who stands motionless outside and beyond the world. According to the *Shivä Âgamä*, "the letter *H* represents Shivä in his aspect as the ultimate principle." "Beyond the creation, beyond all that which can be defined, I am *H*, the Supreme Witness, the sum of all mercy. Having said that, the peace-giver (Shambhu) disappeared" (*Nandikeshvarä Kâshikâ* 27).

With this, Nandikeshvarä's analysis of the *Maheshvarä Sûträ* comes to an end. His commentator adds: "The letter *A*, the first of all the letters, represents light and the supreme deity. The *I* (*aham*) is formed by the union of the beginning (*A*) and the end (*H*)."

The Ego, the center of all individualized consciousness, allows the living being, like universal man, to be the witnesses through whom the divine dream becomes apparent reality; the Gnostic Christians interpreted this formula as Alpha and Omega, the first and last letters of the Greek alphabet.

Creation by the Word

NANDIKESHVARÄ's theory is an attempt to explain the fact that linguistic symbols can be used to define and describe the world of ideas as well as the world of matter, and that they can be the instrument of science and of thought. The way in which the original language was revealed to (or discovered by) mankind is of little importance. Nothing is changed by this revelation being instantaneous or a drawn-out process. Creation develops according to a preestablished plan, like a fetus. It is neither more nor less likely that language stemmed from the Damaru (Shivä's little drum), whose rhythm sym-bolizes the origins of life, than that it was slowly formed in the dull-witted intellect of half-apes: one myth is as good as another. The possibility of language must necessarily preexist its discovery and use. Its point of departure lies not in changing customs but in eternal principles. The extent of our possibilities of knowledge is determined by the limits of language.

Monosyllabic Dictionaries

ONE can find in India monosyllabic dictionaries that analyze the meaning of the various components of a syllable, and the corresponding elements in the various orders of reality.

In the realm of Yogä, particular vowels are associated with specific colors. Color differences are due to the frequency of light waves, just as musical sounds are defined by the frequency of sound waves. These in turn can be placed in parallel with the vowels of the spoken language. Nevertheless, because of the lack of simple instruments to measure the frequencies of the light waves, and because of the limited range in the spectrum of colors, the parallels between sounds and colors are imprecise. According to Raghunundanä Sharma's *Aksharä-Vijñânä* (in Hindi), the fourteen vowels correspond to the following colors:

A = white (*shvetä*)　　　　　Â = cream (*pân̲d̲u*)
I = red (*raktä*)　　　　　　　Î = copper (*tâmrä*)
U = yellow (*pîtä*)　　　　　　Û = faun (*kapilä*)
Ë (*r̲i*) = bluish-black (*kr̲ishnä*)　Ê (*r̲î*) = browny-black (*shyâmä*)
Ü (*l̲ri*) = smoke-color (*dhûmra*)　Û (*lrî*) = orange (*supishanga*)
É = red-brown (*pishangä*)　　È = mother-of-pearl (*trivarna*)
Ó = speckled (*shabalä*)　　　Ò = black or gold (*karvandhurä*)

These letters and colors correspond to those which characterize the cycles in which new human species are born and die. We are currently at the end of the seventh cycle (*manvantara*), which is characterized by the vowel Ë and the color bluish-black.

Modern Indian grammarians have attempted to trace, in the most varied of languages, the origins of certain words, on the basis of the information given in the *Maheshvarä Sûträ*. For example, the word *devä* (god), comes from the root *div*, meaning "shining" (an epithet of the sun). *I* represents *shakti*, or energy. *D* is sight; *V* derives from *U*. *Div* therefore corresponds to "materialized, visible energy."

The root *vid* (from which comes *Vedä*) is the opposite and reflection of *Div*. *Div* is the divine light; *vid* is its reflection —sight, knowledge, revelation. The English word *God* and the German *Gott* derive from the root *go*, meaning "bull," the animal sacred since prehistoric times as the incarnation of Shivä-Dionysos. *G* means "hearing" and *Ó* means "the principle present in its manifestation." *Gó* therefore means "revelation." In the same way, *crown*, a symbol of royalty, comes from the root *krn*, which means "horn" and refers to the divine character of royalty (*K* = Purushä, man; *R* = *agni*, fire; *N* = earth), or man shining out on earth.

Magic Formulae (*Manträ*)

THE meanings given to the different elements of language are not simply attribution. There is a true correspondence between the formulation of the Word and the structures of living beings and the material world. This can be verified by the power of the Manträ(s), or magic formulae.

Some syllables not only have a descriptive value, but can also become a path of action, the means of summoning a subtle principle. The real presence of a divinity can be summoned into his image through the power of a Manträ. A typical example of a Manträ is the Christian formula of consecration, which, in its Aramaic form actually changes the bread and wine into the flesh and blood of Christ; but in translation it can only evoke the mystery. The translation of words that are magical in nature renders the rite ineffective.

The magical power of words is not necessarily linked to

their apparent meaning. This is the case with all Manträ(s): they play an essential role in all magical rites. The syllable with which many mantra(s) begin is the one which opens onto the universal: the syllable *AUM* (or more precisely *AUÑ*, as it appears in Tantric rites).

One section of the *Chhândogyä Upanishad* is devoted to the various correspondences between the components of that syllable and the different aspects of the manifest world. Many other texts discuss the same subject. *AUM* is considered in a symbolic sense to be the syllable from which all others have stemmed. It contains all the elements of language since it is formed from the three points of the triangle (throat A, lips U, and nasal resonance Ñ), within which all the points of articulation and hence the entirety of language are to be found. In day-to-day usage, the Ñ is replaced by M in order to avoid accidentally summoning the magic powers of the Manträ. A represents the principle of the world; U is the manifest principle; Ñ is hearing; *AUÑ* summons the principle of the world manifested in the Word.

Much of the time we use words without knowing their true meaning: yet they have their revenge; for when we use sounds whose meaning is the opposite of what we attribute to them, and regard approximations as realities, we live in absurdity, and the results we obtain are contrary to those we are seeking. This is typical of most modern ideologies, which are based on key words whose meanings are other than what is attributed to them. Language, as the instrument of knowledge, is a powerful weapon whose misuse brings us quickly to disorder.

Elements of the Musical Vocabulary

STEMMING as they do from common principles, the divisions of articulated sound, just like those of musical sound (whose limits define our possibilities for communication), can be found in all the harmonies and proportions that form the universe.

It is through the study of these harmonies—whose most immediate image is the phenomenon of music—that we can have insight into the harmonic nature of the stellar and planetary worlds as well as the structure of atoms, of the subtle and material worlds, both invisible and perceptible; we can then also understand the parallel universe which exists inside us, and which we perceive in the form of sensations and emotions, and whose mechanisms we can, through the introspection of Yogä, analyze and put into arithmetic formulae. The possibilities of articulated sound, like those of musical sound, are limited by inexorable and parallel laws; these are dependent upon the possibilities of our discrimination and perception, which establish the limits of the aspects of the world which we can and *must* perceive.

In the musical language, the intervals, which have a precise expressive significance, are in Indian musical theory called Shruti(s) (perceptible musical intervals). These Shruti(s), which form the base of all the musical languages, are fifty-four in number, just like the phonemes of spoken languages. In modal music like that of India, twenty-two of these intervals have a predominant role in the psychological action of the music.

The Various Forms of Language

SPOKEN language is not the only means of communication. There are linguistic possibilities, means of expression and communication linked to each of the states of matter (*bhûtä*) and each of the corresponding senses of perception and action.

The language of odors, tied as it is to the solid state of matter, is the most elementary. It plays an important part in the reproduction of the species. Odors and perfumes are signals: some animals (wolves, dogs, etc.) mark their territory and recognize their friends and enemies, their prey and food, by means of odors.

We use the language of taste, corresponding to liquid elements, as a guide to the alimentary process, the precondition of life.

The sense of touch, connected to the gaseous element, is rather rudimentary in man, with the exception of the aspect linked to auditory perceptions. The sound vibration is only perceptible to us because it is transmitted by the pressure of air, for our direct perception of the waves of ether is not developed. Some insects are not subject to the same restrictions, but we need a decoder in order to transform radio waves into audible sounds.

Visual Languages

CONNECTED as it is to the element of fire and to light, visual language is almost as important as spoken language. It is the realm of gesture, of symbols, of hieroglyphs and ideograms, and even to a certain extent of the forms of writing, which transpose audible sounds into visual symbols.

The language of Mudrä(s) (symbolic gestures) is used in ritual and dance, and allows the expression of concepts independently of any sound aspect. It is thus not linked to a spoken language. The same is true of ideograms; writing with ideograms, which are formed of visual elements not directly linked to sounds, is on a more abstract level than phonetic writing. Writing tends to alter and paralyze the evolution of a language, even though it is an artificial memory that allows the conservation and transmission of ideas.

A Geometric Language (Yanträ)

THE visual language of symbols makes use of elementary geometric forms, corresponding to the phonemes of the spoken language and to the numerical intervals of the musical language. Through their mathematical connections, the Yanträ(s) reflect the fundamental structures of matter and the principles of life in a more obvious way than does spoken language.

"Einstein and some of his successors, such as Wheeler, when they constructed the theory of general relativity, have put forward the idea that everything is geometric at base" (D'Espagnat: *La Recherche du réel*, p. 81).

Yanträ(s) allow the representation of particular states of being. There is a Yanträ and a Manträ for each god; they are an expression of his nature and enable us to summon him.

Yanträ(s) thus play an essential role in ritual. The anthropomorphic images are proportioned according to canons based on Yanträ(s) and are accompanied by accessories that call to mind the role and the individual characteristics of each god. The Yanträ(s) are essential to all magical accomplishment; they are also the basis of the plans of temples and the proportions of all sculpture. The artist first of all draws the Yanträ of a god and then, within the limits thus established, he brings out of the stone the anthropomorphic image that was concealed within it.

The human body is formed according to particular proportions and harmonies, which are the secret of its beauty. By means of yogic introspection we can perceive geometric diagrams in the subtle centers, connected to the sound symbols which define the body's role and actions. The Yanträ(s) are the expression of the constants that are to be found at the base of all the structures of the world, of atoms as well as of galaxies, of the genetic components of life and the mechanisms of thought. They are also a key to the mechanisms of our emotions.

In musical intervals we can analyze the psychophysiological action of purely numerical relationships that cause emotive reactions in listeners. This suggests the possibility of a mathematical definition of our reactions and feelings.

THE POINT

In the language of the Yanträ(s), the point (*bindu*) represents the transition from nonmanifest to manifest. All manifestation must start from one point. It corresponds in Manträ(s) to Anusvarä, the nasalization of syllables.

THE SPIRAL

The symbol of ether, the principle of the development of space and time, and of the expansion of the universe, is the spiral, which, starting from the initial point, develops indefinitely with circular movements like the universe itself. It corresponds to hearing (hence the labyrinthine shape of its organ, the ear). The corresponding Manträ is *Han*, the guttural semivowel, stemming from A. The spiral is perceived in the experience of Yogä in the center of purity, situated in the throat.

THE CIRCLE

The symbol of the gaseous element of air is the circle, or occasionally the hexagon. It corresponds to nondirectional movement perceptible by touch.

It is from the gaseous state that the other elements are born through orbitation or condensation. It is thus the first manifestation of the energetic principle represented by the Manträ *Yañ*, the semivowel Y, stemming from I (energy, *shakti*). The corresponding color is blue-black. The principle of the gaseous element is achieved in Yogä in the center of spontaneous sound (Anâhatä Chakrä) close to the heart.

THE TRIANGLE

The symbol of the liquid state is the triangle, resting on its point, which is also the symbol of feminity. A simple horizontal line can also represent the liquid state, for water always tends toward a leveling. Its corresponding sense is that of taste. Its Manträ is *Vañ*, deriving from U. In Yogä it is perceived in the center of the Svâdhishthanä, at the base of the sexual organs. Its corresponding color is blue-green. The symbol of the fiery state is a triangle with its point at the top (the masculine symbol), or simply a vertical line: fire tends to rise. The corresponding sense is that of sight; its Manträ is *Rañ*, derived from *Ë* (*ri*). It is perceived in Yogä in the center of the navel (Nabhi Padmä). Its corresponding color is red.

The triangle, symbol of femininity, illustrates the numerical relationship 2 (base) above 3 (triangle) corresponding to (2/3), that is, C–F (Do–Fa), or a fourth in music, a gentle, feminine interval.

The masculine principle shows the relationship of 3/2. In music this is the frequency ratio of the fifth, C–G (Do–Sol), a sparkling, masculine interval. The six-pointed star represents the union of principles, the erect phallus in the vulva.

The cross too is a symbol of the union of water and fire: the union of opposites, which is the origin of the perceptible world.

THE SQUARE

The square is the symbol of the solid element or earth. It corresponds to the sense of smell, to the color yellow, and to the syllable *Lañ* (deriving from *Ü*). It is also the symbol of the god Brahmâ, the shaper of the world, riding on the elephant Airavatä.

THE PENTAGON

The number 5 (Shivä's number) is the symbol of life and of consciousness. At the base of all living conscious structures is to be found the factor 5 (five senses, five fingers, five places of articulation, etc.). The crescent moon, used as a symbol, has the shape of the moon on its fifth night and thus stands for the number 5.

In music the perceptible and emotive intervals are those which include the factor five (harmonic third 5/4, minor third 6/5, harmonic sixth 5/3, minor seventh 9/5, etc. (See Alain

Daniélou, *Sémantique musicale.*) Various aspects of the living being reflect symbolic features: such are the hand (with its five fingers), the erect phallus (the axis or column, symbol of the continuity of species), the eye (the sun), and the ear (a labyrinth).

The Swastika

THE swastika is the symbol of the irrational. It reminds us that the principle which is at the origin of the world, and the universe itself are twisted (*vakrä*). Any explanation that seems to be simple and logical is inevitably wrong. Starting from the nonspatial point (*bindu*), the universe develops in a spatial form; this is represented by a cross, image of the union between Purushä and Prakriti, the masculine and feminine principles. But this space is twisted: one becomes lost in space if either the inner or the outer branches of the swastika are followed. One never reaches the center. It is necessary at a given point to change direction and reject apparent logic. This is why in mathematics the irrational numbers are closest to reality. The prime numbers, which defy simple logic, are the only important ones.

The geometry which we know as Euclidian is merely approximative and has very narrow limits. In music the cycle of fifths, which seems to be a rational base, is exact only until the fifth fifth. Social theories, the relationships between human beings and the rites or relationships with the subtle beings, are never simple. All slogans are by their very nature wrong. For this reason the swastika is a beneficial sign: inscribed on the door of a temple or a house, it reminds us that there is no logical solution to any problem and that all simplification leads to absurdity.

Any science or technology or philosophy or religion that claims to be in possession of the truth is illusory and dangerous.

The god Ganeshä, who is both man and elephant, is the

iconographical equivalent of the Svastikä. He evokes the identity between the macrocosm, the immense being, and the microcosm, the human being. He defies logic. One cannot be at the same time small and large, immortal and mortal, god and man, but nonetheless there exists a fundamental identity between irreconcilables. The divine principle is that in which opposites coexist, and so it is likewise in the divine work, in all the aspects of the created world.

Appendix II

Chronology of the Kali Yugä

The First Millennium (3100–2100 B.C.)

3313   Beginning of the Maya calendar in America

3100   Prithu, the first (legendary) king of India, develops agriculture.

3100   Founding of the First Egyptian Dynasty

3000   Fo Hi, first emperor of China
The first writing: Indus Valley, Sumer, and Egypt
Development of cities in the Indus Valley and in Mesopotamia

2800   First Minoan civilization in Crete

2750   Founding of Troy

2675   Gilgamesh

2100   Megalithic monuments in Europe (The oldest of the megalithic monuments are prior to the Kali Yugä, dating back to the middle of the fourth millennium B.C.)

The Second Millennium (2100–1100 B.C.)

THE DESTRUCTIVE POWERS

2000	Invasion of Sumer by the Amorites and the Elamites
1900	Arrival of the Achaeans in Greece
1800	Destruction of the cities of the Indus by the Aryans
	Birth of Abraham at Ur
	The Aryans import the horse.
1400	Invasion of Knossos by the Achaeans
1300	Babylon taken by the Assyrians
1250	Trojan War

The Third Millennium (1100–100 B.C.)

THE RETURN OF ARIHAT

1100	The Dorian Invasion
1050	The Aryans occupy the Ganges Valley.
1016	David becomes king.
900	First Phoenician alphabet
	The Védä(s) and the Homeric tales transmitted orally
	The Âgamä(s) and Purânä(s) in occult tradition
817–778	Pârshvä, the 23rd Jaïna prophet
705	Hesiod
700	Beginning of the Greek alphabet
600	Midpoint of the Kali Yugä
	Kharoshti (Phoenician) writing appears in India.
630–553	Zoroaster
603–531	Lao Tse
560–484	Makkhali Gosâlä

551–479	Confucius
550–483	Gautamä Buddhä
547–467	Mahâvirä
540	Xenophanes
530	Pythagoras
520	The Indus region annexed by Darius Introduction of Brahmi (Aramaic) writing into India
500	Rome becomes a republic. The grammarian Panini
469–399	Socrates
384–322	Aristotle
356–323	Alexander
274–237	Ashokä

The Fourth Millennium (100 B.C.–A.D. 900)

THE SHAIVA RENAISSANCE

100	Lakulishä
78	Manes, first Scythian king of India
50	Beginning of Mithraism in Rome
50	House of the Mysteries in Pompeii
25 B.C.–A.D. 27	John the Baptist
22	Ambassador of Augustus visits King Pandion of South India. Simon the Magician Growth of the Pashupati cult
19	Herod restores the Temple of Jerusalem and favors the Essenes.
4 B.C.–A.D. 30	Jesus The Gnostics
100	The Gospels are written.
100	Indian ambassador visits Trajan.

The Fifth Millennium (900–1900)

THE DECLINE

Bibliography

In the following bibliography, the publisher's name is not given for texts existing in multiple editions, nor for texts in manuscript form or published only in local Indian editions that are difficult to obtain.

Texts

IN TAMIL

Kâraṇâgamä

Tirukkural of Tiruvallur (V.R.R. Dikshitar, Adyar, 1949)

Maṇimékhalaï (U. V. Svaminath Aiyar, Madras, 1898)

Navakadir

Onbadukadir

Shilappadikâram (U. V. Svaminath Aiyar, Madras, 1927)

Tiruvorriyur Purâṉam

IN SANSKRIT AND IN PRAKRIT

Purâṉä(s)

Kâlikâ

BIBLIOGRAPHY

Kûrmä (Bibliotheca Indica, Calcutta, 1890)

Lingä (Calcutta, 1885)

Mârkandeyä (Bibliotheca Indica, Calcutta, 1862)

Matsyä (Anandashrama, Poona, 1907)

Shivä (Benares, 1930, with Hindi commentary)

Skandä (Venkateshvara, Bombay, 1911)

Vâyu (Anandashram, Poona, 1905)

Vishnu (Gorakpur, 1915, with Hindi commentary)

Mahâbharatä (Kumbhakonam, Bombay, 1906)

Âgamä(s)

Kamikä

Mrigendrä

Parameshvarä

Shivä

Sukshmä

Yogä

Upâgamä(s): Secondary Âgamä(s)

Âtmayogä

Bhaïravottarä

Narasimhä

Sâmkhyä

Shanti

Târakä

Uttarä

Vinashirottarä

Tanträ(s)

Achârabhedä

Damarä

Kulârnavä (Ganesh and Co., Madras, 1965)

BIBLIOGRAPHY

Mahânirvânä (Ganesh and Co., Madras, 1953)

Shaktisangamä (Baroda, 1932–1947)

Shashti

Vedä(s)

Aitareyä Âranyakä

Atharvä Vedä

Chhandogyä Upanishad (Adyar edition)

Kathä Upanishad (Adyar edition) .

Rig Vedä

Shatapathä Brâhmanä

Shvetâshvatarä Upanishad (Adyar edition)

Taïttirîya Brahmanä

Darshanä(s)

Dighä Nikâyä (in Pali): Dialogues of the Buddha (translated and published by Rhys Davids, London, 1890–1911)

Ganä Kârikâ of the Bhâsarvajñä

Nyâyä Sârä of Bhâsarvajñä

Sâmkhyä Kârikâ of Ishvarä Krishnä
  with commentary by Gaudpadä (Poona, 1933)
  with commentary by Varshagânä
  with commentary by Vasubandhu

Sarvä Darshanä Samgrahä of Sâyanä-Madhavä (with Hindi translation, Chowkhamba, Benares, 1964)

Sâmkhyä Pravachanä Sûträ of Asuri

Sâmkhyä Tattvä Kaumudi of Vâchaspati Mishrä

Shaddarshanä Samuccayä of Haribhadrä (with commentary by Gunäratnä, Calcutta, 1905)

Shankarä Digvijâyä of Mâdhavä (with commentary by Unmattä Bhairavä)

Tattvä Sâmasä of Varshaganyä

Vaisheshikä Sûträ of Kanâdä

[269]

BIBLIOGRAPHY

Pâshupatä

Ga<u>n</u>ä Kârikâ of Haradattä (with the Ratna<u>t</u>ika Commentary of Bhasarvajñä, Gaekwar Oriental Series no. 15, Baroda)

Ishvarä-Kart<u>ri</u>-Vâdä of Bonteya Muni

Lâkulâgamä Sâmayä

Pâncharthä-Bhâ<u>sh</u>yä (Commentary on the Pâshupatä Sûträ by Kau<u>n</u>dinyä)

Pâshupatä Sûträ (with Commentary by Kau<u>n</u>dinyä, Trivandrum University, 1940)

Ratnä <u>T</u>ikâ of Bhâsarvajñä

OTHER TEXTS

Âgamä Prâma<u>n</u>yä

Ak<u>sh</u>arä-Vijñânä of Raghunandanä Sharma

Ashtâdhyayi of Pâ<u>n</u>ini

Âvashyakä Sûträ (in Prakrit) with commentary by Jînä Dâsä Gani (Rutlam, 1928)

Bauddhâyanä

Bhagavati Sûträ (Jaïnä) (in Prakrit) (Agamodayä Samiti, Bombay, 1928)

Brahmä Sûträ, with commentary by Râmânujä

Brahmä Sûträ Bhâ<u>sh</u>yä of Sankarâchâryä (with various commentaries) (Nirnayä Sâgar, Bombay, 1938)

Buddhächaritä of Ashvaghoshä (Punjab University, 1935)

Harshächaritä of Bâ<u>n</u>ä (Motilal Banarsi Dass, Delhi, 1965)

Kadambari of Bâ<u>n</u>ä (Nirnayä Sâgar, Bombay, 1920)

Lalitä Vistarä (Mithila Institute, Darbhanga, 1958)

Mahâbhâshyä of Patañjali

Mâlatîmadhavä of Bhavabhûti (Poona, 1935)

Manu Sm<u>ri</u>ti

Nandikéshvarä Kâshikâ

Prabodhä-Chandrodayä of K<u>rishn</u>ä Mishrä (Nirnayä Sâgar, Bombay, 1965)

Rudrä Damaru of Nandikeshvarä

Shabdä aur Arthä of Swâmî Karpâtrî (Revue Siddhantä)

Shankarä Vijayä of Ânandä Giri (Bibliotheca Indica, Calcutta, 1968)

Sharadâtilakä

Shrî-Bhâshyä of Râmânujä (Poona University, 1959–1962)

Siddhantä Kaumudi of Bhattoji, Dikshitä (Calcutta, 1926)

Tripitakä

Vâkyapadîyä of Bhartrihari (Varanasi, 1961)

Vétalä Panchavishati of Jumbhaladattä (American Oriental Society, 1934)

Vishnu Smriti (Adyar edition, 1964)

Vyâkaranä of Kalâpä

Yâjñavâlkyä Smriti (Nirnayä Sâgar, Bombay, 1946)

Yashodharä-Kavyä of Vadirâjä Sûri

Recent Works

Aiyangar, S. Krishnaswami, *Manimekhalai in Its Historical Setting* (London, Luzac, 1927).

Banerjee, P., *Early Indian Religions* (Delhi, Vikas, 1973).

Basham, A. L., *History and Doctrines of the Âjîvikas* (London, 1951; reprinted by Motilal Banarsi Dass, Delhi, 1981).

Bharati, A., *The Tantric Tradition* (London, 1965).

Bhattacharya, Narendra Nath, *History of Shakta Religion* (Delhi, Munshiram Manohar Lal, 1974).

Chakraborti, Haripada, *Asceticism in Ancient India* (Calcutta, Punthi Pustak, 1973).

Golzio, Karl Heinz, *Der Tempel in alten Mesopotamien* (Leiden, Brill, 1983).

Johnston, E. H., *Early Sâmkhyä* (London, Royal Asiatic Society, 1937; reprinted by Motilal Banarsi Dass, Delhi, 1974).

Kramrisch, Stella, *The Presence of Shiva* (Princeton University Press, 1981).

Lorenzen, David N., *The Kâpalikäs and Kâlâmukhas* (University of California Press, 1972).

McEvilley, Thomas, *An Archeology of Yogä* (RES 1, Harvard University, 1981).

Mellersh, H.E.L., *Chronology of the Ancient World* (London, Barrie and Jenkins, 1967).

Narayana Ayyar, C. V., *Origins and Early History of Shaivism in South India* (University of Madras, 1974).

Rao, Gopinath, *Elements of Hindu Iconography* (Madras, 1914–1916).

Sakhare, M. R., *History and Philosophy of Lingayat Religion* (Darwad, Karnatak University, 1978).

Van Duk, J., *Lugal Ud Me-Lam-Bi Nir Gal* (Leiden, Brill, 1983).

Translations

Le Shivä Svarodoyä, translated from Sanskrit by Alain Daniélou (Milan, Arché, 1982, and Paris, Dervy Livres).

Manimekhalaï, partial translation into English by S. Krishnaswami Aiyangar (Madras, 1928).

Shilappadikâram (The Ankle Bracelet), translated from Tamil by Alain Daniélou (Paris, Gallimard, 1981, and New York, New Directions, 1965).

The Epic of Gilgamesh, translated from Sumerian by J. B. Pritchard (Princeton, Ancient Eastern Texts, 1950, and Abed Azri, Paris, Berg International, 1979).

Other Works Consulted

Alexandrian, *Histoire de la philosophie occulte* (Paris, Seghurs, 1983).

Bernard, Jean, *Le Sang et l'histoire* (Paris, Buchet-Chastel, 1983).

Espagnat, Bernard d', *A la recherche du reel* (Paris, Gautier Vilars, 1979).

Maffesoli, Michel, *L'Ombre de Dionysos* (Paris, Meridiens/Anthropos, 1982).

Reeves, Hubert, *Patience dans l'azur* (Paris, Le Seuil, 1981).

INDEX

INDEX

INDEX

[283]

INDEX